Museum Visitor Evaluation

Museum Visitor Evaluation:
New Tool for Management

Ross J. Loomis

American Association for State and Local History
Nashville, Tennessee

Library of Congress Cataloging-in-Publication Data

Loomis, Ross J.
  Museum visitor evaluation.

  Bibliography: p.
  Includes index.
  1. Museum attendance—United States—Evaluation.
2. Museums—United States—Public relations—Evaluation.
3. Museums—United States—Administration. I. Title.
AM11.L58 1986   069'.62'0973   86-22346 ISBN 0-910050-83-X

Publication of this book was made possible in part by funds from the sale of the Bicentennial State Histories, which were supported by the National Endowment for the Humanities.

To
the Museum Visitor,
past, present, and future

Contents

Acknowledgments

Many individuals have been kind enough to take time out of busy sched-
ules to review portions of this manuscript and offer helpful suggestions
to the author. The following persons reviewed plans, outlines, or
individual chapters: Donald Adams, of the Henry Ford Museum and
Greenfield Village; Gene Ball, Yellowstone Library and Museum Associ-
ation; Kent Brown, Longmont Museum; Nancy Glaser, Ringling
Museums; James Hartmann, Colorado Historical Society; Robert Hoel,
Colorado State University; Mark Lane, Witte Museum; the late Glenda
Morgan, Texas Historical Commission; Brian Moroney, Fort Collins
Museum; Arminta Neal and Susan Salazar, Denver Art Museum; Cindy
Sherrell-Leo, Texas Historical Commission; Harold Skramstad, Henry
Ford Museum and Greenfield Village; Vicki Stolzenback, Longmont
Museum; and Patterson Williams, Denver Art Museum.

Beverly Serrell and C. G. Screven reviewed an early draft of the complete manuscript and provided many constructive suggestions for improving the work and helping the author reach his goals.

The author is also indebted to the staff of the American Association
for State and Local History for supporting a project of this kind, offering
many insightful suggestions and waiting patiently for this professor to
get his work done. At different times in the project, Gary Gore and Betty
Doak Elder, each of whom served several years as Director of Publications for AASLH, and Jerry George, the Association's director and chief
executive officer since 1978, contributed their insight to the effort. Editor
Martha Strayhorn worked hard to get a manuscript written by a psychologist into a format useful to both professionals and volunteers in the
historical agency and museum fields.

Nancy Patton, Robin Trent, and Jamie Kenyon typed drafts of the manuscript; and Joyce Patterson helped with graphics.

Preface

Most people responsible for the operation of a museum today are keenly aware that increasing emphasis on museums as viable social institutions make new areas of growth and change imperative: museums today must add to their traditional purpose of preserving and exhibiting objects new programs and services attractive to increasing numbers of visitors who may be depended upon to add badly needed funds to the museum's shrinking budget.

That means that, today, people who run museums are having to make hard decisions about new ways of looking at both the product and those who use it.

Management decisions are critical in determining the viability of any institution, and the kinds of museum visitor evaluation research discussed in this book can be an important aid to such decision-making. To that end, examples of museum visitor evaluation research are cited throughout this book. Insights from recreation research and the field of marketing nonprofit institutions are also drawn upon in discussing the needs of museum visitors and the ways those needs relate to museums as social institutions.

It is not enough, however, simply to review ideas and research about museum visitors. Readers are encouraged to undertake evaluation tasks in their own places and to find out firsthand information about their visitors. Each setting that attracts visitors has its own unique audience profile and dynamics. Firsthand evaluation is the best way to identify who visitors are and to find out whether exhibits and programs are working the way they were planned. This book has been especially written for museum staff people considering or actually doing museum visitor evaluation work.

While much of the book will be focused on the museum visitor, the basic topics in various chapters apply to other public-access settings that have visiting audiences. Readers who identify with zoos, aquariums, parks, historic settings, and nature centers will find common interests in much that is discussed; and, from time to time, an example will be drawn from such places.

A Reader's Guide

Chapter topics have been organized to address a wide range of museum evaluation needs. Those needs are reflected in such questions as these:

•What is the best way to record and report visitor attendance?
•How can I identify the people who are visiting? How many different kinds of visitors use my museum?
•What kind of visitor and nonvisitor evaluation is needed to help make a marketing plan successful?
•Why do some people stay away from museums?
•How can I know what kinds of orientation problems exist for visitors? How can we make visitors feel more comfortable with the museum?
•Is a specific exhibit working the way it was planned, in terms of circulation patterns, visitor understanding of themes and objects, visitor use of labels, and other interpretation aids?
•Can I find out whether a new education program is reaching the intended age level and is viewed positively by students and teachers?

These questions are but a sample of many that could be asked about visitors. Each question reflects different kinds of staff and management needs.

Another aim of this book is to provide useful visitor- information to a number of different people, including directors and other administrators, educators, exhibit designers, special events coordinators, public relations personnel, publicity directors, membership coordinators, fund-raisers, volunteer coordinators, docents and other volunteers who work with the public, business managers, directors of marketing, community relations coordinators, and managers of museum security. Museum executive committees, trustees, and exhibit-planning groups will also find topics of interest in the pages that follow. Other important potential readers are students in museum studies programs, who will find that this book can be read as a text in visitor research.

While some readers may use the book as a text to gain a broad overview, many others may elect to use the various chapters as reference sources to be consulted as different needs arise. Most museums and other public access settings have small staffs—a situation where it is necessary for people to wear more than one hat and to attend to several visitor-related tasks over the course of a year. For this reason, the following chapter overview section is presented to help identify major topics. The index at the end of the book will also help readers find topics of interest. Readers may gain a general overview by reading the whole book, but they are advised, as are museum visitors who plan to tour a large museum in a day, to wear something comfortable and take frequent rest breaks.

All readers are encouraged to begin with chapter 1, which discusses the nature of visitor evaluation and its relationship to management, provides suggestions for using evaluation in museums, and concludes with a brief history of museum visitor research.

Chapter 2. Evaluating attendance is one of the most basic audience study tasks that can be undertaken. Many kinds of management decisions can rest on the number of people who attend exhibits, programs, or special functions. Readers will find in the second chapter a number of different methods for collecting attendance data described, some important evaluation issues presented, and a few practical tips for improving attendance evaluation. The goal of chapter 2 is to help make collecting attendance information a useful evaluation and management tool and not just a routine exercise that is traditionally undertaken, but not always used.

Chapter 3. Surveys can help staff members and management know the kinds of people that visit and use museums and other public access settings. To be effective management aids, visitor surveys must ask questions that reflect staff interests and forthcoming decisions that involve visitors and programming for the public. Well-done surveys can provide valuable information about visitors that can influence such decisions about museum management as hours of operation, special programming for specific kinds of visitors, and the interpretation to be used in exhibits. Chapter 3 provides a basic rationale for undertaking surveys, numerous examples of visitor-survey topics, and guidelines for conducting surveys. Chapter 3 will be useful to those planning a visitor survey, whether they intend to conduct it themselves or ask someone outside the institution to do the work.

Chapter 4. Audience development, applying techniques from marketing to make programs successful, and attracting visitors to exhibits are management activities that have become increasingly important. These activities, however, rely heavily on evaluation of both existing and potential audiences. Chapter 4 shows how a marketing plan for nonprofit organizations needs the kind of evaluation discussed throughout this book. The external survey, conducted in the community rather than at the museum, will be presented as a tool for measuring public perceptions of institutional identity and specific barriers to visitation. Chapter 4 will also focus on ways to analyze the reasons people do or do not visit and suggests ways to develop an external survey to help with audience development.

Chapter 5. The quality of a visit to a museum can be improved through good visitor orientation, and chapter 5 discusses the psychological basis of orientation and provides suggestions for evaluating orientation needs of visitors throughout the course of a museum visit. Included under the topic of orientation are the comfort needs of visitors.

Chapter 6. Does my exhibit work the way I intended? Do circulation patterns support or conflict with interpretation goals? Are visitors reading labels and learning from them? Chapter 6 provides ideas for evaluating questions about exhibits and analyzing whether these very special environments meet the needs of visitors.

Chapter 7. How well does my program work? This question is a variation of the exhibit-evaluation process where events and programs become the focus of attention. Readers responsible for supervising docent presentations and other forms of live interpretation, special events, and school group visits will find chapter 7 useful.

Museum Visitor Evaluation

1

Understanding Museum Visitors:
Evaluation and Management

Museums are places for the safekeeping of *objects*. And, every year, tens of millions of *people* visit museums to see the objects kept there. Museums are also places established for the conservation of objects worth keeping. And the work of conservation requires the investment of millions of hours of time and effort by *people*—both paid staff people and unpaid volunteers. Museums are places for the work of scholars—special people with the knowledge needed to find meaning in the *objects* of the world.

Museums *are* places for *objects*—but just as important, they are *people* places, too. *Objects* cannot be collected, studied, understood, and preserved without the efforts of *people*.

This book is about the people side of museums. Such an emphasis is not new. Laurence Vail Coleman, in his classic three-volume work, *The Museum in America*, clearly understood the importance of people and interacting social factors in the institutional life of museums. He understood that museums could not grow as institutions without undergoing social change. Summarizing the status of museums in the United States just before World War II, Coleman correctly foresaw major changes under way in visitation patterns. One example he recognized was that the growing popularity of the private automobile would open up historical houses and local museums to new audiences. Visitation to urban museums would change also, as broader geographic cross-sections of city populations gained access through use of the automobile.[1] Coleman also brought out a social emphasis in the second volume of his work by considering exhibition as the central function of museums. The character or image of a specific institution rested heavily on the nature of exhibits presented for public use. A strong people-orientation also appears in his description of the museum's educative role for adults and children and his detailed descriptions of "museum people"—those who work in museums, from trustees to preparators. In a chapter on public relations, Coleman speaks of *museum zeal*, the process of finding active roles for the passive institutions of the nineteenth century. That zeal, he notes, changed the character of museums—first, by creating an organized work force to deal with collections, and then through motivating followers to come and see the completed work in exhibitions.[2]

Aware that museum professionals had spoken of the potential of museums as active places for many years, Coleman thought he detected a major effort to involve people following the Great Depression of the 1920s and 1930s. He reasoned that economic hardship of the times prompted museum leaders to look to the public for greater support. A parallel situation may be taking place today. There is much concern just now about the future of museums as viable social institutions.[3] Public financial support for museums will probably continue for many institutions, but possibly not to the degree that it has in the past. Admissions fees appear increasingly the rule rather than the exception for museums in the United States. With admissions and other direct charges levied for visitor programs and services, there is growing interest in marketing the museum, making it desirable to and used by the public. There is some possibility that public relations and marketing promotion might one day seem to require more than its fair share of staff time from the traditional tasks of collections management, conservation, preparation of permanent exhibits, and education. On the positive side, however, current interest in visitor services, community and public relations, and marketing appear constructive ways to deal with social change involving the institutional viability of museums—now an essential central concern. An underlying assumption behind evaluation of museums and their relationship to people is that meeting the needs of people will help to insure that museums will be viable, robust institutions in the future. Viability for museums means not only the ability to draw a loyal audience and secure community support, but also the capacity to collect, study, and care for objects worth keeping. A museum in decline not only fails to meet the needs of people; it is also on the way to being a place unable to care for its holdings.

In today's world, management decisions are an integral part of any good plan to maintain the viability of museums as institutions, and this book discusses the kinds of evaluation research that can be used in making such decisions.

We begin with a look at some ways in which visitor evaluation research can help museum management make sound decisions.

Making Visitor Evaluation Research Useful to Management

What is Evaluation Research?

Edward A. Suchman observes, "An evaluation is basically a judgment of worth—an appraisal of value."[4] The goal of evaluation research is to provide, for busy managers and professionals, information that will help them judge the worth of the commodity they are dealing with and guide their decision-making. Good evaluation can strengthen museum management by providing timely information about audiences, programs, and other items that are part of a manager's responsibilities. Like all research, evaluation is based on data, and established methods must be used for collecting the information needed. This combination of emphasis on data and research methodology gives evaluation a unique contribution. While intuition, tradition, critical review, expert opinion, and group consensus are also means of establishing worth, collecting and interpreting data opens up another aspect of collected information. It is one thing to discuss in a staff meeting what visitors are like; it is quite another to undertake a survey that will determine empirically the kinds of people who are visiting the museum. This distinction between deciding what visitors prefer or do and undertaking actual research to find out what sort of people museum visitors are, what they prefer, and what they do during museum visits was made early in museum evaluation work by Arthur W. Melton in a study made for the American Association of Museums.[5]

Although it draws on accepted methods of research, evaluation is not intended to determine what causes things to happen as they do or to provide the explanations that formal or academic research does. On this point, Carol H. Weiss notes that evaluation research is also distinct from formal research in that it is not done primarily to provide knowledge for publications to be disseminated to a community of scholars.[6] Rather, information gained in evaluation is collected to be used immediately and often is never published in a formal journal or other scholarly outlet.

Evaluation information can be summative—that is, collected after a program or an exhibit is completed and used to assess the worth of the project: did things work out as expected? Is the project worth keeping or repeating? Evaluation can also provide formative information to guide a project as it is being developed. Data can be collected as a program is evolving and mid-course corrections can be made, based on that information. Mock-ups of exhibit labels, for example, can provide feedback about how readable or how attractive a proposed label format is, guiding a final decision about format before costly general label preparation and installation are undertaken. One of the best discussions of summative and formative evaluation for museum research is found in C. G. Screven's "Exhibit Evaluation: A Goal-Referenced Approach."[7]

Does Evaluation Make a Difference?

Any effort to assess the worth of a thing entails assigning to that item personal or intrinsic values. Evaluation does not eliminate personal judgments, but does provide a constructive basis for challenging them and putting limits on intrinsic subjectivity.[8] Effective evaluation arms the decision-maker with additional information for establishing worth and pays its way either by opening up new possibilities, providing validation for existing ideas, or a combination of both.

At a minimum, evaluation of museum visitors provides objective information about visitors' identity, expectations, interests, and motivations. If nothing else, audience evaluation can help staff members understand visitors better and anticipate their needs in planning.

Evaluation research can also clarify goals and purposes needed to make a project successful. The very process of performing an evaluation well requires making goals explicit and expressing in them a form that can be tested. When increased awareness of visitors is added to clarification of goals for specific projects, evaluation takes on added value, even if the results of a specific study argue against making any major changes.

Evaluation work can have more specific outcomes when formative evaluation is combined with a task like exhibit development. C. G. Screven mentions in a current work[9] four such benefits: Results from formative evaluation can increase the chances that exhibits and interpretation will work as planned, making the effort for curators, designers, and everyone else involved much more satisfying; specific design decisions can be based on actual *information* rather than *assumptions* about visitors and their characteristics; evaluation can identify features that do not appear to be working well, are impractical, and/or are too costly to be included in final production; and, ideally, formal evaluation will reduce the number of postinstallation changes—likely to be costly and sometimes embarrassing to staff—that have to be made.

Evaluation and Quality Control

Quality control of visitor experience is another benefit of visitor research. Visitation to a museum, historic site, park, or other public-access setting is a highly subjective experience. Such visits are not hard commodities, like automobiles in a showroom or apples on a grocer's shelf. Visitors will evaluate a visit by the quality and kinds of subjective experiences it provides, and they will compare museums to other settings and activities where they might invest their leisure time. Insuring the quality of visitor experiences is a very important museum management function.

Research into the ways in which recreationists value their experiences in forest lands, parks, and other recreational settings is closely allied to museum evaluation. One idea advanced by recreation researchers is that the satisfaction with a specific recreation experience like camping or skiing may rest on individual reactions to *little* things—politeness of attendants (or lack of it), cleanliness of the area, absence of unnecessary delays, and similar relatively insignificant factors can add to or detract from the total experience. Good management of recreational opportunities calls for attention to details, making sure that minor elements are not overlooked or allowed to become major factors because they are not handled well. A visitor can sense whether or not he or she is welcomed in a museum by the way small amenities are handled. Courtesy and helpfulness of attendants, cleanliness of exhibits, and thoughtful anticipation of orientation needs through well-prepared signs and other aids are specific examples of *little things* that communicate concern and interest to the visitor; neglecting them can present a negative image and spoil a visit.

B. L. Driver, Donald Rosenthal, and Lynn Johnson discuss a "theory of little environmental quality things"[10] whereby many specific features of a setting interact to provide the overall experience or impression gained. A single feature neglected or of unsatisfactory quality may influence the whole impression. Deterioration in the quality of a setting can happen gradually and may not be directly noticed by a visitor. A subtle impression may be conveyed, however, that things are not as they could be or that there is a lack of care in preparing for the visitor and his or her experience. That impression becomes part of the overall image the visitor has of the museum.

Quality control reflected in caring about the visitor's overall image of the museum is consistent with current ideas about effective museum management. In their book *In Search of Excellence*, Thomas J. Peters and Robert H. Waterman characterized successful business organizations as having an "obsession" with quality control.[11] For these authors, quality control included maintaining a consistent level of product or service that customers could depend upon, no matter how many repeat visits they made or how many times they purchased the product. Cleanliness and first-rate appearance were attributes of quality, as was a tendency to pre-test new products or services carefully before introducing them to the public. Peters and Waterman also noted that successful organizations knew their limits and had a sense of identity as to what their purpose was. Given a focus, quality is protected, through not overextending the organization's resources. These various attributes of quality control can be generalized to museums, and they all can be evaluated.

Integrating Evaluation with Management

If evaluation research is designed to help management decision-making, why is there often resistance to the idea of using evaluation? If summative and formative evaluation can provide a more objective basis for knowing visitors, pre-testing exhibits and programs, and insuring quality of visitor experiences, why is such information not put to use more often than it is? One answer is that many people are simply not aware of the potentials of visitor evaluation research.

A more fundamental reason for the lack of application of evaluation information is the nature of the research for it. Because evaluation is "action," or real-life research, it requires cooperation between researchers and nonresearchers. The academic researcher can work independently in the environment of a university or research center, but the *evaluation* researcher is dependent upon others whose primary function is not research. In research settings, the researcher has control over what is studied, as well as *when* and *how* investigation proceeds. Evaluation research, on the other hand, takes place in a setting not planned for researchers, and the work often must be added to an already crowded schedule. Research topics are often suggested by staff people close to the problem—a manager, perhaps, or other staff members—and the evalua-tor is often an outsider. Further, the aim of evaluation is to provide infor-mation for actions or decisions that are not under the control of the researcher at all. A working relationship must develop between those *requesting* and those actually performing an evaluation.

While it is easy to propose evaluation as a tool for management, it is much harder to make the idea a reality. Some managers are not comfortable with evaluation methods or results and find that evaluation does not fit their style of leadership. The ideal remains true, however: *evaluation can and should help management make decisions on topics that involve the museum and its public.*

In theory, evaluation should help any manager by providing information that clarifies problems and helps guide decision-making. In fact, evaluation information is frequently not used, and the whole evaluation process comes to be viewed as an expensive frill, an unimportant task that is of little benefit.

Indifferent use of evaluation information by management is not a problem limited to museums. Often, the results and implications of costly and long-term evaluation projects commissioned by business and government are virtually ignored by decision-makers. The reasons for this lack of utilization do not rest with managers only; problems with the evaluation process, management styles, and properties of the institutional setting are also factors.

Problems with the evaluation process. The very process of conducting an evaluation can sometimes interfere with the acceptance of findings and recommendations. In discussing utilization of evaluation information, for example, Gary B. Cox has mentioned in a paper on managerial style and utilization of evaluation information, that research methods can appear trivial and time-consuming to an action-oriented manager.[12] The time consumed in evaluating can also cause useful information to become available after a decision has already been made. Such delay in assembling information exposes the manager to negative criticism at worst, and stale or outdated results at best. While the evaluator is applying approved research procedures, the busy manager makes decisions, thereby limiting or negating the potential value of the completed research.

Cox observes also that the evaluation process sometimes generates answers to questions no one is asking. Unless managers and other staff personnel are involved in planning an evaluation, it is possible that the research may become independent of the management process. Such divergence could defeat the idea of action or decision-oriented research. Lack of effective communication between evaluator and administrator or staff member is another problem. Formal, research-based reports may be difficult to read, filled with jargon and terminology of little meaning to nonresearchers.

Marilyn G. Hood has criticized the technical merit of some visitor research, especially surveys of museum audiences. Certainly, if decision-makers doubt the efficiency of methods used for an evaluation, they are not likely to be greatly influenced by the results. It is important that the research process of evaluation follow accepted methods. Ms. Hood offers good advice for improving the quality of visitor research in a recent article, "Getting Started in Audience Research."[13]

Management style and evaluation. In his paper on managerial style, Gary Cox also reviews some characteristics of managers and suggests ways to match evaluation more to managerial styles of work. Typically, managers work at an unrelenting pace, keeping work in mind even during nonworking time. Managers engage in work activities that require frequent changes in brief, oftentimes unrelated tasks. Often, the requirements of managerial activity may be attractive to people who prefer action to more contemplative or abstract tasks. Managers are likely to see themselves as individuals who cause things to happen, who know how to accomplish tasks and enjoy meeting deadlines. While managers may be involved with long-term planning, their immediate job is often to carry out concrete, specific tasks. Managers are likely to prefer oral to written communication, because speech is more efficient and less time-consuming than writing. In addition, managers are part of a work linkage that includes people they supervise and others that they are accountable to. Evaluation information may suggest ideas for changes and new or modified programs, but a specific manager or decision-maker may be constrained in what he or she can do. Work linkages are also communications links, and managers are sensitive to information flow—especially to the possibility that they may not be getting important information. That sensitivity can be heightened if the evaluation project involves programs and/or areas of direct responsibility to a manager. Cox notes that most managers prefer to be kept at least partially informed with whatever information or incomplete knowledge is available than to be left with no information at all. It also can be helpful to discuss with managers critical or unfavorable results directly and quickly, rather than have them discover unpleasant news indirectly in reports or notices that appear after long delay and are circulated to other managers and administrators in the organization. It is not hard to see why the results of evaluations may often fail to be utilized by managers or other decision-makers. The information produced must be relevant to people who face a continuous flow of tasks and must think in terms of immediate solutions to specific problems. Cox suggests a number of considerations that can help make evaluation information useful to managers as decision-makers. For one thing, implementation of evaluation results need not be an immediate requirement; possibly it should be held, to wait for a point in an annual cycle of institutional decision-making. A new visitor program may be best started as part of next year's budget. Managers may be encouraged to use evaluation information along with other sources of information— sources that may include what other managers think, for example—and the total pool of information will determine whether it is time to make a particular decision. Evaluation should not be undertaken merely to solve an immediate crisis or problem. It is also important to realize that changes in visitor programs may take time to have any impact. For example, keep in mind that word-of-mouth motivation is a major influence for making museum visits. But word-of-mouth influence takes time to spread through a community. Changes such as special exhibits, new programs, renovations of galleries and permanent exhibits may all have positive impacts on visitation, but the impacts may not be apparent right away. Evaluation that ends too soon may not pick up the impact of planned change. Cox emphasizes that continuing evaluation that can include running records may yield more useful information than a one-time evaluation, since evaluation data collected over time can have an accumulative effect that reveals trends and changes over a longer time period.[14]

Some short-term evaluation information can be useful, especially for topics like exhibit effectiveness and visitor orientation. In these areas, managers want to know how well something is working, and a one-time study may well answer that kind of question. Unfortunately, evaluations of exhibits, programs, and other kinds of specific topics are often requested by outside authorities, and that sort of evaluation does not produce results in the concrete, problem-oriented format that would be useful to managers. A common situation of that type is an evaluation undertaken to meet the requirements of an outside funding agency. The emphasis becomes one of going through the process of evaluation because it is required and producing results that will satisfy the funding agency. The consequence is an evaluation study ignored by staff and, one sometimes suspects, by the agency itself. All evaluation, to be effective in decision-making, must yield information that is problem-oriented for the busy task-oriented manager.

Cox suggests two other implications for fitting evaluation to managers' styles of operation. First, because managers are action-oriented people, they value results that suggest alternatives and concrete choices. Evaluators are likely to be more cautious in interpreting outcomes and use scientific merit as a criterion for determining validity of outcomes. The author has learned that statistical significance of results is a concept that often separates the thinking of managers and evaluators. To the evaluator, results must reach predetermined levels of outcomes or statistical significance as assessed against probability estimates to be considered important or valid. A manager may be willing to act on results that appear to be moving in a particular trend or direction. To the manager, the evaluator seems to be hedging his or her bets by insisting on statistical significance, while the evaluator perceives the manager as willing to take risks. Some managers may well consider risk-taking as part of what they should be doing. Cox concludes with the idea that effective communication of evaluation results to managers is likely to be informal and on a continuous basis. Furthermore, managers are likely to view surprises or unexpected results as threatening, while evaluators find unexpected results interesting and important to report. To be effective in aiding decision-making, evaluation must be communicated in a manner useful and timely to managers.[15]

Evaluation and the institutional setting. Neither evaluation nor decision-making takes place in isolation. Even a small institution has more than one source of influence, including boards of control and private or public agencies. Evaluation data may simply not be as important as the influence of an outside source, such as a trustee board or a municipal budget authority. Evaluation works best in a climate of support for using information to guide decisions. In "Reforms as Experiments," Donald T. Campbell suggests that decision-makers should be rewarded more openly for conducting experiments and evaluations to see which alternatives work best. The trouble with that suggestion is that the decision-maker may be exposed to negative information or documentation of choices that did not work well. Managers are sometimes trapped into covering up problems or adopting a public facade implying that everything is working well, even though they know that is not true, because any admission of failure could be costly. Unless there is a climate that tolerates experimentation and some public airing of problems, managers may find it best not to attempt evaluation.[16] A museum director might like to use evaluation to document existing problems, but feels trustees would interpret relying on evaluation research as a lack of administrative strength or object to documentation of institutional weaknesses. A staff educator might feel that the education program would benefit from evaluation, but is afraid to expose the program to criticism. A curator may read about variations in label content and style, but hold back from experimentation with labels because peers might not approve. In short, evaluation can be helpful in making decisions, but it can also be costly. Information gained from evaluation can reveal skeletons in closets, challenge conventional ways of thinking about visitors and the museum, and sometimes expose managers to criticism. There must be a climate of support for freely looking at problems, and there must be a willingness to take risks through experimentation for evaluation information to aid decision-making. In particular, it is important for the manager who attempts evaluation to feel support from those in authority.

In *Planning for Innovation*, R. Havelock identifies some guidelines for integrating decision-making with evaluation, taking into account organizational dynamics that are a part of most situations.[17] One essential guideline is that there must be strong working links established between evaluators and all the individuals and/or groups within an organization that might use evaluation results. Evaluators are suppliers of information; and institutions like museums are potential consumers of such information. The more contacts that occur between suppliers and users, the more information is likely to be exchanged. Some writers have emphasized collaboration in evaluation efforts and the idea that evaluation must be responsive to staff and institutional needs.[18] Achieving collaboration is one reason for including on design and planning teams an expert in evaluation or having a staff member with some expertise in evaluation. A responsive or closely linked relationship between evaluators and decision-makers can go a long way toward dealing with many institutional problems. Once a strong link is established, evaluators are in a better position to learn the practical needs of managers; and managers are in a better position to know about the kinds of information evaluators can provide. With improved communications, more effective scheduling may be worked out for the timing of evaluation information and demands for decisions.

Identifying Specific Visitor Evaluation Needs

Once a decision is made to undertake some visitor-based research, where does one begin? Evaluation is going to cost something in terms of time, money, and applied energy. What approach will yield the most useful information? Two activities can help to suggest specific evaluation needs and ways to meet them: institutional self-study and a survey of staff members for their perceptions of information needed about visitors and the public.

Institutional Self-Study

Self-study involves an analytical effort to define overall goals and long-range plans for an institution. Self-study can be undertaken during a staff retreat, a series of planning meetings, or a facilitated conference with an outside consultant to lead the group. Exhibit and program planning, publicity, fund-raising, and other museum functions should be brought into line with the long-term goals defined through self-study. Although specific evaluation studies can be a part of any thorough self-study, it is important to keep institutional goals in mind when planning an evaluation and not to expect visitor surveys or other specific evaluation projects to take the place of long-range staff planning.

The grant program for state historical societies instituted by the National Endowment for the Humanities is one useful example of self-study. In "Self-Study," Suzanne B. Schell notes that a period of rapid growth for state historical societies in the 1960s and early 1970s presented a need for better planning for the public's involvement with these organizations.[19] Grants were provided to permit historical societies to examine their programs, survey constituencies served, and consult with outside resource people. Emphasis was placed on planning long-term programs. Self-study was planned as a management tool to help state historical societies determine long-range missions, establish priorities, set goals, and match limited resources to growing public use of the societies.

Any self-study should use such information sources as staff interviews, archival records, meetings with support groups, financial analysis, and visits to similar institutions. Surveys of the public can also be included, and one specific goal of a self-study could be the development of a marketing plan for a historical society or museum. Schell is careful to distinguish between evaluation of programs and the broader analysis of an institution's history, mission, and long-range goals. Institutional self-study pertains to self-analysis based on the institution under study and can often lead to specific evaluation of programs, exhibits, or other public offerings. Self-study cannot be done as a hidden agenda item, and it requires a supportive environment. Sometimes a period of transition in the life of an organization, such as a change in administration, is an opportune time for self-study. Ideally, institutions should look at themselves every five years or so and examine their long-range plans. Schell notes that self-study is used by both business and academic organizations. Funding agencies often require it as part of the application and funding process. One benefit of self-study is that it may help an organization to focus its programs more competitively for soliciting grants or other forms of financial support. The long-range value of self-study is to help nonprofit organizations maximize the impact of what they do while recognizing that resources are going to be limited, perhaps even decreased.[20]

Long-range planning and goals discussed in self-study should include consideration of the images projected to the public by the museum. It can be particularly helpful to consider and compare two questions:

•What do people say about our museum?
•What do we want people to say about our museum?

Dealing with these questions and doing any evaluation research necessary to help answer them can make the self-study responsive to visitor and public needs. In one example, results of a self-study clearly indicated that a number of museums in Texas had a public-image problem related to poorly defined purposes and identity.[21] The study revealed that institutional focus was needed in these museums to match programs more effectively to realistic levels of funding and staff support. For many of the museums, the problem involved trying to do too much and satisfy too many different audiences.

An Evaluation-Needs Survey

Specifying the kinds of evaluation an institution may need can be a part of a self-study conducted over a fairly long time period or a follow-up to such a study. A self-study might indicate that attendance records need to be overhauled and a better system of recording attendance instituted to improve accountability evaluation. Or the most pressing need indicated may be an external survey for a marketing plan project. Visitor orientation may be another need that surfaces from self-study, or the need to evaluate existing exhibits to help plan exhibit renovation.

Staff members can be surveyed directly for their perceptions of visitor-evaluation needs. A staff-based survey may reveal unique needs—one person or one department may bring up a need no one else has mentioned—or identify points of agreement such as overall concern about effective visitor orientation. A key trustee, volunteer, or others might also be included in the survey. A perceived evaluation-needs survey can be a formal or informal exercise, depending on the size of staff involved and the specific situation. D. Geoffrey Hayward provides a good example in *The*

Quadrangle Research Notes, his evaluation work with the Springfield Library and Museums Association, involving four institutions.[22] Planning for visitor research began with a meeting of staff people representing each institution to discuss evaluation needs. Following the meeting, a brief survey sheet was sent to each staff member, permitting individual staff people to list their interests and the group to pool needs to see what consensus existed among staff members. Two kinds of evaluation needs were assessed: staff people answered questions about such basic evaluation needs as public images of the museum, descriptions of visitor demographics, and exhibit evaluation, and each listed specific research topics that he or she would like to see investigated. In each instance, the participants were asked to rate the importance of an item as an index of their interest in that topic of visitor-related research. Hayward summarized the responses for the Springfield museums, and the results were reported to the staff for their consideration. Results of such a survey might show, for example, that priority topics for evaluation in the minds of the various staff members included knowing something about the benefits people gained from a visit to any of the museums, program evaluation, assessment of the museums' images, and description of visitor demographics. Less interest might be shown in orientation or patterns of use by visitors and in exhibit evaluation, comparisons with other museums; and testing the visitor's knowledge of the museum and interpretation might be topics for later study. Survey results would assist the evaluator and staff in assigning priority to evaluation needs. Table 1.1 displays a sample survey that could be used to measure staff perception of major visitor evaluation needs.

Museum Evaluation and Visitor Research: A Little Bit of History

A rather unusual article appeared in the first issue of the *Scientific Monthly* for 1916. Entitled "Museum Fatigue," the article had been written by museologist Benjamin I. Gilman. A highlight on Gilman, from Ed Alexander's *Museums in Motion*, notes that Gilman coined the word *docent* and had been interested in providing interpretation experiences for patrons of the Boston Museum of Fine Arts.[23] It is not so surprising, then, that Gilman should write a paper about museum-visitor fatigue. What is interesting is that in the paper Gilman described a museum-evaluation project. The project was quite modern in technique and far-reaching in its implications for exhibit design.

Table 1.1
Sample Survey for Staff Input
on Perceived-Visitor Evaluation Needs

Topic	Indicate how important you feel each topic is to collect information on planning for visitors:				
	Extremely important				Not important
1. Assessment of the museum's image with the public	1	2	3	4	5
2. Evaluation of visitor expectations for a visit	1	2	3	4	5
3. Study of visitor interest and knowledge of various exhibit content areas	1	2	3	4	5
4. Study of visitor orientation needs and problems	1	2	3	4	5
5. Assessment of visitor satisfaction with basic facilities (i.e., gift shop, food service, parking, visiting hours)	1	2	3	4	5
6. Overall assessment of visit experiences (what did they get out of a visit?)	1	2	3	4	5
7. Research on how visitors compare the museum with other local cultural institutions	1	2	3	4	5
8. Descriptive survey of who visitors are	1	2	3	4	5
9. Community marketing study of interest in the museum	1	2	3	4	5
10. Exhibit evaluation study	1	2	3	4	5
11. Program evaluation study	1	2	3	4	5
12. Membership survey	1	2	3	4	5

Source: Survey items used by permission of Jeffry Hayward, of People, Places, and Design Research, Northampton, Massachusetts.

Gilman had deduced that viewer fatigue could result, in part, from poor exhibit case design. Visitors were compelled to exert special effort to see the objects displayed in the traditional storage type of exhibit case then widely used. Viewers frequently assumed awkward positions to look at the artifacts and read the labels. Such efforts unnecessarily increased fatigue and would leave the visitor with little inclination for careful exploration of the museum and its contents.

To provide evidence for his point of view, Gilman had an individual seek answers to a set of questions that required looking for specific objects and reading labels. The physical effort needed for this task was recorded in photographs taken as the "visitor" bent, crouched, twisted, looked up, and stretched to view the exhibits. Gilman had anticipated by many years the contemporary technique of using photography to evaluate human response to environmental design.[24]

The photographs provided documention of Gilman's thesis that considerable effort was needed actually to examine the various objects on display. Such effort could contribute to viewer fatigue and cause the visitor to take a noticeably superficial approach to the visit. Gilman showed us that museum fatigue could be avoided, or at least reduced, by redesigning exhibit cases.

Actually, Gilman concluded his 1916 paper with an even more dramatic suggestion: public exhibits serve a purpose clearly different from that of storage galleries, and exhibitors should consider some of the physical needs of visitors. Gilman made specific suggestions for designing exhibit cases, observing that they should be scaled to human height, given enough depth to display objects without obscuring them, be placed so that visitors could view the contents at distances safe for the artifacts and comfortable for the viewer, and display a limited number of artifacts. It is hard to realize that such a seminal effort in museum evaluation appeared in print so many years ago.

A brief overview of visitor research since the time of Gilman's paper follows. Its purpose is to reveal major trends, and it is selective, not exhaustive. Examples of visitor research in the United States are given, as well as some mention of the international interest in museum evaluation and visitor research.

About the time Gilman's article appeared, a cartoon in Punch[25] (see figure 1.1) displayed a very unflattering image of museums: a carefree lad yields to impulse and blows his breath on the outside glass of a window display at the British Museum. As his breath condenses on the glass, he starts to write a comment there—and is seized by an outraged policeman—tried, sentenced, and jailed for many years. . . The cartoonist probably reflected the mood of a great many people of that time who perceived museums as austere, oppressive places. That view, of course, presented only one side of the picture; in fact, a definite concern about the public or social role of museums was evolving at the time, and Gilman's efforts were only one example of that concern.

In "An Introduction to Museum Visitor Research," Margaret Bouslough Parsons suggests that the origins of modern-day museum evaluation work should be traced back to those who founded public museums and to others who followed and tried to "reform" the work of the founders. She presents evidence that both groups of museologists felt that museums had an obligation to meet the needs of their visiting public. Founders— people like Joel Poinsett, Martin Brimmer, George Brown Goode, and George Fiske Brown—were instrumental in the necessary entrepreneur-

Fig. 1.1. Sample frames from "The Boy Who Dared to Breathe on the Glass of the British Museum," a 1916 Punch cartoon by H. M. Bateman. The artist pokes a brilliant and badly needed bit of fun at the notion then prevalent that museums were awesome, rather sacrosanct places, never to be lightly thought of.—Reprinted, by permission, from Punch, 1916.

ial activities of founding and developing great museums. They were criticized by a group oriented more toward education—people such as John
Cotton Dana, Frank Jewett Mather, Rositer Howard, and Charles J.
Douglas—who believed the founders were too preoccupied with collections, research, and preservation, at the expense of public education. Parsons is not sure that that was an intentional oversight by the early founders
of public museums; it may have been more a question of priorities in
getting struggling institutions started. She cites statements from different founders, in which an educational mission for public museums is
clearly advocated.[26] Whatever the case, a definite period of criticism about
the lack of visitor consideration in the design and operation of museums
existed, at least up to the time of World War I.

Topics that particularly drew the attention of critics included the poor
design of galleries that made understanding the collection impossible
and the need to have separate collections for public viewing and for study.
Behind any specific criticisms, however, was a far more extensive concern with the nature of museums that made the commentary of the *Punch*
cartoonist seem mild indeed.

Basically, the reformers accused museums of being places of gloom,
isolated, both mentally and physically, from their publics—"dead" institutions that needed to be changed from "cemeteries of bric-a-brac" to
"museums of living thought."[27]

Although they said it in different ways, what the criticism of the
reformers and the goals of the founders added up to was a two-fold public function envisioned for museums: an educative role to instruct the
public in the technical knowledge of collections; and a cultural role of
uplifting communities through the presence and programs of museums.
This second function is reflected in an early annual report of the Colorado
Museum of Natural History, eventually to become the Denver Museum
of Natural History:

We cannot occupy ourselves in two ways at the same time. The evenings spent
in the library or museums are not spent on the street or in a bar room. A young
man who takes up any of the sciences and has a museum for reference loses all
taste for dissipation.[28]

Parsons, in her thesis, emphasizes that, while many people talked
about the public missions of museums, few realized that the actual needs
of the public were not so obvious, and that some kind of empirical
research was necessary to define audiences and their requirements of
museums. This definition of visitor-related problems and topics is exactly
what museum evaluation and visitor research efforts should provide. Par-

sons concluded from her review that the origins of museum evaluation in the United States were heavily influenced by the growth of interest in making museums public institutions.[29]

A word of caution is in order. This apparent dominance of American evaluation studies over the years may merely reflect difficulties encountered in rendering translations from works in languages other than English and finding sources available in different countries. The bibliographical work done through the International Council of Museums (ICOM) has been important in locating evaluation studies from different countries. (See annual issues of the ICOM *International Museological Bibliography*; visitor studies appear in these annual volumes under a variety of headings.) A Working Party on Visitor Research and Communication, made up of members of ICOM's Committee for Education and Cultural Action and led by C. G. Screven, has sponsored research and bibliographic activities over the past several years. One thing certain about current trends in museum evaluation is that major interest in the area exists in West Germany, England, France, and Holland. West Germany not only is conducting evaluation research, but has sponsored major interdisciplinary colloquiums, seminars, and lectures in recent years.[30]

Early Efforts: A Search for the Educational Value of Museums

From the late 1920s until the onset of World War II a concerted effort was made to document the educational value of museums. No specific work was more complete than that of two Yale psychologists, Edward S. Robinson and Arthur W. Melton. Working under the sponsorship of the American Association of Museums and financially supported by funds from the Carnegie Foundation, both Robinson and Melton initiated formal psychological studies of the behavior of museum visitors as a way of documenting the educational role of museums.

Robinson believed museums offered the public a unique educational opportunity that could be realized only if museum exhibits and programs were innovative. Furthermore, it was essential to evaluate any innovations made, to assure that the public really did benefit. It is difficult to read a contemporary source like *The Art Museum as Educator* and not reflect on the fact that Robinson's practical philosophy of empirical experimentation was a very good match for the early philosophical statements of museum founders and reformers about the public missions of museums.[31]

Both Robinson and Melton used—some might say *overused*—an interesting method to estimate the educational value of museum visitation. They had visitors observed, unobtrusively, throughout gallery visits, with the observers noting the viewers' patterns of movement, the location and number of stops made, and the exits taken. This technique resulted in a map of gallery areas most frequently visited and gave reliable indications of specific gallery features drawing the most attention.

Whether their work can be considered definitive in establishing the educational value of museums may be debated; but they were able to define a wide variety of visitor-related topics for evaluation, and they showed that these topics could be investigated with at least one empirical method—unobtrusive observation.

At the heart of much of this work was the assumption that the way objects and content were presented to visitors through interpretation was very important. Typical visitors were very dependent upon habitual patterns of movement and exploration used in other settings, along with cues from the gallery architecture to guide their progress through an exhibit hall. In addition, they had to deal with fatigue, especially when visiting large museums. Where an artifact was installed within the overall architectural layout of a gallery could often determine the likelihood of its being viewed by the average visitor. Melton summarizes the focus of much of this work in a single sentence: "The gross behavior of the museum visitor is relatively independent of the qualitative differences in the objects exhibited."[32]

Melton was convinced that what he termed "the nonaesthetic factors in the museum environment"—location of exhibits; shape of the gallery; installation practices (the manner in which objects were grouped); the level of museum fatigue—played a much more important role in an exhibit's educational effectiveness than was generally realized. Through systematic study of these nonaesthetic variables, one could discover ways of increasing the educational value of exhibits. It was from this orientation that a rather remarkable array of evaluation topics was generated in the projects undertaken by Robinson and Melton (see Table 1.2).[33]

Museum professionals of that time also employed methods of unobtrusive observation to estimate educational value. C. Hay Murray, director of the Liverpool Public Museums, tried to gain an estimate of what visitors had learned from their visit by interviewing them as they exited. He was unsuccessful, because it was difficult, on the spur of the moment, for people to think of things they had just learned or seen.

Discouraged, Murray turned to a rather clever alternative means of estimating the educational value of exhibits. He instructed the museum clerk who checked umbrellas and coats at the front door to record the length of time people stayed in the museum. Murray then calculated the

Table 1.2
Sample Findings from Early Museum-Evaluation Studies

Museum Architecture

1. Small museums may be a more desirable size than large ones in terms of reducing fatigue and maximizing exploration. (See Robinson, 1928).

2. Right-hand walls of rectangular galleries are typically the most explored locations for the majority of visitors. (See Melton, 1933)

3. Number and location of exits have a marked influence on visitor circulation patterns within and out of a gallery. (See Melton, 1935)

4. The majority of visitors "short-cut" their movement through open space rectangular galleries by using a direct pathway from entrance to exit. (See Melton, 1933)

Museum Fatigue

1. Museum fatigue is more than a physical variable and can be caused by psychological satiation with viewing too many objects of a similar nature within a short time period. (See Robinson, 1928; Melton, 1935)

2. Museum fatigue can be reduced somewhat by intentionally designing points of variation in galleries as contrasted with putting many similar items together. (See Robinson, 1928; Melton, 1935)

Exhibit Installation

1. How objects are grouped in terms of density (number of items) or similarity-difference can influence visitor attention. (See Robinson, 1928; Melton, 1935)

2. As a general rule, objects exhibited alone or in small groupings draw more attention than when exhibited in a more complex context. (See Melton, 1935)

3. Period room installations draw surprisingly low levels of attention from visitors when the large number of objects on display is considered. (See Melton, 1935).

Exhibit Interpretation

1. Labels containing printed information may increase visitor memory for objects. (See Droba, 1929)

2. Placement of labels can influence whether or not they are read and how much they compete with objects for visitor attention. (See Melton, 1936)

Sources: Edward S. Robinson, *The Behavior of the Museum Visitor* (Washington, D.C.: Publications of the American Association of Museums, no. 5, New Series, 1928); Arthur W. Melton, "Studies of Installation at the Pennsylvania Museum of Art," *Museum News* 10 (January 1933); Arthur W. Melton, *Problems of Installation in Museums of Art* (Washington, D.C.: Publications of the American Association of Museums, no. 14, New Series, 1935); Arthur W. Melton, "Distribution of Attention in Galleries in a Museum of Science and Industry," *Museum News* 14 (June 1936); D.D. Droba, "Effect of Printed Information on Memory for Pictures," *Museum News* 7 (September 1929).

time it took a person simply to walk through the museum without stopping to look at any of the exhibits. From these two time calculations, Murray prepared a ratio he called the *value factor*. The value factor was the
visitor's circulation time (as observed by the clerk) divided by a *standard* comparison time needed just to walk through the museum. Murray reasoned that if the museum held anything a visitor considered to
be of value, the reflected value factor should be greater than one. The
more the visitor was attracted to the exhibits presented, the longer it
would take to complete a visit and the higher the value factor would
become. Murray also observed that the factor was influenced by the
weather and by visiting the museum as part of a group.[34]

An American museologist, Louis H. Powell, provided some validation for Murray's value factor when he used it to estimate visitor response
to a number of renovated galleries. For Powell, at least, the value factor
worked well to document his theory that renovated galleries in his
museum drew greater attention than their older versions.[35]

Not all museologists were impressed with what Carlos E. Cummings,
in *East is East and West is West*, called the "stopwatch methods" of unobtrusive observation. In a book-length report, Cummings described the
observations and evaluation of a panel of museum experts who toured
the two world's fairs of 1939. Cummings and his fellow reviewers identified a wide array of topics relating visitors and exhibits. They included
considerations of the entertainment value of exhibits; importance of a
story line to conceptual understanding; use of live demonstrations; relation of subjects to a visitor's own life and experience; uses of light and
color; dynamics of visitor participation; traffic flow; and use of labels.
Perhaps most important about the Cummings report was its detailed
description of exhibit design in the late 1930s and the way that design
related to visitors.[36]

Other efforts at determining the educational value of museums
included assessment of the educational effectiveness of a series of public health exhibits. In a study on use of ratings to evaluate exhibits, Homer
N. Calver, Mayhew Derryberry, and Ivan H. Mensh asked visitors directly
to rate exhibits in terms of their clarity of information, general attractiveness, and other aspects of presentation. They also asked visitors to
indicate the exhibits they preferred most and least. Despite all their efforts
at collecting ratings, however, these three authors pronounced their method a failure. They concluded that no meaningful pattern of ratings
emerged, whether experts or the general public were used as judges.
While they interpreted the lack of consistency in ratings as a failure of

the method, it is well to consider the possibility that real differences may exist both within expert and lay audiences over what constitutes a "good" exhibit.[37]

Years after the Calver-Derryberry-Mensh experiment, other researchers would still find the task of rating exhibit features a difficult one that produces a great deal of variability across raters.[38]

What can be concluded about these early efforts at museum evaluation and visitor research? For one thing, a number of different efforts at collecting empirical data or data-based information about visitors had been completed by the time of World War II. Data were also collected for other evaluation topics, including use of the museum by school children, attendance, use of self-guidance materials such as gallery pamphlets, and visitor surveys.[39] There was a definite option to merely speculating about visitor use of museums. The hope of early museologists that museums would be responsive to their audiences could be given concrete expression through evaluation studies.

Another benefit of these early works was that a number of specific topics were defined through evaluation. These topics did not provide a conclusive answer to the broad question of the educational value of a museum, but they did point to specific ways museums and exhibits could be made more effective in reaching their audiences.

A Middle Period: Visitor Surveys and Expanded Exhibit Evaluation

Although somewhat arbitrary, it is useful to describe the evolution of exhibit evaluation studies and the coming of visitor-survey efforts as major topics in museum evaluation in the two decades or so following World War II.

For many, a survey describing the visitors that come through the front door is synonymous with museum evaluation. Actually, surveys were not the first major efforts at museum evaluation, at least in the United States. It was not until the late 1950s and early 1960s that a definite evaluation topic of audience description became highly acceptable. That acceptance was due in great part to the work of two men: David Abbey, psychologist, and Duncan Cameron, museologist, who collaborated on a series of survey reports for the Royal Ontario Museum. Their reports helped establish visitor description as a viable evaluation topic. The Royal Ontario survey dealt with the problems of sampling museum audiences that can change as the seasons of the year change. The unique sampling strategy needed and survey topics suitable for museum audiences were developed by these authors. They also looked at problems associated with attendance recording, admission charges, and other issues associated with a museum's relationship to its public.[40]

Cameron and Abbey were not alone in their interest in museum-visitor surveys. Arthur Neihoff in Milwaukee reported on survey efforts at the Milwaukee Public Museum. Among other topics, Neihoff emphasized the importance of contrasting winter- and summer-season audience characteristics. Still other survey efforts appeared in the twenty years after World War II, including exit interviews of visitors and contrasted regional patterns of museum attendance. By the close of the 1960s, the on-site museum survey had become an accepted—though perhaps not always appreciated—evaluation activity.[41]

A variation in the focus of surveys evolved during this time. Because of the prevalence of government-sponsored traveling exhibits, interest developed in measuring public attitudes and reactions to these special exhibitions. There was also interest in determining whether exhibits had any measurable influence on attitudes or opinions. A series of efforts to measure visitor attitudes about the United States Information Agency traveling exhibits were carried out in a rather unimaginative manner. How valid these efforts were at measuring visitor opinions was a matter of some debate.[42]

One of the more interesting and better-performed evaluation efforts on influence of exhibits on attitudes was conducted by Howard Leventhal and Patricia Niles, who explored the question of whether fear aroused by viewing health-related exhibit materials would increase the effectiveness of messages relating lung cancer to smoking. Another attitude evaluation effort completed during this time examined whether attending an exhibit depicting cultural information would reduce or increase ethnic prejudice toward the people featured in the exhibit.[43]

Visitor surveys in the United States during this period served a decided evaluation purpose, since they were commissioned to describe audiences for a specific museum. On the average, little could be generalized about other settings from such surveys. In contrast, surveys in Europe have tended to focus more on a sociology of cultural institutions, have looked at the perceptions people had of museums as social institutions, and have investigated motives for visiting or not visiting museums. Hans-Joachim Klein and Monika Bachmayer note, in their *Museum und Offentlichkeit*, that a major European study investigated the role of museums in the cultural life of citizens as early as 1908.[44]

By the mid-1960s, a variety of techniques had been developed to study visitor reactions to exhibit settings. Much of the development of exhibit evaluation was due to the fact that *exhibits* were more often studied than were museum galleries as such. The Seattle World's Fair and traveling government exhibits were special targets of evaluation efforts. In these studies, it became common to use a variety of measures orchestrated into a battery of evaluation tasks. Unobtrusive observation, now aided by photography or closed-circuit television, was combined with interviews, structured tests, ratings, experimental mock-ups of planned galleries, and other assorted tools.[45]

By the end of the 1960s, a strong emphasis on exhibits as learning environments appeared, reflected in the work of such researchers as Harris Shettel and C. G. Screven. Shettel developed a collection of specific techniques to use in multimeasurement evaluation efforts, and helped to point out the need for stated criteria by which to measure what an exhibit should accomplish in visitor communication. He also suggested specific factors that contribute to exhibit effectiveness. To Shettel, the old unobtrusive observation measures of Robinson and Melton were really indicators of visitor attention to specific exhibit features. Successful exhibits should have both attention-drawing (attraction) and attention-maintaining (holding) factors. In addition, they should have a learning factor—some demonstrable sharing or gain in comprehension of information should be passed on to the visitor whose attention the exhibit holds. This emphasis on a learning factor really has its roots in the original evaluation efforts to demonstrate the educational value of museums in the 1920s and 1930s. It also helped to spur interest in exhibits as learning environments, a topic that would gain strength rapidly in years to come.[46]

Screven's work reinforced Shettel's emphasis on exhibit evaluation and also brought a fresh look to the old issue of the educational potential of exhibits. Planning objectives for designing exhibits, he stressed, should include ways to involve visitors more actively with exhibit content. Screven suggests using numerous ideas and methods from educational technology and the psychology of learning, including the use of interactive exhibit features such as visitor-response devices that would permit answering questions or solving problems. The important aspect of Screven's work was not the development of "push-button" exhibits, but the realization that educational objectives for exhibits could be defined in ways that permitted measurement. With measurement would come the possibility of developing exhibits that enhanced visitor learning and participation in many ways, from the preparation of labels to more elaborate opportunities for participation, as provided by self-testing response panels and other interactive displays.

No review of exhibit evaluation topics of the 1960s should fail to mention Stephan de Borhegyi and the Milwaukee Public Museum and the work done there on visitor surveys. Borhegyi was a strong and effective advocate of visitor considerations in museum design and operation. His insightful papers on the topic ranged from use of exhibit design in relation to visitor use of space to testing a self-teaching exhibit case. A bibliography and anthology he prepared with Irene Hanson also served to give recognition to visitor research.[48]

Present Times: A Multitude of Evaluation Tasks

From the early 1970s to the present time, there has been considerable activity in museum visitor research. Consistent with the goal of enhancing the educational mission of museums, C. G. Screven has compiled an extensive bibliography of educational evaluation research in museums and a large proportion of the works cited have appeared since 1970.[49] He identifies several categories of research from the work of many investigators, reflecting a developing maturity in the field of visitor research. They provide a good synopsis of what has been going on in recent times:

1. *Evaluation research and methods* continue to be major concerns, with considerable interest in using formative evaluation to guide exhibit development. There is also interest in testing different kinds of interpretation features, to develop improved learning opportunities. Program evaluation is also included in this category. The main thrust of this research is finding out how well things work.

2. *Audience surveys* continue to be popular, with the descriptive study of visitors giving way to more marketing or community-based survey efforts. Major surveys that sample regional or national thinking about museums still seem to be more common outside the United States, with the exception of larger-scale surveys of fine arts audiences that sometimes contain limited information about museums.

3. *Behavior studies* of visitors to zoos, museums, and similar institutions are popular with some researchers and usually do not attempt to evaluate the setting, but concentrate on the descriptive studies of the ways in which people react.

4. *Experimental studies* attempt to control features of a situation, such as the type of field trip planned or the label format for an exhibit. While these studies contain evaluation, they try to control research variables so that it is possible to generalize beyond the specific situation being studied.

5. *Theory papers,* while not a common contribution, do appear occasionally. Theory issues may center on such topics as ways to evaluate an exhibit, prepare labels for visitors, or discuss visitor learning—a topic certain to stimulate theory discussions in the future.

Screven also cites a number of background references that, while not specifically about visitors, provide assistance for undertaking visitor research.

Another development that speaks well for visitor research is the commitment of individual institutions to *programmatic* use of evaluation research that extends over time and involves more than an isolated study. A recent article by Toni Gardner describes nine examples of such commitments that cover a variety of art, history, natural history and science institutions.[50]

One of the most significant institutional efforts has taken place at the British Museum (Natural History), where exhibit planning makes use of summative and formative evaluation. It was recognized that visitor learning from exhibits could not just be assumed to happen, and evaluation was needed to assess the potential for learning. What is especially significant is the use of evaluation for each exhibit planned for reinstallation.[51]

Edward Robinson envisioned a time when every major museum would have a staff person to evaluate visitor programs and experience.[52] To a great extent, his ideas have been realized through departments of education, visitor services, or community outreach. Visitor research has also evolved as a field of inquiry and, as Robinson hoped for, provides a source of help for those who work with the visitor.

NOTES

1. Laurence Vail Coleman, *The Museum in America: A Critical Study,* 3 vols. (Washington, D.C.: American Association of Museums, 1939), 1:3-44.

2. Coleman, *The Museum in America,* 2: 297-316.

3. See Susan Bertram, "Hard Times," *Museum News* 61 (February 1983): 20-25; Migs Grove, Sibil Walker, and Alexandra Walsh, "The Uses of Adversity," *Museum News* 61 (February 1983): 26-35.

4. Edward A. Suchman, *Evaluative Research* (New York: Russell Sage Foundation, 1967), p. 11.

5. Arthur W. Melton, *Problems of Installation in Museums of Art*, Publications of the American Association of Museums, New Series, no. 14 (Washington, D.C., 1935), pp. 8-13.

6. Carol H. Weiss, *Evaluation Research: Methods of Assessing Program Effectiveness* (Englewood Cliffs, N.J.: Prentice-Hall, 1972), pp. 6-9.

7. C. G. Screven, "Exhibit Evaluation: A Goal-Referenced Approach," *Curator* 19 (December 1976): 273-276.

8. Suchman, *Evaluative Research*, pp. 11-12.

9. C. G. Screven, "Exhibitions and Information Centers: Some Principles and Approaches," *Curator* 29 (June 1986): 109-137.

10. B. L. Driver, Donald Rosenthal, and Lynn Johnson, "A Suggested Research Approach for Quantifying the Psychological Benefits of Air Visibility," in *Proceedings of the Workshop in Visibility Values, Fort Collins, Colorado, January 18-February 1, 1979*, United States Department of Agriculture, Forest Service, General Technical Report No. WO-18, ed. Douglas Fox, Ross J. Loomis, and Thomas C. Green, Washington, D. C., August 1979, pp. 100-105.

11. Thomas J. Peters and Robert H. Waterman, *In Search of Excellence: Lessons from America's Best-Run Companies* (New York: Harper & Row, 1982), pp. 171-182.

12. Gary B. Cox, "Managerial Style: Implications for the Utilization of Program Evaluation Information" (Paper read at American Psychological Association Annual Convention, September 3-7, 1976, Washington, D. C.), 18 pp.

13. Marilyn G. Hood, "Getting Started in Audience Research," *Museum News* 64 (February 1986): 25-31.

14. Cox, "Managerial Style," pp. 5-9.

15. Cox, "Managerial Style," pp. 5-9.

16. Donald T. Campbell, "Reforms as Experiments," *American Psychologist* 24 (1969): 409-429.

17. R. Havelock, *Planning for Innovation* (Ann Arbor: University of Michigan, Institute for Social Research, 1971), pp. 3-27.

18. See Weiss, *Evaluation Research*, pp. 92-109. For a general discussion of museum leadership and evaluation, see Robert L. Wolf, "Enhancing Museum Leadership through Evaluation," *Museum Studies Journal* 1 (Spring 1984): 31-33.

19. Suzanne B. Schell, "Self-Study," *History News* 38 (October 1983): 13-16.

20. Suzanne B. Schell, "Taking a Hard Look: Strategies for Self-Study in Museums," *Museum News* 63 (February 1985): 47-52.

21. Gerald George, "Looking Forward: Professionals Examine Future Directions for Texas Museums," *History News* 38 (December 1983) 14-17.

22. D. Geoffrey Hayward, *The Quadrangle Research Notes: Springfield Library and Museums Association*, unpublished research report no. 1 (Northampton, Mass.: People, Places, and Design Research, 1982), pp. 2-6.

23. Benjamin I. Gilman, "Museum Fatigue," *The Scientific Monthly* 12 (1916): 62-74; Edward P. Alexander, *Museums in Motion* (Nashville: American Association for State and Local History, 1979), p. 12.

24. G. David and V. Ayers, "Photographic Recording of Environmental Behavior," in *Behavioral Research Methods in Environmental Design*, ed. W. Michaelson (Stroudsburg, Pa.: Dowden, Hutchinson, and Ross, 1975), pp. 235-279.

25. "The Boy Who Breathed on the Glass in the British Museum," drawn by H. M. Bateman. Published in *Punch*, October 4, 1916, p. 251; reprinted in *Curator* 11 (1959): 259-268.

26. Margaret Bouslough Parsons, "An Introduction to Museum Visitor Research" (Thesis, State University of New York at Oneonta, Cooperstown Graduate Program, 1975), pp. 1-8.

27. John Cotton Dana, *The New Museum* (Woodstock, Vt.: Elm Tree Press, 1917), p. 15; Charles L. Hutchinson, "The Democracy of Art," *The American Magazine of Art* 7 (August 1916): 398.

28. John T. Mason, *First Annual Report* (Denver: Colorado Museum of Natural History, 1901), p. 8.

29. Parsons, "Introduction to Visitor Research," pp. 3-5.

30. For an international annotated bibliography that combines visitor research with sources on museum education and social programs, see Ilse Baer, *Zur Offentlichkeitsarbeit der Museen* (Berlin: Verlag, 1978). See also Hans-Joachim Klein and Monika Bachmeyer, *Museum und Offentlichkeit: Fakten und Daten-Motive und Barrieren* (Berlin: Verlag, 1981), pp. 1-87.

31. Edward S. Robinson, "Experimental Education in the Museum: A Perspective," *Museum News* 16 (February 1933): 6-8; Barbara Y. Newsom and Adele Z. Silver, *The Art Museum as Educator* (Berkeley, Calif.: University of California Press, 1978).

32. Arthur W. Melton, "Studies of Installation at the Pennsylvania Museum of Art," *Museum News* 10 (January 1933): 8.

33. Refer to Table 1.2, Museum Architecture: (1) Edward S. Robinson, *The Behavior of the Museum Visitor*, Publications of the American Association of Museums, New Series, no. 5 (Washington, D. C., 1928), pp. 15-30; (2) Melton, "Installation at the Pennsylvania Museum," pp. 6-7; (3) Arthur W. Melton, *Problems in Art Installations*, pp. 92-150; (4) Arthur W. Melton, "Some Behavior Characteristics of Museum Visitors," *Psychological Bulletin* 30 (1933): 720-721. Museum Fatigue: (1) Robinson, *Behavior of the Visitor*, pp. 31-42; Melton, *Problems in Art Installations*, pp. 262-265; (2) Robinson, *Behavior of the Visitor*, pp. 48-52; Melton, *Problems in Art Installations*, pp. 187-214. Exhibit Installation: (1) Robinson, *Behavior of the Visitor*, pp. 43-52; Melton, *Problems in Art Installations*, pp. 151-186; (2) Melton, *Problems in Art Installations*, pp. 151-161; (3) Melton, *Problems in Art Installations*, pp. 218-252. Exhibit Interpretation:(1) D. D. Droba, "Effect of Printed Information on Memory for Pictures," *Museum News* 7 (September 1929): 6-8; (2) Arthur W. Melton, "Distribution of Attention in Galleries in a Museum of Science and Industry," *Museum News* 14 (June 1936): 8.

34. C. Hay Murray, "How to Estimate a Museum's Value," *Museums Journal* 31 (1932): 527-531.

35. Louis H. Powell, "Evaluating Public Interest in Museum Rooms," *Museum News* 11 (February 1934): 7.

36. Carlos E. Cummings, *East is East and West is West* (Buffalo, N. Y.: Buffalo Museum of Science, 1940), pp. 374-376.

37. Homer N. Calver, Mayhew Derryberry, and Ivan H. Mensh, "Use of Ratings in the Evaluation of Exhibits," *American Journal of Public Health* 33 (1943): 709-714.

38. Harris Shettel, "An Evaluation of Existing Criteria for Judging the Quality of Science Exhibits," *Curator* 11 (June 1968): 137-153.

39. Early evaluation work on children and museums included Katherine Gibson, "An Experiment in Measuring Results of Fifth-Grade Class Visits to an Art Museum," *School and Society* 21 (1925): 658-662; Marguerite Bloomberg, *An Experiment in Museum Instruction*, Publications of the American Association of Museums, New Series, no. 8 (Washington, D. C., 1929); Nita Goldberg, "Experiments in Museum Teaching," *Museum News* 10 (February 1933): 6-8; Arthur W. Melton, Nita Goldberg, and Charles W. Mason, "Experimen-

tal Studies of the Education of Children in a Museum of Science," Publications of the American Association of Museums, New Series, no. 15 (Washington, D. C. 1936). An early attendance summary was prepared by Paul Marshall Rea, "How Many Visitors Should Museums Have?" *Museum News* 8 (January 1930): 9-12. Reports on evaluation of gallery guides and pamphlets can be found in Robinson, *Behavior of the Visitor*, pp. 53-65, and Mildred C. B. Porter, *Behavior of the Average Visitor in the Peabody Museum of Natural History,* Publications of the American Association of Museums, New Series, no. 16 (Washington, D. C., 1938), pp. 16-27. An example of an early visitor survey was "Pennsylvania Museum Classifies its Visitors," *Museum News* 7 (February 1930): 7-8.

40. A number of papers and articles were prepared by Cameron and Abbey, with the Ontario survey summarized in three reports: David S. Abbey and Duncan Cameron, "The Museum Visitor: I-Survey Design," Reports from Information Services, no. 1 (Toronto: Royal Ontario Museum, 1959); Duncan F. Cameron and David Abbey "The Museum Visitor: II-Survey Results," Reports from Information Services, no. 2 (Toronto: Royal Ontario Museum, 1960); David S. Abbey and Duncan F. Cameron, "The Museum Visitor: III-Supplementary Studies," Reports from Information Services, no. 3 (Toronto: Royal Ontario Museum, 1961).

41. Arthur Niehoff, "Characteristics of the Audience Reaction in the Milwaukee Public Museum," *Midwest Museums Quarterly* 13 (1953): 19-24; Arthur Niehoff, "Audience Reactions in the Milwaukee Public Museum: The Winter Visitors," in *The Museum Visitor*, ed. Stephan F. de Borhegyi and Irene A. Hanson (Milwaukee: The Milwaukee Public Museum, 1969), pp. 22-31. A well-done survey of this time period is described in David Johnson, "Museum Attendance in the New York Metropolitan Region," *Curator* 12 (March 1969): 201-230.

42. Twenty studies of various trade fair audiences are listed in Pamala Elliot and Ross J. Loomis, *Studies of Visitor Behavior in Museums and Exhibitions: An Annotated Bibliography Primarily in the English Language* (Washington, D. C.: Smithsonian Institution, Office of Museum Programs, 1975). A critical review was provided by Vergil D. Reed, "Report and Recommendations on Research Methods Used to Determine the Impact of and Reactions to U. S. Official Exhibits in International Trade Fairs with Special Emphasis on an Evaluation of the Usual Methods as Applied at the Tokyo Fair" (Washington, D. C.: Office of International Trade Fairs, United States Information Agency, 1957).

43. Howard Leventhal and Patricia Niles, "A Field Experiment on Fear Arousal with Data on the Validity of Questionnaire Measures," *Journal of Personality* 32 (1964): 459-479; William Cooley and Terrence Piper, "Study of the West African Art Exhibit of the Milwaukee Public Museum and Its Visitors," in *The Museum Visitor*, ed. De Borhegyi and Hanson, pp. 144-165.

44. Hans-Joachim Klein and Monika Bachmeyer, *Museum und Offentlichkeit: Fakten und Daten-Motive und Barrieren* (Berlin: Verlag, 1981), pp. 57-59.

45. Two examples of this type of exhibition evaluation include James B. Taylor, "Science on Display: A Study of the United States Science Exhibit, Seattle World's Fair, 1962" (Seattle: University of Washington, Sociological Research, 1963); and Harris H. Shettel, Margaret Butcher, Timothy S. Cotton, Judi Northrup, and Doris Clapp Slough, "Strategies for Determining Exhibit Effectiveness," Technical Report no. AIR-E95-4/68-FR (Pittsburgh, Pa.: American Institutes for Research, 1968). This report is also available as ERIC Document ED 026718.

46. Shettel's approach to exhibits and visitor learning is well summarized in Harris H. Shettel, "Exhibits, Art Form or Educational Medium?" *Museum News* 52 (September 1973): 33-41, and in a vigorous exchange with M. B. Alt in *Curator*: M. B. Alt, "Evaluating Didactic Exhibits: A Critical Look," *Curator* 20 (September 1977): 241-258; and Harris H.

Shettel, "A Critical Look at a Critical Look: A Response to Alt's Critique of Shettel's Work," *Curator* 21 (December 1978): 329-345.

47. Screven's early work is well represented by C. G. Screven, "The Museum as a Responsive Learning Environment," *Museum News* 47 (June 1969): 7-10. A good review of Screven's work of the late 1960s and early 1970s is in C. G. Screven, *The Measurement and Facilitation of Learning in the Museum Environment: An Experimental Analysis* (Washington, D. C.: Smithsonian Institution Press, 1974).

48. Borhegyi's interests in visitor research are reflected in Stephan F. de Borhegyi, "Space Problems and Solutions," *Museum News* 42 (November 1963): 18-22; also Stephan F. de Borhegyi, "Testing Audience Reaction to Museum Exhibits," *Curator* 8 (March 1965): 86-93; Stephan F. de Borhegyi, "Test your Knowledge," *Midwest Museums Quarterly* 25 (1965): 10; and Stephan F. de Borhegyi and Irene Hanson, *The Museum Visitor: Selected Essays and Surveys of Visitor Reaction to Exhibits in the Milwaukee Public Museum* (Milwaukee: Milwaukee Public Museum, 1968). In addition, the February 1964 issue of *Museum News* carried a chronological bibliography of visitor studies, pp. 39-41.

49. C. G. Screven, "Educational Evaluation and Research in Museums and Public Exhibits: A Bibliography," *Curator* 27 (June 1984): 147-165.

50. Toni Gardner, "Learning from Listening: Museums Improve their Effectiveness through Visitor Studies," *Museum News* 64 (February 1986): 40-44.

51. R. S. Miles and M. B. Alt, "British Museum (Natural History): A New Approach to the Visiting Public," *Museums Journal* 78:4 (1979): 158-162; R. S. Miles, M. B. Alt, D. C. Gosling, B. N. Lewis, and A. F. Tout, *The Design of Educational Exhibits* (London: Allen and Unwin, 1982).

52. Robinson, "Experimental Education in the Museum," p. 8.

2

Evaluating Attendances: Making Figures Count

In an article titled "How Many Visitors Should Museums Have?" Paul Marshall Rea recognized, more than fifty years ago, the importance of evaluating museum attendance figures:[1] by collecting and interpreting attendance data, administrators could demonstrate accountability by showing how much a museum was visited by the public. Not only does evaluation of museum attendance provide evidence of community use; it can also help document the impact of changes in museums, such as new or expanded collections, new buildings or galleries, publicity campaigns, special events, educational programs, or experiments in marketing.

Effective evaluation of attendance figures depends upon the effectiveness of the method used to record the number of visitors in order to use the method most appropriate for a particular situation. Once attendance figures are collected, they must be organized to make interpretation possible. Such routine steps as checking for inaccuracy of figures or noting the distinction between visits and visitors will improve the accuracy of figures being evaluated.

Attendance evaluation can also help in planning a more extensive survey of visitors. For one thing, attendance variations evident at different seasons of the year should be taken into account in determining samples to use in a questionnaire or an interview survey. And a well-documented attendance evaluation can help determine the kinds of questions to be used in a survey. For example, what kinds of visitors come during peak or low attendance periods? How did tourists learn about the museum and find their way to it? These are two examples of survey questions closely tied to attendance patterns. Using attendance figures as an evaluation component is the first step toward knowing the audience who make museums a part of their lives. And how does one collect attendance figures? Seven methods are listed below.

Seven Methods for Collecting Attendance Figures

Attendant counts. Perhaps the most common method for collecting attendance figures is to have an attendant record the number of visitors seen entering the museum. Receptionists, volunteers, guards, and museum shop attendants are often called upon to operate a hand counter or other means of keeping a daily running tally of the museum's visitors. There may be considerable variation in counts—not simply because of different methods used by different attendants, but also because of different practices needed to count users of separate entrances for business visits and those attending special programs or events separate from actual gallery traffic.

Electromechanical counts. A second common method is use of mechanical or electromechanical devices to record attendance. Turnstile counters, devices activated by foot traffic, and photo-eye counters are common substitutes for human observers. As with human attendants, mechanical devices can be prone to errors. Adventuresome children may discover a photo-eye cell system and enjoy running up a "good" score by dashing back and forth within its range for a while.

A hodometer gallery. A third method is the hodometer gallery—really an elaborate application of electromechanics and more of a research tool than a practical means of recording attendance. Conducting such research, which he later wrote about, Robert B. Bechtel placed pressure-sensitive pads underneath the entire floor of a small art gallery and recorded visitor movements. Through this device, which he called a *Hodometer,* it was possible to estimate not only attendance, but the pattern, amount, and rate of visitor movement throughout the entire gallery.[2]

Simple observation is a fourth and much more practical method of counting visitors.[3] Obviously, attendant counting of visitors is a form of observation, but a distinction is intended with this fourth method: here, observation involves some preplanned system for coding observations. One of the simplest systems is to have observers note, for example, whether visitors appear to be alone or in a group. Such a system of observation can reveal ways in which both group and individual attendance patterns change across the months of the year. Sex and age estimates can also be made through observation.

Simple observation may involve developing special indicators of visitation. In a study at the Denver Museum of Natural History, this writer and Carl F. Hummel noted the home state (or county, for in-state vehicles) origin of automobiles parked in visitor areas of that metropolitan museum.[4] Visitors' auto tags were checked twice a day, to get a sample of morning and afternoon visitors. The auto-plate survey was undertaken at an opportune time, since there had been a gasoline shortage the previous summer. A question of interest to the museum administration was whether people from outlying areas some distance away would use private vehicles to get to the museum, as had been true in the past. In this tally, the unit of measure was not *visitors*, but *registration origin of vehicles*. Any museum dependent upon tourist travel could find the auto-tag tally a simple, low-cost way to find out where visitors are coming from, and could estimate the general rate of visitation for any setting highly dependent upon automobile transportation. A running record of school buses in the parking lots could also be kept in such a tally.

Visitor registers—entries in a guest book or guest register—can provide both a running estimate of attendance and indicate visitors' places of residence. Obviously, there is a selection process operating in terms of visitors who are willing to "sign in." Placing guest registers in easily seen, well-lighted locations can encourage their use. Cards with blanks for visitors' comments or guests' registration can be used instead of a register or a guest book. Cards may be handed to visitors by attendants or volunteers or enclosed in guide-pamphlets.

One variation of the registration book for visitors is a U.S. map, on which visitors are asked to place a pin in the name of the place they are from. While such a device will not be helpful in recording the number of visitors in groups attending from the same place, it does give an estimate of attendance and geographical background of the general visiting audience. Multiplying the number of pins by a factor of two or three could compensate, to some extent, for the fact that most visitations to museums are made in small groups. Registers can also yield some evaluative comments from guests, although such comments are often somewhat superficial.

Paid admission. Probably one of the most accurate methods available is through paid admission data. Cash register receipts or ticket stubs can provide a very useful running record of attendance, although care should be taken in interpreting attendance trends this way soon after instituting a fee for admission: what might be interpreted as a drop in attendance due to a new system of fees could really be sounder figures reflecting a more accurate system of counting visitors. Attendance on free days, group admission tickets, and annual membership programs that provide free daily admissions are all factors that could interfere with the accuracy of using admissions revenue records as an indicator of attendance; but correction values for these factors can be estimated, so that records for paid admissions will reflect a fairly accurate running tally of audience support for a museum.

Archival records are the seventh key to attendance figures. Sometimes meaningful sources of information have already been collected and put in storage. Such sources as past attendance-count summaries and/or older guest-register books can sometimes provide practical answers to questions about attendance over extended periods of time, indicating the best periods to schedule special events, such as traveling exhibits, for maximum attendance. Archival records can also provide documentation as evidence of accountability. For example, an analysis of records kept for the scheduling of nearly three thousand school tours to a natural history museum in an urban location revealed a number of trends, such as the relative popularity of different tours and the location of the school scheduling each tour.[5] A major use of the organized school-tour data was to show officials of the school system and the city the impact of the school group visitation program. In numbers alone, the program represented about fifty thousand visitations annually. This sort of information is very useful in talking with government executives and school officials about the scope and the impact of museum programs.

Other running records that may be discovered in archival materials include visitors' addresses, required by some museums when visitors check out audiophones or other self-guidance devices. These records not only indicate the extent to which the audiophone system is used; they also show the geographic distribution of visitors and possibly the change in number of tourists or out-of-town visitors throughout the seasons of the year. Naturally, these data and any interpretation based on them are limited to those visitors who use the self-guidance system. Such visitors, by their interest in additional interpretation, are an important group to document. As with all archival materials, an important advantage to these specialized records is their low cost, since the actual data have already been collected.

There is the possibility of error associated with most of the methods used to count visitors to museums. Error may take the form of bias sampling, as is true of registers that reveal only those visitors who take the time to sign them. Error can also occur when the attention of attendants doing the counting is diverted or disrupted and they miscue in tallying. Attendance data can be very useful, despite the possibility of error, and methods for checking attendance figures for accuracy appear in the last part of this chapter.

Organizing Meaningful Attendance Figures

Reams of accumulated attendance data stored *somewhere* within a museum do no one any good, however, until they can be brought to light and organized in ways that can justify programs and/or suggest helpful changes.

Attendance data are routinely organized in two principle ways: either as running records, or as limited-duration special studies. Running or continuous records may span many years, and some museums can trace annual attendance back to the year in which the institution was chartered. Typically, running-record attendance data serve an evaluation purpose of accountability. Trustees, school boards, program sponsors, and government officials are all possible reviewers of this continuous kind of information about visitation.

By contrast, organizing attendance data into specific studies can provide important insights and technical assistance. Short-term evaluation projects may help a museum staff plan programs by yielding specific information about attendance.

Running Records and Attendance Trends

Time-period trends. One of the most basic ways of organizing museum attendance figures is by each hour of public operation. Hourly counts are somewhat costly to take and may not be necessary, unless such program features as live demonstrations or lectures are used. Science centers, parks, and historical sites might also find it useful to know hourly crowd flow statistics, so that optimal scheduling of presentations can be made.

An alternative to keeping an hourly count is simply to *estimate* the hourly flow by subjecting the *daily* count to a formula suggested by Duncan F. Cameron and David S. Abbey:

$$\text{Turnstile Traffic Per Hour} = \frac{\text{Daily Visitor Count}}{\text{Total Public Hours (Daily)}}$$

This formula could be used with daily totals already collected to determine periods of heavy use when additional demonstrations might be scheduled.[6] It is not possible from this estimation to discover what hours during the day might be the most used by visitors.

It may be desirable to organize attendance by days of the month, in order to make comparisons, such as weekday-to-weekend rates of visitation. Usually, attendance is summarized for a given day, and it is easy to go back and look at daily figures. As with hourly data, the most useful function of daily attendance figures may be to anticipate staff and program needs for peak periods of visitor use and avoid overstaffing during slack times. Keeping track of hourly attendance requires special effort that may be practical for only the limited time period required to do a special study of attendance.

For many situations, the most useful time period is monthly, with attendance figures reported across years (see figure 2.1). Data like these can be used to detect long-range growth or decline in attendance and also to reveal seasonal changes in attendance—very useful information for planning.

Louis Powell years ago realized and wrote about the usefulness of organizing monthly attendance data and provided an example that is still very helpful.[7] Powell combined attendance in general with weather information, formal group attendance data, and visitor registration that showed which visitors were local and which were from out of town (see figure 2.2).

The evaluation use to which Powell put these attendance trends is of interest here. By organizing his measures into a number of indicators, Powell was able to set up an annual planning guide for managing periods of group visitation and staffing for the highest periods of general attendance. He was struck by the predictable annual pattern of attendance and the fact that *group* and *general audience* peaks did not occur at the same times. This lag in high-use periods permitted staff members to alternate between school group and general audience needs. Powell also felt that weather played an important role in encouraging both of the high attendance peaks for general visitation. Also, by determining when tourists are in attendance, Powell and his staff were able to identify times when the exhibit program should remain fairly static and other times when specific lectures could be used to provide changes and new features for local visitors.

Gallery load trends. An alternative to emphasizing time intervals as a means of organizing attendance data is to calculate gallery-load trends.

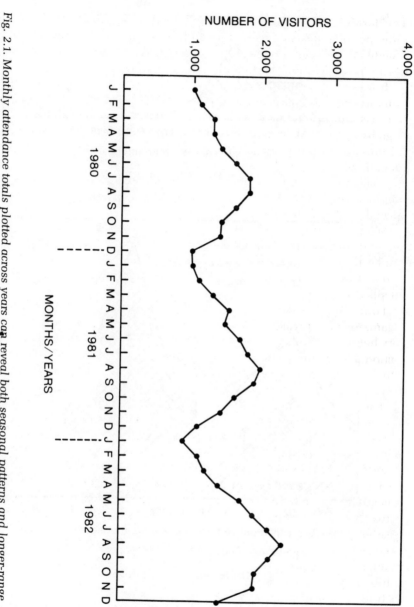

Fig. 2.1. Monthly attendance totals plotted across years can reveal both seasonal patterns and longer-range growth or decline in attendance.

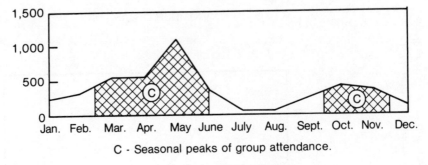

C - Seasonal peaks of group attendance.

GROUP ATTENDANCE

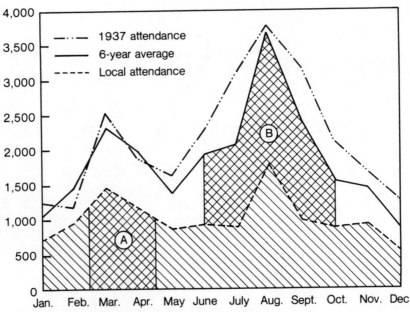

A - Local attendance peak following end of severe weather.

B - Tourist peak. August has brief local peak.

GENERAL ATTENDANCE

Fig. 2.2. Attendance patterns organized to show seasonal trends of group and general audiences. Note that peak periods, local attendance, and a six-year average are also indicated.—Reprinted, by permission, from Louis L. Powell's "A Study of Seasonal Attendance at a Mid-Western Museum of Science," Museum News 16:3 (1939): 7.

This estimation can be useful in situations where there is seasonal fluctuation in attendance and/or live demonstrations, films, or other special events used as part of a museum's programs. Gallery-load trends can be a technical-assistance evaluation to help plan programs that make maximal use of attendance patterns.

As a rule, gallery-load calculations are based upon hourly tallies of attendance. It should be noted that archival records of hourly attendance, if they exist, can be analyzed to reveal past trends. Cameron and Abbey, in their work with attendance statistics, suggested using the following formula to estimate visitation per thousand square feet of gallery space:[8]

$$\text{Gallery Traffic Per 1000 Sq. Ft.} = \frac{\text{Visitors Per Hour}}{\text{Total Square Feet of Exhibit Space}} \times 1000$$

If hourly attendance figures are not available, one could estimate the hourly rate called for in the formula by dividing daily attendance by hours of operation or take the time to collect a sample of hourly figures. If the formula is calculated on a daily basis, a seasonal pattern should emerge that will identify those periods of highest gallery traffic. Such periods are good times for special events or additional activities to accommodate larger crowds and also increase the number of people who attend such events. Calculations made every hour can reveal a pattern throughout the day and identify daily periods of highest and lowest use. Identifying low gallery use times could suggest that some operating hours are not really necessary and that other hours should be expanded. Identifying hours of maximal use can help in arranging staffing patterns for security and live presentations.

Larger museums with multiple galleries can calculate individual gallery attendance. Michael O'Hare writes about visitor behavior in an art museum, after conducting a special study of gallery-attendance load by having guards take readings every fifteen minutes for a minimum of fifty days out of the year.[9] His work is a good example of the practice of taking a limited number of time samples when a running record of attendance by gallery was not available. The requirement of fifteen-minute readings would be excessive for most running-record tallies, but would be acceptable on a short-term basis, and his study was conducted in an art museum, where it is common to have attendants stationed in each gallery. Patterns of attendance could be compared on a gallery-by-gallery basis; O'Hare's data, for example, revealed that gallery utilization declined in proportion to distance from the museum entrance.

This writer performed a simplified version of the method used by O'Hare for adaptation to a science museum.[10] In this case, one individual walked through the   museum on an hourly basis and recorded the number of people in each gallery. The direction of the walk and the time (on the hour or the half-hour) sampled were randomly mixed during course of the study. The study was performed on randomly selected days during a peak-visitation season. Results showed which galleries usually had the most and least numbers of visitors, and the pattern of visitation throughout the hours of the day was also described. A number of practical decisions for operating a museum can be related to the hourly gallery-load data. For one thing, museums that install participative exhibits have a crowd-pacing problem, in dividing large groups of people into "viewer-sized" units, since such exhibits often can be operated by only one or two people at a time. Crowding in some galleries could be reduced by limiting the number of interactive exhibits and adding visual material to occupy the time of those waiting their turn. Museums sometimes use live demonstrations, and the gallery-load data this writer has collected supported scheduling concurrent presentations when the museum was very busy. Holding demonstrations in galleries less often visited could also balance building loads during peak attendance time. It did not take a major investment of staff time to collect gallery-load data that provided technical assistance for scheduling and planning programs.

Combining Indicators of Attendance

As a rule, it is helpful to use more than one indicator of attendance based on running records. In an example already mentioned—Louis Powell's work on seasonal attendance—recall that Powell kept track of attendance by group as well as by individual and differentiated between local people and tourists visiting. Table 2.1 reveals a number of ways in which records can be organized into indicators that would give a fairly complete annual summary of attendance. All of these indicators used together are probably more than the average situation would require. Which indicators are actually used would depend upon what kind of evaluation is needed, as well as what methods of attendance-recording are available and in use.

Figures shown in Table 2.1 have been organized for a hypothetical museum with 40,000 individual visits recorded. This organization is based on the work with attendance statistics (noted earlier) by Cameron and Abbey.[11] The hypothetical museum was supposedly established in a community of 66,000. By asking visitors to indicate whether they were

Table 2.1
**Suggested Indicators for a Complete Annual Summary
of Museum Attendance**

Total Voluntary Visits:	40,000	
Total School Group Visits:	12,360	Number of Tours: 412 (average of 30 per tour)
Total Other Organized Visits:	3,225	Number of Tours: 159 (average of 20 per tour)
Subtotal (voluntary and group):	**55,585**	**Number of Tours: 571**
Total of Special Group Events:	3,225	Number of Events: 129 (average of 25 per event)
Grand Total of Museum Utilization:	**58,765**	**Groups/Events: 700**
Annual Hourly Turnstile Rate:	15	
Gallery Traffic per 1000 sq. ft./hour:	6	
Local Response	11.7%	
Local Voluntary Visits:	21,000	
Nonlocal Voluntary Visits:	29,000	
Rate of Repeat Voluntary Visits:	2.72	

Source: Adapted from Duncan F. Cameron and David S. Abbey, "Toward Meaningful Attendance Statistics," *Bulletin of the Canadian Museums Association*, no. 12 (1960), pp. 6-10. See text, pages 40, 44-46, for various indicators.

local residents or from outside the community, it was possible to record the 21,000 local-visit figure. In addition, by finding out from visitors how many previous visits they had made, an average could be calculated— shown in Table 2.1 as the repeat visit rate of 2.72. By dividing local visitation (21,000) by the repeat-visitation rate (2.72), the number of *different* local visitors could be estimated (7,721); and dividing this number by the community population (66,000) yields an indicator of local response. In Table 2.1, this figure is a percentage—11.7 percent; that is, it is estimated that about 12 percent of the local population visited the museum during the past year.

Unless visitors are required to register and list place of residence as well as number of previous visits during the year, it would not be possible to do the kinds of calculations shown in Table 2.1 without sampling visitors from time to time to determine the rates for local and repeat visitors. If such information cannot be collected all the time, occasional sampling can suffice to estimate these rates. In fact, even reported figures on previous visits have to be treated as estimates, since some visitors will have trouble remembering for certain when, or just how many, previous visits have been made.

The hourly turnstile entrance attendance shown in Table 2.1 is also an estimate. To arrive at the figure of 15 shown on the table, the 40,000 total voluntary visits was divided by 2600, used to represent the museum being opened an average of 50 hours each week of the year. Note that hourly turnstile traffic becomes 22.6 if the total museum attendance for all reasons is included; and the value drops to 21.4 if school tours and other organized visits are used but attendance to events other than gallery tours are excluded. Keep in mind that this rate of hourly turnstile traffic is an *average* and not an indicator of high and low hourly use.

The turnstile traffic indicator is the numerator of the gallery traffic formula discussed above. Suppose that the hypothetical museum had 2500 square feet of gallery space. Applying the gallery traffic formula from page 43 to the hourly turnstile rate based on 40,000 voluntary visits would yield a gallery traffic estimate of six visitors per 100 square feet per hour. If the total of voluntary and group attendance figures is used (shown in Table 2.1 as a subtotal of 55,585), the rate of gallery traffic will be higher, as a figure of 8.5 is obtained. Since the presence of groups in a gallery is a definite factor in crowding, the latter figure is appropriate to use in estimating overall gallery load.

It is possible to look at annual attendance by voluntary attendance, total school visitation, other visitation by organized groups, and event visitation to programs and meetings with the Table 2.1 indicators suggested by Cameron and Abbey. This last figure is kept separate, since it does not necessarily entail use of the gallery space. A grand total combines both voluntary or general visitation with organized group visits and attendance to special events. Group use of the museum is also shown by three different totals for a number of school tours, other organized groups, and annual events.

Often, attendance figures are reported as a factor of both budget projections and goals set for the museum. Museums that are part of a larger public institution, such as a city government, may have to show accountability with information that combines indicators of attendance with stated goals or objectives for a given year. Figure 2.3 displays monthly percentages for each of three attendance indicators (total museum utilization, total guided tours, and number of program events) and budget expenditures. The illustration was set up as "in progress" and follows through the month of September. It is possible that some indicators will go above the goal projected for a given year, and that can be shown in this procedure. It can be seen that the three indicators move toward the annual goal at different rates: tours showed a major advancement in the spring, while voluntary visits increased the total museum utilization indicator during summer months. The events indicator (in terms of number held) climbs at a fairly regular rate because staff intentionally space the timing of events across the months of the year.

Since the data of figure 2.3 comprise monthly reports, it can be helpful to have a short, to-the-point narrative accompany them for busy administrators to read. The narrative is needed to point out why the attendance and group use figures are changing at the rates shown. *It is important not to overemphasize numbers while informing key decision-makers about qualitative things that are happening.* Thus, accounts of special shows, changes in the museum, and school tour use can be described in the narrative. The monthly narrative should also call attention to the volunteer hours donated each month, as a reminder that the public described in the data could be served only with community volunteer help.

While the particular procedure just described came about because of government demands for accountability, staff members learned to use the indicators for technical assistance in overall planning.[12] For example, planning special exhibits and events could be done not only on the pattern of last year's trends, but with an additional event or two included in later months of the year if attendance and budget figures were running behind expectation. The success of encouraging school personnel to schedule fall tours can also be monitored in the attendance summary.

The need to interpret trends. To make any of the attendance indicators based on the running record meaningful, it is necessary to monitor them over time. All of the specific examples discussed thus far can, in one way or another, involve looking for *trends* in attendance data. There are, however, a number of caveats to be watched for when considering

	TOTAL MUSEUM ATTENDANCE	GUIDED TOURS	PROGRAMS/ EVENTS	EXPENDITURES
	58,765	571	215	Approx. $140,000
ABOVE GOAL 100%				
90%	51,126 - 87% Sept.			
80%	47,012 - 80% Aug.	463 - 81% Sept. 451 - 79% Aug. 423 - 74% July 405 - 71% June	183 - 85% Sept.	
70%			155 - 72% Aug.	
60%	37,021 - 63% July	343 - 60% May	129 - 60% July	77,959 - 56% Aug.
BELOW GOAL 50%	27,619 - 47% June	263 - 46% April	110 - 51% June 99 - 46% May	68,931 - 50% July 59,107 - 43% June
40%	21,743 - 37% May		71 - 33% April	49,477 - 36% May
30%	15,279 - 26% April	160 - 28% March	52 - 24% March	35,752 - 29% April 26,677 - 23% March
20%	10,578 - 18% March			
10%	5,877 - 10% Feb. 2,938 - 5% Jan.	69 - 12% Feb. 23 - 4% Jan.	32 - 15% Feb.	15,394 - 14% Feb.

Fig. 2.3. Example of plotting monthly attendance and budget indicators as a function of predetermined goals.

attendance trends. For one thing, what appears to be a trend may in reality be only a random or chance fluctuation around an average that is remaining constant or changing very slowly.

Another potential problem for interpreting trends is attributing the cause of any changes not due merely to chance fluctuations. While the staff naturally would like to consider any positive growth in attendance as the result of museum programs, such gains may in fact be due to the opening of a new shopping center in the area or a change in highway routes. Declines in attendance may also be due to factors apart from the museum. Over the years, for example, declining school-group attendance has reflected fuel conservation and cost-cutting decisions by school systems more than it has indicated a change in the way people evaluate the merits of a school visit to a museum.

A third potential problem with trend interpretation relates to the time interval used to sample a trend. Sufficient time should be allowed for assessing the effectiveness of changes, such as the addition of evening visitation hours. Efforts to recruit new audience segments for a museum may also take time to bear fruit. Word of new opportunities and experiences typically circulates on a person-to-person basis in addition to whatever formal program of publicity is undertaken. Thus, time is needed to pass the word around and give any innovative process time to take its course. What appears to be the absence of a trend may eventually turn out to be a viable change if observed over a long enough time period.

A number of sophisticated techniques exist for determining whether real change is taking place in a museum's running record. A detailed account of such techniques is beyond the scope of this book, but some awareness of the possibilities is useful. One such technique is the *time-series* comparison. This technique provides a way of systematically testing for trends over a period of time by taking a series of measurements at different intervals. H. L. Ross and D. T. Campbell demonstrated that what appeared to be a reduction in the number of traffic deaths due to one state's tougher police enforcement policy was more likely to be part of a long-range decline in that area's traffic deaths possibly due to improved highway designs.[13] Only by checking a trend over an appropriate period of time could a better estimate of causation be made.

As mentioned earlier, museum running records such as those for attendance data can show considerable instability or fluctuation *that does not reflect real change.* Changes in museum audience policy might have little or no effect on attendance although, if one looked only at a short-

term fluctuation in attendance, the appearance of change would be evident. Similarly, there is a natural tendency for running data to recede
or "regress" from a high peak solely as a function of statistical dynamics.
At a practical level, museum attendance following an unusually high
period, caused by such things as a blockbuster temporary exhibit or a
higher-than-average number of visitors during tourist season, will appear
to be declining when, in fact, the figures are reflecting merely a return
to more normal levels. One should expect, therefore, that attendance
would drop after a very high year. Time-series analysis is one procedure
for detecting such sources of instability in attendance trends.

The real value of time-series analyses is to detect what might be causing a trend. After studies in that area, Gene Glass, Victor Willson, and
John Gottman suggest some specific ways of detecting causation through
time-series tests.[14] One could follow up Louis Powell's idea, mentioned
earlier, that weather was a factor in seasonal attendance fluctuation. Such
an analysis would be testing for concomitant variation: do weather
changes influence museum visitation? Chances are, they do, as Powell
suspected; and a time-series tested trend can document the ways in which
seasonal weather shifts, including rainy Sundays, influence museum-
going in a specific community. Glass, Willson, and Gottman also explain
that time-series analyses are well suited for after-the-fact or archival
attempts to identify causation in trends. The use of existing records of
past attendance throughout years or months can be subjected to a time-
series breakdown. Past changes in museum practice, or major develop-
ments in buildings, collections, exhibits, and/or programs can be treated
as experimental interventions, and thereby some estimate of cause and
effect can be secured.

Planned changes to come can also be investigated by the time-series
technique. For instance, initiation of evening hours, or an experiment with
different times for free admission—if there is an admission charge—are
innovations that could be evaluated by taking observations of attendance
for periods before and after a change was initiated.

Use of time-series comparisons can present some technical problems,
and for that reason professional guidance in applying them is advised.
Sophisticated evaluation tools do exist for testing the validity of changing trends, whether in attendance rate or some other audience measure.
Use of these techniques can enable museum staff members to evaluate
the results of various tests or trial runs with visitation variables—such
as changed hours, new education programs, publicity in the media, or
a branch location.[15]

While the use of formal techniques for determining the validity of
attendance trends just mentioned may not prove practical in every set-

ting, one means of estimating whether a trend is occurring is available to anyone—thanks to the invention of the modern pocket calculator. Any calculator with functions for business analyses is likely to have instructions for performing a trend analysis. Attendance figures can be subjected to this analysis and checked against projections of what a continuing trend should look like. A specific illustration of checking trends can be provided by looking at attendance figures of twenty, eighteen, twenty-one, twenty-three, and twenty-two thousand visitors for each of five years for an imaginary small local museum. The figures do not appear to be changing much, and one could question whether the small museum is gaining attendance over the years. A projection of the next five years' attendance can be made with the trend analysis function of the pocket calculator and would be based on the five actual attendance tallies. Performing the analysis for the figures just given reveals that a growth rate of between 3 1/2 to just under 4 percent per annum would be needed to keep the trend established in the first five years. If such a trend continued, the museum would have an attendance of some twenty-seven thousand visitors by the fifth year. The point of this illustration is that *figures by themselves do not necessarily reveal a trend.* Highly dramatic changes may be self-evident, although their *actual* cause may not be so evident. More subtle changes can be overlooked, and an example of small changes in attendance was specifically chosen for this illustration.

Why should one bother with checking out trends, anyway? The whole exercise may seem a bit academic—and in many situations, it probably would be. However, there are likely to be increasing numbers of situations where a high degree of accuracy in reporting indicators of public accountability will be expected. The growing competition for public resources, often between agencies within the same community, is likely to stimulate requests for precise documentation of reported trends. Another reason for greater sophistication in reporting the direction of attendance figures is that government agencies may commission their own evaluation studies, which will use more sophisticated analyses of information about public use of museums. This last reason is typical of the modern-day interest in accountability evaluation where public funds are involved. The local museum whose income includes public funds may not have to render unto Ceasar anything but an accounting, but it may have to learn to live with Caesar's system of evaluating accountability.

Special Studies of Attendance

In contrast to an evaluation from running records, attendance can be evaluated for a specified period of time to provide information on topics such as the desirability of evening hours or the impact of admission fees on attendance. Short-term studies of attendance can provide technical assistance to help in decision-making and, in contrast to running records, may often entail collecting such detailed information as hourly attendance, since the effort is sustained for only a limited time.

Are evening visiting hours worthwhile? Kenneth Barton in *Museums Journal,* provides a good example of using specific attendance evaluation studies to adjust museum visiting hours for maximum visitation and more efficient scheduling of security personnel and building operations. His study, focused on a change in operating hours for different museums located in Portsmouth, England, was part of a comprehensive analysis of running records of attendance at that city's museums. It became evident from a comparative analysis of attendance at the different museums that some operated most efficiently with afternoon hours, while others needed evening access to draw the most visitors. In one instance, evening hours were changed from 6:00 P.M. to 8:00 P.M. and then, based on attendance assessment, were extended even later.[16]

Museologists have surveyed museums and visitors about the desirability of evening hours and found no clear-cut pattern of success.[17] That is why a specific study of changing operating hours is needed to decide whether evening hours are worthwhile in specific situations. Many factors can spell the difference between success or failure of evening hours, among them good use of publicity, a combination of such special programs as floor lectures and concerts, proximity to holiday shopping areas, dining facilities within the museum, a central location, tourist or holiday crowds, and activities of local clubs or support groups. An additional important point is made by those who have looked at the problem of evening hours: patience is often needed, to allow time for changes in museum opening hours to become known throughout a community. Rate of use may increase gradually, over time, and a premature cessation of evening hours could mask their ultimate success.

Evaluation of paid admissions. A good opportunity for studying attendance is the period just after an admission change has been instituted. In the last decade, more and more museums have found it necessary to charge admission. What do such charges do to attendance?

One evaluation method used surveys to ask people whether they were willing to pay admission. Tim Mason, for example, in a study at Manchester, England, found that 66 percent of the visitors surveyed at the

Manchester Museum indicated they would be willing to pay a moderate admission fee. He excluded students and old-age pensioners from the sample, since they would be logical groups to be exempt from a fee. Mason was aware of a major limitation in connection with this kind of evaluation: how could one know that people would *do* what they *said* they would do? The problem is not so much that people are inconsistent, as that they may judge things differently, from one situation to another. Thus, a person who is merely answering a survey question may honestly feel that a fee is justified, but when confronted with the request to *pay* admission, that individual may decide to spend the money on some other activity.[18] A better strategy than using survey results to determine any impact from admission charges is to treat the charge as a form of experiment and monitor attendance directly, to see who is coming and paying admission.

Duncan F. Cameron and David S. Abbey did such a follow-up survey after a minimal charge for adult visitors was instituted at the museum studied. Their findings suggested that the composition of the visiting audience in terms of education level, sex, and income did not appear to change after the fee was required. The researchers drew that conclusion because *they had comparative visitor-descriptive data that had been taken before the admission fee was started.* Earlier surveys had also measured the amount of money that visitors were willing to pay, and that information guided the decision to keep the admission fee quite low, a fact that may have contributed to the lack of change in audience composition before and after the fee was instituted.[19]

The Cameron and Abbey study revealed a major problem that is not unusual with evaluation of attendance: several changes occurring at the same time make it hard to know what incident most influenced attendance. In addition to initiating an admission fee, officials of the museum Cameron and Abbey studied also authorized a major construction job involving the entrance and made a change in the museum's visiting hours. For purposes of evaluation, it should be kept in mind that a number of visitor-related changes occurring in close time proximity will make it difficult to determine which one most influenced attendance.

In another study monitoring attendance before and after a fee was initiated, findings suggested that attendance could be adversely influenced by fees, at least on a short-term basis. Paul Huszar and David Seckler surveyed visitors at a California institution and monitored attendance in two-month periods before and after fees were charged. As in the Cameron and Abbey study, the amount of the fee instituted was not large. Young children continued to be admitted free. A dramatic drop in attendance occurred during the period of the investigation, but the authors were careful to note that *all* of the decline in attendance could not be attributed to admission fees. Charging admission provided a mechanism for a more accurate count than that obtained with the pneumatic foot-pedal counter previously used, and that accounted for some change. Also, a mild national economic recession appeared to reduce museum attendance in general throughout the investigation period. In spite of the attendance drop, the admission fees raised enough added revenue to remove an operating deficit and to pay for the cost of collecting fees. To that good news the investigators added other information, seriously questioning whether there was a net gain from the admission fees.[20]

For one thing, the authors pointed out that if a dollar value was given to the social cost of patrons not served because of lower attendance, such a cost would offset the increased revenue realized. Furthermore, their survey questions did show that local residents at lower income levels who walked or rode a bus to the museum used the museum less often after fees were charged.

The Huszar and Seckler evaluation suggested that admission fees might discriminate against citizens at lower income levels. Making museums less accessible by charging for admission is a major concern when use of fees is considered; but at least one study—conducted by Michael O'Hare—has suggested it may be possible to strike a balance between free accessibility and paid admission revenues.

Effective use of free hours combined with experimental use of different fee-collection methods could enable an institution to collect revenue while still permitting access to a fairly wide audience spectrum. Michael O'Hare experimented with admission costs, both as a problem of generating revenue and as a potenial barrier to museum attendance.[21] What makes the O'Hare study a good example of museum evaluation is that it begins with a set of clearly articulated goals about the museum's attendance policies. Included in these goals were the establishment of open hours to maximize public use of the museum while at the same time encouraging attendance during hours of ordinarily low usage to achieve efficient operation. Another goal recommended collecting revenue from those able to pay, but providing access to those of limited financial means and even subsidizing specific groups to insure their attendance. One goal was to maximize, within limits, revenues realized from admission charges.

In contrast to what Huszar and Seckler reported, O'Hare indicated that it was possible to keep the existing level of attendance while increasing net revenue and paying for additional open hours from admission fees. A number of adjustments suggested by evaluation were made to accomplish these goals. Free hours were changed from Tuesday evening to Sunday when the study revealed that those using the Tuesday free admission were capable of paying a fee. Other adjustments included providing an admission subsidy, in the form of a five-dollar pass program, for students, artists, and the elderly; increasing evening hours; and raising the price of admissions. To estimate the effect of variables other than admission fees on visitation, O'Hare looked at a nine-year period that included years before there was an admission charge. A form of trend analysis was used to estimate ways in which evening hours, special exhibits, and the dollar amount of admission charges influenced monthly attendance. Significantly, the analysis also found that special exhibits did stimulate additional visits.

O'Hare also investigated the manner in which visitors responded to paying a voluntary fee for a special exhibit within the museum. Before O'Hare's study, the museum had requested voluntary contributions for some special exhibits as visitors entered the exhibit area. O'Hare changed the procedure so that the request for a contribution was made as visitors left the special show. In addition, a sign installed at the exit explained that the contribution could be whatever the visitor wished to give, listed the cost of a previous exhibit, and informed visitors of the ticket price for other popular leisure-time events. This procedure resulted in a modest increase in giving over the usual before-the-show collection at the entrance. It is important to point out that a sign at the entrance did inform incoming visitors that a contribution was expected. Unfortunately, it was impossible to determine from O'Hare's study whether it was the prompting of the entrance sign or the placement of the request for donations at the exit of a special exhibit that might have stimulated increased giving.

A number of other topics related to the admission charge could be studied through evaluation. In their survey, Huszar and Seckler kept track of the length of visits made and compared the average length of visit before and after institution of the charge. Since no difference was found in the visit lengths—visitors paying admission did not stay any longer than those not asked to pay—the authors questioned whether admission payment increases the perceived value of museum visitation.

Reduced vandalism is another topic that could be related to admission fees. Cameron and Abbey suggested in their admission charge study that the museum experienced less vandalism after the charge was instituted.

One benefit, reduced crowd levels, was documented by Huszar and Seckler in their study at the California Academy of Science. To the extent that admission fees reduced attendance, they *could* cause a positive side effect of lowering congestion and crowding in galleries.

The Milwaukee County Zoo may have devised an optimal balancing of the various benefits of admission charges and serving a broad public interest. Free hours are available at the zoo every morning for county residents. Those who come early are rewarded with free admission. The institution thereby has open access every day, yet collects revenue every day. The combination of free times and cost times also helps balance the crowd load between morning and afternoon hours.

Points to keep in mind in evaluting possible effects of admission fees on attendance are summarized below:

1. Surveys asking people whether they will pay fees, and how much, are a very limited method. If used, questions should be planned by marketing researchers who understand the problems associated with measuring willingness to pay and who know how to estimate what prices people will pay.[22]

2. Looking at running records of attendance before and after instituting a fee can reveal changes, provided enough time is allowed to determine long-range effects. It is possible for attendance to drop, at first, then increase as the public adapts to having to pay for what was previously free. Trend analysis is important, as is making sure that the running-record indicators of attendance report needed information.

3. Short-term descriptive surveys of types of visitors completed before and after initiation of admission fees can help determine what specific groups of visitors (i.e., repeat visitors, those of lower income, students, the elderly) are affected.

4. Many things—from weather to popular special exhibits—can influence attendance. For that reason, it is best to minimize the number of changes in public programming during the start-up period of an admission fee (or a major change in the level of fee asked) to permit evaluation of the admission charge.

5. Short-term experiments with signs to prompt donations, list free hours, and inform visitors of other admission-related topics can be useful planning tools, provided they are evaluated.

Changing methods for supporting cultural institutions—such as the use of cultural vouchers—may bring about new topics for evaluation. Museums of the future may develop visitor programs designed to attract voucher use by different community groups. Under a voucher system, public support for cultural programs would be given directly to the consumer rather than the institution that supplies cultural opportunities. In such a system, museums would need to encourage the public to invest their voucher support in the musem, and there would be some competition between various institutions.

Gary R. Bridge has studied ways in which a limited-voucher system might work. Ten community groups in New York City were given government funds that they could then direct according to member interests. The cultural interests available to the participants ranged across a variety of New York museums as well as a Botanical Garden and Zoological society. In addition, the type of contract with a cultural institution could range from payment of general admission fees to much more intensive services, such as study courses in and involvement with on-site museum training opportunities. The New York experience with a cultural voucher program described by Bridge revealed some interesting findings. First, the voucher money did seem to stimulate museum attendance from within groups of people who would not ordinarily use a museum. Among the community groups were Native Americans, elderly people, families with emotionally disturbed children, and various groups involved with youth and youth problems. Second, the community groups elected to use their voucher funds to procure more intensive experiences, such as museum courses and in-museum training, rather than general admission or special tours. Finally, Bridge reported that an effective management relationship between community groups and cultural institutions took only a few meetings to iron out problems.[23]

There are many pros and cons involved in a voucher program of public support. Perhaps what is most important to realize is that if a voucher system ever became widely used, museums and other institutions would then need to adapt to that form of financial support if they wished to participate and use evaluation information to insure the success of voucher-based programs.

Improving Evaluation of Attendance

Selecting appropriate methods for collecting attendance data, organizing attendance figures into meaningful indicators for running records and/or special studies are all important steps in making evaluation useful. A number of other things can also be helpful.

Check for Inaccuracy in Attendance Figures

It is wise to expect some error in whatever method for recording attendance is used, whether that method be mechanical counter, simple observation, guest registers, or something else. A short-term study of accuracy of counts should therefore be undertaken, whatever methods are in use. While every method can have some error, it is possible to determine the extent (as a percentage of reported attendance) and direction (over- or underestimation of actual attendance) of error. Two general sources of error should be kept in mind.[24]

First, errors can be constant or systematic in nature. Imagine a museum attendant or a guard stationed at the museum entrance to keep a tally on a hand-counter during a regular duty shift. Such a person may learn to anticipate the count as the crowd flow changes. Predictions made in this way may be conservative or liberal—underestimations or overestimations of crowd size—depending upon the person on duty. Boredom is likely to result in the attendant's recording a routinely high number when a crowd of visitors passes by and a routinely low number for light traffic. These predictable errors produced by anticipation and boredom can build up, over time.

Second, errors can be random or variable in nature. The attendant may be interrupted and the count lost for a while. Fatigue or distraction of attention can also produce variable error. Using different attendants may help counter individual sources of error, but can also produce variable error as different people perform the task.

Two procedures can help detect errors. First (for attendant-based counts), a second set of counts can be made of the same crowd by another attendant; or, for automated counts, a second mechanical counter may be used. These second countings would be made for a limited time and compared with the first or usual counts. The two counts should yield similar results, unless some error is detected.

Second, one method can be compared with another. Some museums use a back-up method, so there may already be a couple of sources of attendance data for the same time periods. If, for illustration, comparisons between mechanical counts and attendants' counts show that the mechanical count is always higher by 10 percent, it would then be possible to look for the reason for the discrepancy. It could be that mechanical factors or children playing with the automated counter caused the difference. If no cause is found, one choice would be to take the average of the two methods as the official count.

As another example, suppose a local historical house uses a guest register as the only means of attendance counting. Taking time to record actual counts of visitors entering over a series of sample periods might reveal that only about half the visitors sign the register. If it is not possible to use the more accurate, observed-count method permanently, at least the register number can be doubled to give a more realistic estimate of total attendance.

Another thing that can be done to improve accuracy of attendance figures is to discuss accuracy with staff members or volunteers who record attendance; they may be able to suggest ways of collecting a more accurate count, and they may also benefit from a full discussion of the problems of constant and variable error.

Finally, it may be necessary to change to a more reliable method. The turnstile counter used for years may be ready for retirement—or it may need overhauling. Guest-book registration may be too insensitive, and a more complete attendance count should perhaps be tried, instead. If there is a change in method, it is important to be aware that, in a trend analysis, a different way of counting visitors might look like a change in attendance behavior. It is not unusual in social science data for trends to be influenced by a different method for recording data.

Visits or Visitors?

Duncan F. Cameron and David S. Abbey focused on an important distinction when they observed that it is usually impossible to tell whether reported attendance figures are based on numbers of visitors or visits.[25] Most attendance data is not broken down in terms of first-time patrons and those who visited earlier in the same year. As a consequence, much of the attendance measured is really based upon the annual total of visits recorded, *not* on different visitors. Cameron and Abbey argue that this global or unrefined measure can obscure important features of attendance patterns. If attendance figures are used simply to estimate a rate of usage, counting visits is probably adequate. If, on the other hand, it is important to talk about the actual number of visitors, such as would be done in documenting that the museum is drawing more visitors, global attendance figures should be corrected for visitors repeating within the year. It can also be useful to know the rate of return visitors as mentioned earlier in the chapter. As a specific example, Cameron and Abbey determined from survey results of their interviews with visitors to the Royal Ontario Museum that attendance figures for the year of the survey could have overestimated the actual number of individuals using the facility by as much as 50 percent. Of their survey sample, 44 percent had visited the museum at least twice during a twelve-month period.

How much of a factor repeat visitors are in annual attendance data would vary with institutions. Those frequented by a large tourist audience would likely have a lower rate of repeat visitors.

Make Use of Existing Resources

A practical tip for undertaking any project in museum evaluation is to make effective use of existing resources, rather than treating evaluation as something totally different from other museum work. Existing records can be used to show past attendance trends for holiday periods and/or different seasons of the year. It may also be possible that usable records—such as a study of cultural institutions commissioned by a city government or chamber of commerce—may exist through community sources. Old copies of annual reports for a museum may also yield a running record of attendance figures across the years covered in the reports. Past copies of visitor registers may have been kept in storage.

Staff and/or volunteer time is another important resource to be used carefully in attendance evaluation. Help is needed to collect both running attendance data and limited or special study material. Collecting meaningful attendance data need not take a great deal of staff time. Even hourly counts can be sandwiched into the daily routine, for a limited period of time, in order to sample gallery loads and/or shifts in attendance during various periods of the day. A few minutes a day can add up to quite a bit of attendance data collected in a fairly short time. Attendants or volunteers who normally work in the galleries or at desks or counters in public areas are also an existing source of potential help in collecting various indicators of attendance. They can be used to prompt visitors to fill out guest registers, and they can take counts directly or read the tallies recorded on any mechanical or electromechanical counters being used.

Existing resources can also include people with time and/or expertise in preparing attendance data so that it can be useful for interpretation. Volunteers, or spouses of volunteers or trustees, may have training in the social sciences or in business management fields that could be useful in interpreting trends. If archival data sources are to be organized and interpreted, a volunteer project to do the task of coding and tabulating data could be instituted. Students from nearby schools may be looking for community projects that would enable them to practice skills in data analysis and interpretation. Social science programs and business schools are likely settings for finding such students, as well as faculty resource people who would lend their expertise in exchange for opportunities to give their students field or practicum experiences.

Museums linked to government agencies may also get evaluation help through staff and other resources, such as computer facilities attached to government agencies. Assistance in management-related evaluation may also be available through local banks and business institutions. A current trend in some communities is for business and commercial organizations to donate management assistance skills as a contribution to the community's cultural institutions.

An Attendance Evaluation Checklist

As mentioned earlier, many factors can influence museum attendance: special exhibits, including record-setting "blockbuster" shows; changes in the weather, including rainy days; onset of the tourist season; new admission fees; a remodeled building; a changed location; promotion and advertising; the school calendar; special events; free admission times. Visitation hours and holidays are just *some* of the things that determine how many visitors come through the doors on a given day. Evaluation is needed to determine which of these factors might be operating at a given time and help in making plans and decisions. Summarizing what is said here, the following checklist could be used to plan attendance evaluation for a specific museum.

Planning Attendance Evaluation

1. List the attendance recording method(s) (hand counter, guest registers, etc.) currently in use:

   _____

   _____

   _____

2. Is attendance recorded by ☐ visits? ☐ Visitors? ☐ Or both?
3. Has a check been made on the accuracy of any methods being used? ☐ Yes ☐ No
4. Has a search been made for any archival records of past attendance figures? ☐ Yes ☐ No
5. Have attendance figures been organized into useful running records of indicators, such as monthly totals or gallery-load trends? ☐ Yes ☐ No
6. Have trends in attendance indicators been plotted and analyzed? ☐ Yes ☐ No
7. Have special studies of attendance and operating hours or admissions fees been conducted? ☐ Yes ☐ No
8. Have staff and volunteer work assignments been reviewed for help available to better record and evaluate attendance? ☐ Yes ☐ No

NOTES

1. Paul Marshall Rea, "How Many Visitors Should Museums Have?" *Museum News* 8 (May 1930): 9-12.

2. Robert B. Bechtel, "Hodometer Research in Museums," *Museum News* 45 (March 1967): 23-26.

3. For a discussion of simple observation as a general method of evaluation, see E. J. Webb, D. T. Campbell, R. D. Schwartz, and L. Sechrest, *Unobstrusive Measures: Nonreactive Research in the Social Sciences* (Chicago: Rand McNally, 1966), pp. 112-141.

4. Ross J. Loomis and Carl F. Hummel, "Observations and Recommendations on Visitor Utilization Problems and Potentials of the Denver Museum of Natural History" (Working Paper no. 1, Denver Museum of Natural History, Denver, Colorado, 1975), pp. 3-5.

5. Ross J, Loomis, Carl F. Hummel, and Martha N. Hartman, "Archival Documentation of School Tour Utilization for a Natural History Museum" (Working Paper no. 2, Denver Museum of Natural History, Denver, Colorado, 1981), pp. 2-9.

6. Duncan F. Cameron and David S. Abbey, "Toward Meaningful Attendance Statistics," *Bulletin of the Canadian Museums Association* 12 (1960): 6-10. These authors distinguish between voluntary versus group visitors, a distinction that should be kept in mind when using the formula.

7. Louis H. Powell, "A Study of Seasonal Attendance at a Mid-western Museum of Science," *Museum News* 16 (June 1939): 7-8.

8. Cameron and Abbey, "Toward Meaningful Attendance Statistics, " p. 8.

9. Michael O'Hare, "The Public's Use of Art: Visitor Behavior in an Art Museum," *Curator* 17 (December 1974): 309-320.

10. Ross J. Loomis, "Visitor Floor Count in Selected Areas," Summer Working Report no. 6 (Oak Ridge, Tenn.: American Museum of Atomic Energy, 1977), pp. 1-5.

11. Cameron and Abbey, "Toward Meaningful Attendance Statistics," p. 10.

12. This example was provided by Brian Moroney, manager of the Fort Collins Historical Museum, Fort Collins, Colorado.

13. H. L. Ross and D. T. Campbell, "The Connecticut Speed Crackdown: A Study of the Effects of Legal Change," in *Perspectives on the Social Order: Readings in Sociology*, ed. H. L. Ross (New York: McGraw-Hill, 1968), pp. 30-35.

14. Gene V. Glass, Victor L. Willson, and John M. Gottman, *Design and Analysis of Time-Series Experiments* (Boulder, Colo.: University of Colorado Press, 1975), pp. 71-118.

15. Glass, Willson, and Gottman, *Design and Analysis of Time-Series Experiments*, pp.53-70. Helpful discussions on evaluation tools are found in Donald T. Campbell's "Reforms as Experiments," *American Psychologist* 24 (1969): 411-420; Donald T. Campbell, "From Description to Experimentation: Interpreting Trends as Quasi-Experiments," in *Problems in Measuring Change*, ed. Chester W. Harris (Madison, Wis.: University of Wisconsin Press, 1967), pp. 212-242. Other sections of *Problems in Measuring Change* describe additional methods for measuring change.

16. Kenneth Barton, "Recording Attendances at Portsmouth City Museums: The Method and its Effect," *Museums Journal* 73 (1974): 167-168.

17. See, for example, Erwin O. Christensen, "Evening Hours for Museums: A Preliminary Statistical Survey," *Museum News* 43 (November 1964): 40-41; also Arthur Niehoff, "Evening Hours for Museums," *The Museologist* 69 (1958): 2-5.

18. Tim Mason, "The Visitors to Manchester Museum: A Questionnaire Survey," *Museums Journal* 73 (1974): 153-157.

19. Duncan F. Cameron and David S. Abbey, "Museum Audience Research: The Effect of an Admission Fee," *Museum News* 41 (November 1962): 25-28.

20. Paul C. Huszar and David W. Seckler, "Effects of Pricing a 'Free' Good: A Study of the Use of Admission Fees at the California Academy of Sciences," *Land Economics* (1974): 364-373.

21. Michael O'Hare, "Why Do People Go to Museums? The Effect of Prices and Hours on Museum Utilization," *Museum* 26 (1974): 134-146.

22. See Philip Kotler, *Marketing for Nonprofit Organizations*, 2nd ed. (Englewood Cliffs, N.J.: Prentice Hall, 1982), chapter 13. This chapter provides an overview of decisions about pricing nonprofit services and opportunities and begins with an example of museum admission fees.

23. Gary R. Bridge, "Cultural Vouchers," *Museum News*, 54 (March/April 1976): 26-60.

24. See David D. Avery and Henry A. Cross, *Experimental Methodology in Psychology* (Monterey, Calif.: Brooks-Cole, 1978): 180-183.

25. Duncan F. Cameron and David S. Abbey, "Visits Versus Visitors: An Analysis," *Museum News* 39 (November 1960): 34-35.

3

The Visitor Survey

"While guessing, mixed with a small portion of common sense, would tell us that there is more than one kind of museum visitor, the same type of guessing might not fare so well in attempting to discover how many types of visitors there are." So said Edward E. Robinson, in "Exit the Typical Visitor," some years ago.[1]

Robinson was concerned that museologists would fall prey to the very common human tendency of stereotyping people. In this instance, that natural tendency was to draw a much too generalized picture of the museum visitor. Robinson questioned the utility of thinking in terms of a "typical" visitor. In reality, people bring with them to museums a broad continuum of interests and abilities. There is no easy, arbitrary way to divide such a continuum. Some kind of first-hand or empirical information about the visitor must be made available. A visitor survey conducted at the museum, or as a post-visit follow-up phone or mail effort, can provide such empirical information.

Years after Robinson wrote his warning about stereotyping the visitor, David S. Abbey and Duncan Cameron provided research evidence indicating that museum staffs may not always have accurate impressions about the visiting audience. In completing a survey of the Royal Ontario Museum audience, these investigators obtained estimates of visitor characteristics from about two-thirds of the museum staff. Results of the survey were still in preparation, so that there was no way staff members could have received advance information. A comparison between staff perceptions and the completed survey revealed some important differences. Staff members were low in their estimates of grade-level placement for school children visiting and the overall educational achievement of adults attending the museum. They also underestimated the percentage of visitors who walked to the museum from the local area. Perhaps even more important was these authors' observation that staff people were consistent in their perceptions of visitors, irrespective of the amount of actual visitor contact, years employed at the museum, or position of employment.[2] This latter observation is really at the heart of Robinson's concern. Staff people, without ever intending to do so, can form, encourage, and perpetuate among themselves images of the audience that misrepresent the visitors. An objective visitor-description survey can help correct many such misperceptions.

The following pages deal with planning a visitor survey, suggesting specific survey topics and providing an overview for completing an evaluation of the visiting audience.

As with attendance evaluation, a successful visitor survey can demonstrate accountability by providing a factual description of the public served by the museum. In addition, such surveys can inform the staff about the kinds of people their visitors are and outline some general visitors' reactions to the museum and its programs.

While visitor surveys have not always been used, or appreciated, there was early recognition in the United States of their useful potential. In the late 1920s, glowing claims were made for one of the very few intramuseum surveys then completed. Public-opinion measurement was a new fascination for American institutions and business corporations at that time. Fiske Kimball had undertaken a year-long audience survey for the Pennsylvania Museum of Art.[3] The survey asked respondents to describe themselves in terms of occupation, residence, and the means used to get to the museum, as well as factors that prompted them to make the visit. Museum features that they liked best were also recorded. Most intriguing about the reporting of this early visitors' survey was the positive reaction of newspaper editors to the effort. Their comments suggested that the museum had gleaned useful evidence demonstrating that an art museum was more than a tourist attraction, that it contributed daily to the educational and cultural life of the Philadelphia community. Commentators were particularly impressed with survey data that showed businessmen as a major visitor group to the museum. This finding challenged the stereotype that an art museum reflected only feminine interests and was used primarily by artists and students. Recall that *a major use of a survey is to challenge existing stereotypes about the visitor.* The Pennsylvania Art Museum survey also generated information about visitor preferences for educational programs, evening hours, and a number of other technical assistance topics.

Surveys Surveyed

While the visitor survey has been a popular evaluation tool in modern times, and the potentials for it envisioned by Kimball have been realized in many specific instances, it has also proved disappointing to some. As an example, Frank A. Taylor and Katherine J. Goldman were disappointed to discover that existing surveys by the late 1960s could not identify the percentage of visitors of pre-college age. Most surveys did not even include an age category for younger visitors. Taylor and Goldman were seeking survey information to document a thesis that pre-college-age science education was being provided to the public through museums. Unfortunately, the existing surveys of that time were of virtually no help in providing technical assistance on that point. Lack of standardization in survey questions was the major problem Taylor and Goldman encountered; and that remains true: because most museum audience surveys are idiosyncratic efforts undertaken by individual institutions, there is a lack of consistent format and information categories.[4]

The complaint about the lack of standardized procedures is echoed by Paul DiMaggio, Michael Useem, and Paula Brown, who reviewed surveys in the United States. These three researchers compiled results for a sample of surveys to reveal the average (median) values for a number of visitor descriptors (see Table 3.1).[5] Keep in mind that the values reported in the table are medians for the surveys reviewed. Just as important as the medians reported are the estimates of variability or range to the statistics summarized. For example, while the overall pattern was for 46 percent of the audience surveyed to be male, note from Table 3.1 that individual survey results ranged from 30 percent to 71 percent male respondents. This variability in visitor characteristics probably results from use of a mixture of differences in method in conducting the surveys and real differences in audience composition.

Some very real differences in audience composition probably exist between different museums. The DiMaggio, Useem, and Brown summary suggests, for example, that men may outnumber women attending science museums, while the converse is true for art institutions. It is unfortunate that there is not a better body of evidence to help us understand the nature of possible differences between museum audiences in the United States.

As a generalization, audiences attending the cultural institutions are better educated, are of higher occupational status, and experience greater incomes than the American population as a whole. Women may have

Table 3.1
Selected Median Demographic Statistics
for a Number of Visitor Surveys (Summarized)

Demographic	Median Percentage	Percentage Range
Men in Audience	46	30-71
Women	54	10-29
Education Level		
Below High School	9	4-57
Some or All of High School	27.6	8-69
Some College	72.3	30-93
College Graduate	41.1	10-66
Some Post-Graduate	17.5	6-35
Occupational Category		
Professional (Including Teachers)	42.2	12-73
Managerial	9.6	4-27
Teachers	23.1	15-33
Clerical and Sales	14.3	5-28
Blue-collar	8.5	0-45
Homemakers	14.5	6-26
Students	22	0-57
Retired & Unemployed	5	1-21
Age Level	Median Age	Range of Median Ages
	31	19-51
Income Level	Median Income	Range of Median Incomes
(1976 Dollars)	$17,158	$13,394–30,618

Source: Paul DiMaggio, Michael Useem, and Paula Brown, "Audience Studies of the Performing Arts and Museums: A Critical Review" (The National Endowment for the Arts, Research Div. Report no. 9, Washington, D.C., November 1978).

Note: Medians were compiled by DiMaggio, et al., across a number of different surveys they reviewed. An overall median and the range of medians across the different studies are both shown in the table. See text for details. The number of surveys sampled varied from characteristic to characteristic and ranged for figures in this table from 6 to 49 studies reviewed.

greater representation in the arts audience, but that is a tentative conclusion. Sex composition of audiences appears to vary from situation to situation. In general, the median age of the arts audience is fairly close to that of the nation overall, although the average museum visitor in general is somewhat younger than the national median age. Racial and ethnic minorities would appear to be underrepresented in the arts and museum audiences.

Most interesting is the observation that museum visitors may be a little more representative of the general American public than other arts or cultural audiences. Data of Table 3.1 can be used as a limited overview to the museum audience. DiMaggio, Useem, and Brown also caution that visiting groups can vary in composition from season to season, as well as according to the day of the week and time of day. This last caution is consistent with a point made earlier, on the importance of organizing attendance data to reveal trends. Not only is the audience changing over time periods in the rate of attendance; it changes also in terms of people who come in at different times.

There is a need for more standardized information based on samples taken at a number of museums. Hans-Joachim Klein has completed such a standardized survey for a sample of thirty museums in a region of West Germany. His report provides a good working example of the way a standardized survey program can provide the basis for noting general characteristics of museum audiences as well as identifying important differences between museums.[6] Information from this kind of evaluation can be used to develop marketing or audience development plans for the museums.

Topics For a Basic Visitor Survey

One reason that museum visitor surveys have not been standardized is that there are so many different topics that could be included in a survey. Thus, while readers are encouraged to standardize as many questions as possible with examples provided in this book or other surveys that have been done, it is also important to tailor a specific survey to the needs of a particular situation. Some suggested topics and examples of survey information gained from a variety of studies follow.

Donald Andrew Newgren, in "A Standardized Museum Survey . . . ," has emphasized that a visitor survey should gather decision-oriented information—information that should be gathered *in advance* of a forthcoming decision so that questions about the relationship of visitors to that decision can be answered. Newgren's philosophy is especially useful for technical assistance evaluation efforts where help in planning future program and exhibit activities is desired.[7]

And the present writer has noted that most museum visitor surveys have focused around descriptions of the visitor, descriptions of the visits, and general visitor reactions to the institution and to its exhibits, programs, and services.[8] These three categories of survey information can all help in making decisions for public programs and exhibits. Figure 3.1 displays a sample visitor survey with questions intended to measure each of the three categories of survey information. Readers are free to use some or all of the items shown, and when possible, the items have been standardized with Klein's work in West Germany.

Visitor Description

Most people are willing to provide information about themselves if they feel there is good reason for providing such information and if the questions are not offensive. However, there is a modern tendency to overburden the public with too many surveys and, not surprisingly, there is a growing resistance by people to participate. For that reason, survey questions should be selected carefully and related to information that can be of value. Visitor description can be broken down into two categories: general demographics and more specific visitor-background characteristics, including visitor expectations for the museum and the visit.

Demographics. Items one to five in figure 3.1 all ask visitors to describe themselves. For the sake of this discussion these items have been placed at the start of the sample survey, but in actual practice, some survey researchers prefer to ask demographic questions last. Two forms of questions have been included for items two and four, to illustrate that some researchers prefer to collect open-ended answers for these characteristics, while others prefer visitors to answer by indicating an alternative or category that is easy to tabulate. Open-ended versus structured or category questions is a basic choice in item preparation. The open-answer format lets a respondent provide a specific answer, but then the answers for all respondents must be organized and sorted into categories. For that reason, some prefer to organize the categories ahead of time, to facilitate quick scoring of answers. Still other researchers like using both question formats as a way of cross-checking the responses; or, in the case of naming hometown or city, as a means of performing a more detailed analysis of the place visitors are from.

One interesting variation of an open-ended question is asking visi-

Fig. 3.1. Sample questions for a basic visitor survey.

PART ONE: Visitor Demographics

1. What is your home residence?

   Town or city _____

   State or country _____

   What is your postal zip code? _____

2. What is your age? Please give exact years _____ and check the appropriate alternative below.

   ☐ 14-19 yrs.   ☐ 50-59 yrs.

   ☐ 20-29 yrs.   ☐ 60-69 yrs.

   ☐ 30-39 yrs.   ☐ 70-79 yrs.

   ☐ 40-49 yrs.   ☐ 80 and older

3. What is your sex?   ☐ Male ☐ Female

4. What is your occupation? Please indicate the name of your *primary* occupation

   _____

   and check the classification below that best fits your current employment:

   ☐ Professional   ☐ Homemaker

   ☐ Managerial   ☐ Student

   ☐ Clerical/Sales   ☐ Retired

   ☐ Labor/Technical   ☐ Unemployed

5. What level of schooling have you completed? (Check appropriate level.)

   ☐ 0-8 years

   ☐ 1-2 years high school (include junior high 9th grade)

   ☐ 3-4 years high school

   ☐ 1-2 years college

   ☐ 3-4 years college

   ☐ More than four years of college

   ☐ Other kinds of schooling—please specify: _____

PART TWO: Visitor Background/Expectations

6. Are you a member of this museum's member association?

   ☐ Yes   ☐ No

7. If you completed post-high school education, which *one* of the following fields best describes your academic major:

   ☐ Business/professional   ☐ Science

   ☐ Arts-humanities   ☐ Engineering

   ☐ Social sciences   ☐ Other

8. If you were visiting a city and someone suggested visiting a museum, which *one* of the following types would be your *first* choice?

   ☐ A natural history museum   ☐ A children's museum

   ☐ An art museum   ☐ A historical site or museum

   ☐ A technology/science museum

9. Below is a list of expectations one might have for a visit to a museum. Using a "1" for first choice, "2" for second, and so on, indicate the order of expectations you have for your visit:

   ☐ To add to my present knowledge

   ☐ To do something with others . . . to share an experience

   ☐ To be entertained

   ☐ To experience something different

   ☐ To see objects of great value

   ☐ Other (please specify) _____

PART THREE: Visit Description

10. Is this your first visit ever to this museum?

    ☐ Yes   ☐ No

    If you answered *No* to the above question, how many visits have you made in the *last year*? (Check one.)

    ☐ 0 ☐ 1 ☐ 2 ☐ 3 ☐ 4 ☐ 5 or more

11. Are you accompanied or alone in your visit today? (Check one.)

    ☐ Alone

    ☐ With a spouse or friend

    ☐ With a group of friends

    ☐ With a family group

    ☐ With a group of both family and friends

    ☐ As part of an organized tour group

12. How did you *first* learn about this museum? (Check as many alternatives below as apply.)

    ☐ Comments from friends or family

    ☐ Comments from employees at other attractions, hotels, or restaurants

    ☐ Read a magazine or newspaper article

    ☐ Saw an advertisement

    ☐ Read the museum's tourist brochure

    ☐ Read about the museum in a tourist guide

    ☐ Noticed a road sign for the museum

    ☐ Saw the museum building and stopped

    ☐ Other (Please specify.) _____

13. How did you get to the museum today? (Check one.)

    ☐ On foot (or bicycle)

    ☐ By private automobile

    ☐ By taxi

    ☐ By public transportation (bus, subway, etc.)

14. Of the possibilities listed below, check as many as you will include as part of today's activities.

    ☐ Visiting other museums

    ☐ Having lunch or dinner at a restaurant

    ☐ Shopping

    ☐ Sightseeing tourist attractions

    ☐ Completing a business engagement

    ☐ Visiting friends

    ☐ Other (specify) _____

PART FOUR: General Reactions to the Museum

15. For each set of words below, circle the one word of the two that best describes your impression of this museum:

dark - light	complex - simple
interesting - boring	clear - confused
new - old	unfriendly - friendly
cold - warm	stimulating - dull
small - large	

16. In a few words, describe the way you feel about your visit to the museum today.

_____

_____

_____

17. Using an "X," indicate in the appropriate spaces below your approximate degree of satisfaction with each museum feature listed on the left.

	Very satisfactory	Satisfactory	Somewhat satisfactory	Somewhat unsatisfactory	Unsatisfactory	Very unsatisfactory	No opinion
The museum shop							
Restaurant							
Information desk							
Gallery demonstration							
Courtesy of security guards							
Places to rest							
Direction and orientation signs							
Museum parking							

18. Below is a list of exhibits currently in the museum. Using a plus sign ("+"), indicate the exhibit you enjoyed *most* and using a minus sign ("−") indicate the exhibit you enjoyed the *least*.

☐ Early American Hall   ☐ Jones's Rifle Collection Exhibit

☐ Memories of the 1950s Exhibit   ☐ Nineteenth-century Exhibit

☐ Local History Hall   ☐ The Hall of Pioneers

---

tors for their postal ZIP codes. The postal service has maps showing where different zones are located. The postal ZIP code system is a convenient way to organize home-residence information, on either a national or a more local basis. Codes can also be useful for identifying percentages of visitors from different metropolitan regions. If a museum draws tax-based support from more than one government entity, it can be very important to show that visitors are coming from different tax districts or areas.

What is the most important information to learn about visitor demographics? The answer is highly dependent upon specific situations. But the visitor's sex, age level, occupation, and place of residence are all useful indicators. Their utility is increased if a survey can include more than one sample to detect change in audience composition for different time periods. Racial, ethnic, and/or religious backgrounds might be important demographic indicators if there is concern about the access of minority groups to the museum. Political affiliation indicators might make useful information for a museum devoted to the history of political parties and/or individuals. Membership in community groups (i.e., historical societies, service clubs, hobby groups) could be a useful indicator for a museum contemplating a membership drive. Identifying community groups that visitors already have membership in could suggest community sources for new members.

One obvious demographic variable that is not included in figure 3.1 is income. Some researchers feel that income is very difficult to interpret, since there is wide disparity in salaries paid for different jobs. A semiskilled worker with minimal formal education in a union job may make a higher salary than a professional with graduate training who works in a museum. Residence, level of education, and type of occupation tend to be more useful sources of information than income. Another problem involving income figures is that some people are hesitant to give this kind of information; and people with either very high or very low incomes may, instead of listing the actual amount of income received, report what they perceive to be a typical middle-income figure. If income is called for, it is very important to make it clear whether individual or household income is to be reported. A structured income question could be:

Please check the alternative below that represents your gross annual household income last year.

☐ under $5,000   ☐ $40,000 to $49,999
☐ $5,000 to $9,999   ☐ $50,000 to $59,999
☐ $10,000 to $19,999   ☐ $60,000 to $69,999
☐ $20,000 to $29,999   ☐ $70,000 to $79,999
☐ $30,000 to $39,999   ☐ $80,000 and over

One general use of demographic information is to compare results with local and/or national census data. Demographic comparisons can inform museum staff members of the degree to which their audience is representative of the larger community. Specific uses of demographics depend upon questions that a specific museum staff in a particular museum may have in mind. For example, a local history museum or a historic site might be dependent upon tourist visitation for support. Knowing where the tourists come from can provide both documentation of the influence of the museum and guidance for publicity efforts. A public museum might need to document the ratio of those in attendance who live in the museum's tax district to those who are nontax support visitors.

Visitor surveys help correct stereotypes of "typical" visitors by providing a more objective basis for audience description. Other investigators have found the situation mentioned earlier of staff members working with a definite misperception of some audience characteristics. For example, a 1966 New York State Museum survey revealed that staff members had greatly overestimated a specific audience group. Prior to the survey, there was the belief that nearby government workers frequented the museum during lunch periods or after work. Survey results revealed that the actual attendance level of this group was only around 1 percent of the total audience.[9] Perhaps nearby workers and users of governmental facilities *should* make up a major audience segment, but efforts at audience development would be necessary to make that outcome a reality.

Ted Cramer, in "Marketing the Museum," provided a good working illustration of the way a particular misperception about visitors can be turned into constructive audience development. Survey evaluation at the North Carolina Museum of Art revealed that 60 percent of the visiting audience was between the ages of eighteen and thirty-four. Staff members, when questioned, had estimated the majority of the audience to be over forty.[10] *An important factor contributing to a more youthful audience was the weekend attendance by area college students.* This latter point about the audience is significant, because it both identifies a group of users and the time period during which they are likely to be in the museum. In another age-related finding, the investigators discovered the museum was not getting its share of tours by school children. Interviews with teachers disclosed that touring the museum was thought to consume too much time, compared to the time needed for other field-trip activities. The museum responded by creating a gallery for the school tours that highlighted the institution's collection and kept the group visit within a workable time period so that school leaders could include the museum on field trips.

Before proceeding further, it would be helpful to point out some reasons for staff people's forming inaccurate estimates of audience composition. Social psychologists are aware of sources of bias when people perceive others in relationship to personal needs.[11] One might like or feel comfortable with a mature audience and thereby accentuate that kind of visitor in estimates of visitor groupings. A more subtle source of bias is a tendency to underutilize or to ignore realistic estimates of base rate information. For example, a staff member may have little contact with or interest in a child's involvement with the museum and may fail to realize that children comprise a large portion of the audience. Such an individual will tend to underutilize the actual rate of children in the audience, when thinking about visitors. Surveys can help establish the actual attendance base rates for different groups of visitors. Those documented base rates can be used as information for planning and decision-making.

Another source of bias is the tendency for people to remember experiences that have actually occurred and to weigh their expectations by those memories. Thus, if a staff member happens to meet a couple of tourist visitors while in the galleries, that individual may tend to overestimate the percentage of tourists visiting the museum. That kind of implicit or heuristic bias explains why casual conversations with visitors from time to time cannot substitute for a more objective survey effort.[12]

Demographic information can be even more useful if additional samples are collected. For example, one of the earliest visitor description surveys, by Arthur Niehoff, included a summer and winter sample. Niehoff describes the Milwaukee Public Museum's drawing of two samples of the 1952-1953 visiting audience. While there were a number of technical limitations to this early survey, it illustrated well the need to think about the ways a survey could be focused. While sample size and time periods were limited, the completion of a summer and winter survey provided for both comparisons between seasons and combined results. The seasonal comparisons suggested that more repeat visitation occurred during the fall and winter, in part because most tourists visited in the summer. Combining results of the seasonal surveys disclosed a low level of representation by the elderly and also by rural residents.[13]

In terms of occupations, this early Milwaukee survey showed students and housewives (homemakers) to be the two most frequently represented groups. Interestingly, their relative numbers were opposite for the two seasons: students were more in attendance during the winter, while a larger percentage of housewives attended in the summer sample. Findings like this inverse ratio between groups over two sampling periods can raise specific questions about audience composition. Do homemakers appear more often in the summer because they are traveling with tourist families and/or are in charge of summer-time family events, such as a planned trip to the local museum? Is the greater percentage of students in the winter sample due mostly to college students being back in school and high school students visiting to work on homework assignments? Michael O'Hare used a seasonal sampling strategy in a survey of an art museum audience—the Museum of Fine Arts, in Boston—and like the earlier Niehoff work, documented seasonal differences in types of visitors attending.[14]

Background and expectations. Another form of visitor information, more specific than demographics, can be tailored to an individual museum. For example, Walter S. Brown asked visitors to the Seattle showing of the Tutankhamen exhibition some very specific background questions. Questions included recalling when they first heard of the exhibit, prior exposure to Tut-related materials, and their perceptions about the functions of art museums.[15] Specific questions can reveal visitor expectations, interests, and other background characteristics that pertain to a special show or to unique features of a given museum. Individual background questions can include information about attendance to other museums and various cultural institutions. Visitors can also be asked about time spent watching television, reading, and about listening preferences, as well as hobbies and leisure-time interests. A profile of these visitor background characteristics can provide insights for program planning and efforts at publicizing the museum.

Because background questions have an unlimited range of possibilities, it is impossible to provide a basic summary, as can be done with visitor demographics. A number of ideas for surveying background or life-style characteristics appear in chapter 4 as part of external surveys of the public at large. Items 6 to 9 in figure 3.1 illustrate some general background questions that could be used in many visitor surveys. Item 8 has been prepared as a general-interest question. It could be modified to a list of more specific interests, to fit the needs of art, history, science.

Measuring expectations for the museum can be done on a general level as illustrated by item 9 in figure 3.1. A variation of that item could be:

I expect a museum . . . (check the *one* alternative below that best describes your expectations)
☐ to be educational
☐ to be a place to share with others
☐ to be entertaining
☐ to be a place with important objects

Expectation questions can also be tailored to features of a specific museum, as with an art museum, as illustrated below:

I expect to find in this museum
1. Examples of French Impressionist paintings   ☐ Yes   ☐ No
2. Examples of contemporary art   ☐ Yes   ☐ No

3. Examples of early American art	☐ Yes	☐ No
4. Examples of Oriental art	☐ Yes	☐ No
5. Examples of modern photography	☐ Yes	☐ No

The advantage of this latter approach is that it can identify the degree to which visitors understand what is available. As a question asked at the entrance, this item can identify what people thought they would find at the museum. As an exit or post-visit item, it can assess what people saw. Michael O'Hare, for example, had people identify from a list of museum galleries the three exhibits they expected to visit at the Museum of Fine Arts in Boston, and then (as they left) indicate which exhibits they did visit.[16] This kind of expectation/actual-choice question can be quite insightful, provided visitors are not confused by the different alternatives and/or do not have difficulty remembering choices made between exhibits that appear very similar.

Expectations about what can be found at a museum—or what one expects to gain from a visit—can reveal, less directly, the way one views the museum in general. Marilyn S. Cohen, in a survey she made of visitors to the Yale University Art Gallery, made the "expectation" question specific when she asked visitors to indicate whether they came to see specific works and exhibits or for more general reasons—to relax, to meet someone, to browse in sales shops, or whether they visited on impulse, since the gallery was near other attractions. Interestingly, a large number of respondents indicated that they visited because they wanted to relax and it was pleasant to visit an art museum, or simply that they made a spontaneous decision to visit because the museum was in the vicinity. Some respondents even took the trouble to write in the comment that they came to the museum because it was fun! Cohen's data revealed a visitors' image of the art museum as an enjoyable place to visit on impulse because it is part of a broader university setting. While some of her sample perceived the museum as a location of specific works of art, it is significant that at least one-third of the visitors came without a specific exhibit or object in mind.[17]

Steven Griggs and K. Hays-Jackson conducted a novel study on visitor expectations by having visitors to the British Museum (Natural History) indicate how applicable different statements were for describing a sampling of institutions, such as an opera, a zoo, a cinema, and, of course, a natural history museum. Statements included different expectations—for instance, "has something of interest of everyone," "a place to go for an educational visit," "a place to take the children." The survey combined measurement of visitor expectations with overall perceptions of different leisure-time institutions. Results revealed that the people surveyed would be more inclined to go to the theater with friends and that they would be more likely to visit the natural history museum with children as part of the group.[18]

Visit Description

One factor that makes the intramuseum survey different from surveys in general is that intramuseum surveys can provide information about the museum visit itself. Five visit characteristics are of primary importance: repeat visitation, size of visiting group, reasons for making a visit, access problems in getting to the museum, and visit-related activities (see items 10-14, figure 3.1).

Chapter 2 discusses first-time visits and repeat visitation as measures of accountability and ways of documenting the need for programming. No matter how the question is phrased ("Is this your first visit to the museum?" "How many times have you visited the museum this past year?") the rate of repeat visitation is an important measurement.

Visiting alone or as part of a group is also an important visit characteristic. People typically go to museums as part of a social occasion and absorb their early information about a museum directly from other people. It may be of value not only to learn the relative distribution of group visitations to those made alone, but also to determine the percentages of people attending as couples, families with children, informal student groups, formal school tour groups, tourist groups, and so on.

As with demographic indicators, surveying over different periods of time can reveal seasonal patterns to group visitation and concentrations of repeat visitors. Tourist visitors may concentrate in periods when vacation travel is common. Tourist families are likely to pass through *before* school opens, while retired persons may intentionally wait to travel until *after* school begins.

The value of learning what prompts a visit has been known for a long time, as shown in Fiske Kimball's survey of the Pennsylvania Museum of Art mentioned earlier in this chapter.[19] Overall, the sample indicated that learning about the museum from someone else led to a visit. Newspaper announcements, advertisements in streetcar ad frames, and mailings from the museum also prompted visitation. Questions about reasons for visiting can help a museum staff determine the value of efforts at publicity. For instance, a local history museum might assess the value of motel and restaurant tourist pamphlet racks as a source of visit-prompting. The number of visitors indicating they learned of the museum from such pamphlets could be compared to those indicating that they learned about it from road signs, radio announcements, travel guides, or other information sources used by the museum.

Kimball's Pennsylvania museum survey also showed that the single most common way of getting to the museum was the private automobile . . . an interesting social finding for the late 1920s. Public transportation was also heavily used by visitors, and a significant number came by foot. This latter finding is important, because it demonstrated that the museum provided off-the-street access to a portion of its audience. This audience segment may typically include neighborhood residents, shoppers drawn to nearby stores and restaurants, tourists from a hotel district, and office workers making a lunch-time or after-hours visit.

In his survey of the Boston Fine Arts Museum in the 1970s, Michael O'Hare found that travel on foot, in private automobiles, and by public conveyance were still the major methods of getting to an urban museum. Private auto, however, was far and away the means most often used to reach the museum.[20]

Access-based questions can focus on problems of finding museums, adequacy of museum parking spaces, adequacy of public transportation, and convenience of the museum's operating hours. A museum that depends heavily on visitors traveling by automobile—a historic house, for example—needs an effective sign and publicity program to promote visits and guide travelers to the museum. It has been long recognized that a combination of signs, maps, and travel literature is important in attracting visitors to historic houses and small local museums.[21]

A fifth aspect of the visit that can be evaluated through visitor surveys is the understanding of activities related to visitation. Visits to urban museums are likely to be combined with special shopping trips and occasions for dining out. Holiday excursions to an urban museum may include visits to other museums, or to parks or zoos. David Johnson documented that activities such as stopping for lunch at a restaurant were part of the average overall planned trip into the city that also includes a visit to a favorite museum.[22] Museum staff members need to remember that the museum, in effect, shares the visitor with other institutions and activities that help justify the expense and effort of visitors' traveling into the city.

One variation of a related-activities question asked visitors to indicate where they had been just before they came to the museum. Another way of identifying activities related to visitation is to have visitors give reasons for coming to town that day.[23] Analysis of responses was com-

pleted in terms of whether respondents were from out of town, from the
district immediately around the museum, and whether they were first-
time or frequent visitors. Analysis of those four types of visitors provided
an even more interesting documentation of related activities. For example, *frequent visitors* were most likely to have just come from home, but
they also came from such nearby areas as a library, shops, or work-places.
First-time visitors were more likely to be from hotels or on sight-seeing
expeditions.

Local museums are likely to be visited as part of travel and vacation
activities. Gene Ball, in Cody, Wyoming, developed an intramuseum survey sensitive to tourist-related activities involving area facilities, such as
motels, stores, and restaurants. Results of his surveys reflect the reliance
of a local history museum on summer visitation.[24] Compiling visit-related
information about ways in which tourist visitors contribute to local business is a good example of accountability evaluation. The museum can
become a contributing resource by attracting tourists to the community.
Sample items related to community support include:

Was the museum the *primary* reason you stopped in the city today?
☐ Yes
☐ No
Indicate which (if any) of the following you plan to do while in the city today:
☐ Buy gasoline
☐ Eat at a restaurant
☐ Visit curio shops
☐ Stay overnight at a motel
☐ Other_____
☐ Will make no other stops in the city today

Ball also asked visitors whether they had planned at the start of their
travels to visit the museum and whether planning to visit the museum
had influenced them to stay overnight in the community. About a third
of the respondents indicated that they *had* planned to visit the museum,
even before starting their trip. One-third also answered that the museum
was a factor in their deciding to stay overnight.

Measuring General Reactions to the Museum

An intramuseum visitor survey can be used to solicit visitor evaluation of a museum as an institution, as well as visitor comment on the
museum's specific exhibits and goods and services.

Reactions to the institution. George Nash asked a sample of visitors to the Whitney Museum of American Art to pick adjectives that described their impression of the museum. Positive adjectives, such as *contemporary* and *comfortable,* were among the most frequently chosen; far fewer negative words (such as *cold, austere, confusing*) were selected.[25] Bipolar adjective responses of this type are one of several kinds of questions that can describe visitor impressions.[26]

In a survey of visitors to the Smithsonian Institution in the 1960s, Carolyn Wells asked visitors to answer an open-ended question and describe the way they felt about their visits. Individual responses had to be coded in some manner, and Wells coded visitor comments in terms of the degree of positive or negative feeling visitors had about their visit. She concluded that most visitors felt positive or favorable and the pressure of trying to see several large museums within too short a time was a major cause for negative statements.[27]

O'Hare, in his study of the art museum audience, used an open-ended question to let visitors indicate specific disappointments.[28] While an open-ended question can often reveal things that are bothering or disappointing visitors, a structured-question format using a checklist, such as the one below, is more likely to cause visitors to evaluate specific features staff people may be concerned about:

From the alternatives below, check any feature of the museum you think should be improved:
□ Courtesy of museum personnel
□ Parking facilities
□ Directions, signs, visitor information
□ Cleanliness of museum
□ Knowledge of personnel
□ Quality of interpretive materials
□ Restroom facilities
□ Merchandise in gift shops

Items included in the checklist could vary, from survey to survey, to reflect staff planning needs.

Figure 3.1 contains another format for a general assessment question (see item 17) that asks visitors to indicate their level of satisfaction with each museum feature and thereby requires visitors to pay specific attention to each feature listed. People are often hesitant to make negative comments, and asking for estimated degrees of satisfaction is one way of getting them to evaluate features without having to list negative comments.

General assessment questions can be made even more specific for measuring reactions to parts of a museum visit and also can measure intentions for using different facilities, as illustrated in the following two items from a museum survey conducted in New York State:[29]

	Agree strongly	Agree moderately	Hard to say but if I must choose: Tend to agree	Tend to disagree	Disagree moderately	Disagree strongly
If the museum had a restaurant or coffee shop I would have used it today.	( )	( )	( )	( )	( )	( )
There are plenty of restful areas and places for people to sit down in this museum.	( )	( )	( )	( )	( )	( )

Needless to say, an item or two on a general visitor survey cannot take the place of a more complete study of needs for rest areas or the feasibility of adding food service. Survey items can, however, identify some general interests or problems that could be studied in more depth to help decision making.

Exhibit/program evaluation. Visitor surveys can provide helpful information about visitor reactions to exhibits and/or programs—discussed at length in chapters 6 and 7. Our discussion here will be a sort of preview, focusing on a couple of examples of measuring visitor reactions to exhibits through a general survey. One kind of question can list different exhibits and ask visitors to indicate the exhibit they enjoyed the *least* and the one they enjoyed the *most* (see item 18, figure 3.1). O'Hare used this kind of question in his study of the Boston Fine Arts Museum audience in which he found that visitors had different preferences among the range of exhibits. He was correct in noting, however, that such questions give only a very superficial evaluation, since visitors are making a global judgment of exhibits. It is impossible to know just what specific objects or exhibit design features influence the choices for "least-enjoyed" and "most-enjoyed" exhibit.

In her survey of the Yale Art Gallery, Marilyn Cohen focused exhibit evaluation questions on a single topic—labeling.[30] Such a focus is good strategy over very general questions, since all of the items can be written around a single topic and more complete information gained. For example, Cohen was able to compare visitor preferences for types of labels; check visitors' estimation of the importance of labels to paintings versus those for sculpture; compare the impact of label information with that of museum catalogues or information sheets; investigate completeness of labels; and, finally, assess perceptions of labels as a source of interference with the study of the art objects themselves.

Surveys of Specific Audiences

Visitor surveys can be focused on specific subgroups within the overall audience for a museum. Three examples of this kind of survey focus include surveys of visitors to special exhibits, surveys of museum membership, and surveys tailored to different kinds of museums.

Surveying the Special-Exhibit Audience

When Walter Brown surveyed the audience attending the Seattle Art Museum's Tutankhamen exhibition in 1979, Seattle was one of the few cities hosting the special exhibit, which had received considerable national publicity and had attracted large crowds in other cities. Brown found answers to a number of questions that challenged over-negative stereotypes of the audience attending the Tutankhamen exhibition. His data, prepared for the Seattle Art Museum, revealed that visitors to the exhibition were very similar to museum visitors in general and to Seattle Art Museum members in particular. For example, respondents in Brown's study had high levels of education, high incomes, and upper-level occupations. More pertinent to questions about the kind of audience attending a special exhibition was the finding that a substantial majority were aware of Tutankhamen before the exhibition's tour was announced and had already been exposed to Egyptian art and archaeology. The visiting public had also taken advantage of opportunities to experience a variety of Tutankhamen-related events after the tour was announced. Nearly 90 percent of the visitors surveyed had visited an art museum before the special exhibition, another characteristic typical of museum-goers in general. Brown's study also combined unobtrusive observations of visitor behavior in the exhibition to elaborate further on the questionnaire survey findings. One clever use of observation was to answer the question of whether or not visitors were more attracted to gold artifacts than those not containing gold. One stereotype bantered about at the time was that people were attracted to the exhibition merely to look at gold. Results of the observation measure failed to support the notion that visitors came because of gold fascination: visitors observed showed no preference for gold objects over non-gold objects on display. Brown concludes that the result of his survey work should be interpreted in relation to the specific appeals of the Tutankhamen exhibit.[31] Visitor interest, at least in Seattle, was more than superficial for this particular collection and historical heritage.

Since one way of gaining access to the exhibition was to become a member of the museum, Brown also surveyed the membership to answer questions about the types of people taking out memberships. Findings from the member survey were that people who joined the museum because of the Tutankhamen exhibition were very similar to existing members. It was Brown's expectation that, over the years, many of the members brought in by King Tut would be indistinguishable from existing members.[32] Much of the work in these two surveys by Brown centered on the idea of looking at audience surveys as a tool for marketing the programs of a museum. However that may be, it is important to note here that Brown's efforts provided the administration of the Seattle Art Museum with tangible evidence about the audience attending a special exhibition.

It is interesting to compare the findings from Brown's work with an earlier survey of visitors to a special traveling exhibit at the Seattle Art Museum. Robert Bower and Laure Sharp surveyed visitors to a Japanese art exhibit shown in Boston, Chicago, and Seattle on a tour during the 1950s.[33] In general, they also found that visitors to a special exhibit were similar to museum-goers overall. As in the case of the Seattle Tutankhamen audience, most people who came out to the special Japanese exhibit were likely candidates for museum attendance, anyway. However, times change; and the Seattle of the 1950s was not the same community as the Seattle of the late 1970s. Likewise, the public's interest in and need for museums can change, over time. A closer look at the Bower and Sharp study suggests some interesting comparisons between the two time periods involved—the 1950s and Brown's late 1970s.

As was true with the Tutankhamen show, a great deal of publicity informed Seattle residents about the Japanese art exhibit in the 1950s. At that time, Seattle had only one major museum, and that was the art museum. Considerable civic pride was generated over the city's being chosen to host the Japanese exhibit, and the extensive publicity emphasized that community pride. Apparently, the Seattle showing was visited by more people who were not on familiar terms with art museums or knowledgeable about what to expect from an art exhibit than were the Boston or Chicago showings of the same art. Bower and Sharp reported that the Seattle respondents were the most dissatisfied with the exhibit. The researchers reasoned that many of the people who came to the showing did so out of a sense of civic obligation and in response to publicity, rather than from a personal interest in art. Respondents also complained about the lack of interpretive material available, a complaint compounded by the visitors' lack of experience with art museums, in the case of the Seattle sample.

The interesting point of comparison between the two Seattle surveys is that results could support more than one point of view. The 1970s survey corroborated the notion that highly publicized, blockbuster exhibits are a desirable stimulant to museum attendance: those who come attend museums, anyway, and bring a commitment to the material on exhibit. On the other hand, the 1950s survey of the Japanese art exhibit revealed that, while it was possible to stimulate the attendance with publicity, some who came would be disappointed with the exhibit. Brown, in the 1970s, may have discovered a key element to the success of the special exhibit when he emphasized the broad interest appeal of the Tutankhamen topic. Dramatic objects and intriguing stories were combined to create a wide audience following. The change in Seattle should also be mentioned. Success of a special show depends upon the availability of a target—or interested—audience. The larger and more cosmopolitan Seattle of the 1970s would provide a greater potential audience for special shows than the Seattle of twenty years earlier. A key lesson from these surveys is the importance of matching special exhibit content to potential audience interests.

Special exhibits can also provide economic benefits to a community by bringing in visitors who spend money on travel, shopping, food, and lodging. Surveys have been used to estimate the economic impact of special shows, including "blockbuster" exhibits.[34]

Surveying Museum Members

Like visitors who make repeat visits to museums, people who invest in museum membership demonstrate a loyalty to the museum that is an important form of support. In times of economic slowdown, member support can be of special value in helping a museum keep programs operating. In recognition of the significance of member loyalty, some museums have surveyed their memberships, not only to find out more about the people who become members, by also to learn how members evaluate their museum memberships.

Figure 3.2 contains a number of questions that could focus a descriptive survey around reasons that motivate visitors to take membership in a museum. Such motivation is a basic concern, and the questions could yield information helpful to staff people in assessing ways members learned about joining, reasons for becoming a member, and perceptions of which member benefits are most valued.

The questions of figure 3.2 could be used in conjunction with member description items and also questions about activities and preferences of members:

Member Characteristics
> Sex, age
> Marriage status, family size
> Occupation, income
> Residence (area, type of dwelling, length of residence)
> Educational level
> Memberships in other cultural organizations

Leisure-Time Activity Preferences
> Use of museums
> Use of other cultural institutions (libraries, theater, etc.)
> Use of other leisure institutions (parks, sports, zoos)
> Hobbies
> Reading preferences
>> Type of reading material (magazines, newspapers, books)
>> Preferences for specific magazines, books, etc.
> Television preferences
> Radio preferences
> Travel interests and experiences

Leslie Buhler reviewed the process or business of operating a successful membership organization and noted that a museum membership can help raise unrestricted funds, develop a support constituency, develop new and/or expanded audiences, and inform the public about the museum and its programs. She mentions a specific use of questionnaires to accompany follow-up letters to those who do not renew annual memberships. Nonrenewing members would be asked to indicate reasons for letting their memberships lapse. A short, conversational interview by telephone to a random sample of nonrenewing members could be an alternative to a mail questionnaire.[35]

Some years ago, Elliot Mittler and Walter Wallner foresaw the kind of situation Buhler deals with, when they were conducting a well-planned member survey for the Los Angeles County Museum of Art. Looking at new members, continuing members, and those who had let their membership lapse, Mittler and Wallner compared members' reasons for joining, evaluation of benefits, and other items. The advantage of such a survey focus is that potential problems in membership programs might become evident in a routine survey of membership rosters. Although the Mittler and Wallner work is an old study, it remains an excellent working model of a member survey.[36]

An interesting point found in some membership surveys is that desire to support a museum, civic pride, and interest in the topic illustrated by the museum's holdings (history, art, etc.) are given as frequent reasons for joining. An unpublished membership survey conducted by the Denver Art Museum in 1979 showed support for the museum as the top-ranked reason for joining the membership and was ranked above such reasons as gaining a discount in the museum shop, free admission to a blockbuster temporary exhibit, and learning about art. While the high ranking of support for the museum may reflect some social desirability or efforts to make the most socially acceptable responses to surveys, supporting a museum through membership is a benefit worth additional investigation. A major benefit of membership may well be the personal satisfaction of contributing to a worthwhile cause, as well as identifying with an institution believed to be important and of social value. Another finding is that memberships are often begun because of a visit to a museum. Actual visitation may be one of the best promptings to increasing membership, especially if an appeal to support the museum is made as part of membership promotion.

Surveys of Different Kinds of Museums

Questions can be selected and shaped to focus a survey on the specific features of a particular museum. For instance, several surveys focused on art museums have included various survey aspects mentioned here— such as characteristics of visitors and visits and evaluations of programs and services. What finally gave each of these efforts a specific focus were questions devoted to art museums and/or their content.

In the O'Hare survey of the Boston Museum of Fine Arts, mentioned above, three questions clearly focused the effort on art museums. Respondents were asked whether they practiced art as a hobby, and specific types of hobbies were itemized; they were asked the value of any fine art they had purchased in the last two years; and a self-description ques-

Fig. 3.2. Sample questions for a survey focused on museum membership.

1. How did you learn about a museum membership? (Check the most appropriate response in the list below.)

    ☐ From a friend

    ☐ From radio/TV announcements

    ☐ From a visit to the museum

    ☐ From a mail announcement

    ☐ From the newspaper

    ☐ Other (Please describe)_____

2. Please indicate the three most important reasons you took out a museum membership. (Place a "1" by the most important, a "2" by the next, and a "3" by the third most important reason.)

    ☐ To attend receptions

    ☐ To support the museum

    ☐ To gain free admission to exhibits

    ☐ To meet people

    ☐ To receive a discount at the museum shop

    ☐ To receive monthly newsletters about the museum

    ☐ Interest in (art, history, science, etc.)

    ☐ Other (Please describe)_____

3. Have you been, in past years, or are you presently, a member of another museum?

    ☐ Yes   ☐ No

4. Please indicate what you think are the five most important benefits available to members of this museum. (Place a "1" by the most important, a "2" by the next, and continue numbering up to a "5" for the fifth most important benefit.

    ☐ Member's discount in the museum shop

    ☐ Monthly museum newsletter

    ☐ Preview receptions for special exhibits

    ☐ Repeat museum visitation without charges

    ☐ Staff consultation privileges about personal collections

    ☐ Travel events for members only

    ☐ Reduced rates on museum films, lectures, classes

    ☐ Other (Please describe)_____

5. Have you visited the museum since taking out your membership?

    ☐ Yes   ☐ No

6. Please indicate the kind of membership you have:

    ☐ Single   ☐ Sponsor

    ☐ Family   ☐ Patron

    ☐ Student   ☐ Benefactor

    ☐ Senior citizen

7. When due, is it your intention to renew your membership?

    ☐ Yes   ☐ No   ☐ Uncertain

    Reason for answer:

---

tion was included, made up of different categories of art-related professions, including student and amateur involvement. Through such questions, O'Hare collected information revealing visitor characteristics and found that about 15 percent of those surveyed considered themselves amateur artists; more than 40 percent pursued some art-related hobby; and approximately 25 percent had purchased art objects of monetary value during the last couple of years. Information of this variety begins to identify the audience more completely as a function of the content of a museum.

Edward P. Alexander's book *Museums in Motion* is a general source reviewing the historical roots of different types of museums. Chapters on various types of museums—art, natural history, history, science and technology—may provide background information to suggest a survey focus. Further reading in classics about the nature and history of museums can provide additional background information that could lead to questions about visitor perceptions of a museum's image and/or function.[37]

Other surveys of the field focus on specific kinds of institutions. Beverly Serrell asked visitors to an aquarium to make suggestions for the institution's future improvement. She found that respondents were interested in more labels around individual specimen tanks, classes or workshops, and—of unique value to an aquarium visitor—special clinics for home aquarists. Serrell noted that most of the suggestions given were compatible with plans the staff had in mind. Visitors surveyed also felt it important for an aquarium to lead in education about ecology and environmental problems, including local environmental issues. Related findings also revealed that the kinds of television shows preferred by aquarium visitors were those about nature and environmental topics.[38]

In coordinating a survey project for a university-based museum of anthropology and archeology, Rochelle H. Prague documented a major disadvantage of a university museum: *the public may not know it exists.*[39] Visitors to the university museum studied tended to be local scholars, and the museum was not well known to the broader community. The survey did establish that people who had ties with the university were the major audience component, obviously an important audience group for such a museum. Additional publicity would be needed to involve people outside the university.

Overview for Planning a Visitor Survey

Organization—a key element in completing any visitor survey—is discussed in this section. Figure 3.3 shows a flow chart or checklist of the tasks needed to complete a survey, in the order in which they should be done. Any text or handbook on survey methodology contains a similar kind of flow chart for completing survey tasks. In *The Sample Survey,* for instance, Donald P. Warwick and Charles A. Lininger note that tasks for conducting a survey are highly interdependent. Once a sample is determined and questionnaires are printed up, it is very costly to change plans. Each task in planning predetermines much of what is to follow. These authors stress that a survey plan must also work backward, in the sense that the audience for the final report must be anticipated in advance.[40]

Task One: Initial Planning

Heavy emphasis on visitor survey topics is needed in any discussion of museum evaluation, and it all leads up to the planning task. It is sometimes a temptation to be too concerned about method, or the way to get a survey done, when the first consideration should be the sort of information (survey topics) that will be most useful to the people who are going to make decisions based on the survey results. It is also necessary to determine early the exact focus of the sample to be completed, the costs that will be incurred, and the resources available to deal with those costs. Reviewing any existing survey information about the museum's visitors and soliciting staff input are important aids in completing initial planning for a survey.

Who will use the survey information? Surveys can fail as useful evaluation tools because of problems connected with the way staff people relate

TASK 1 INITIAL PLANNING

_____ Define the audience who will use the survey
_____ Solicit staff input
_____ Review existing visitor-survey reports
_____ Determine survey content focus
_____ Determine sample focus
_____ Estimate costs and resources available

TASK 2 DESIGNING A SURVEY

_____ Prepare a survey design
_____ Determine a sample strategy
_____ Select type(s) of survey instruments
_____ Determine data analysis needs
_____ Complete pilot work

TASK 3 ORGANIZING FIELD WORK

_____ Prepare final forms of survey instruments
_____ Finalize survey administration procedure
_____ Select and train survey workers

TASK 4 COLLECTING FIELD DATA

_____ Initiate and supervise data collection
_____ Code field data
_____ Complete quality control checks

TASK 5 ANALYZING SURVEY RESULTS

_____ Complete data coding
_____ Process data
_____ Prepare results summary

TASK 6 REPORTING THE SURVEY INFORMATION

_____ Complete oral briefing
_____ Circulate summary report(s)
_____ Write a major report

Fig. 3.3. Flow chart for tasks required to plan, administer, and report a visitor survey.

to and use them. Staff members' lack of interest, turnover of staff personnel, and staff hostility to survey strategies can destroy a survey's usefulness. One of the surest ways to avoid that sort of potential failure is to plan ahead for the audience most likely to use the survey results. It is important to know what interests potential readers of the finished report have in mind, and it would be helpful to know the kind of specific visitor-related questions are to appear in it. The more ways one finds to involve potential users of survey information, the better. It is well worth the time it takes to talk with staff members who have visitor-related concerns before designing a survey instrument; and it is always wise to keep interested persons involved with the progress of the project.

It is also wise to keep potentially new survey-report audiences in mind. At the center of the widening circle are those closest to the department or the individual initiating the survey. The sphere widens as one moves from the initiator of the survey to the community, the city, the state, the region, or possibly the nation. The important point is that *potential audiences could exist in any sector of the circle,* and some thought must be given to which of these overlapping audiences will make the greatest use of the survey results. A list of potential audiences for survey information might look like the following:

1. Initiating staff or department (i.e., Office of the Director, Membership Coordinator, Public Relations Director, Education Department)

2. Other staff (i.e., curators, security chief, Office of Development)

3. Special audience-support groups (i.e. volunteers, members, school teachers)

4. Trustees and/or patrons; key community benefactors

5. The larger community (i.e., businesses, chamber of commerce, cultural organizations, government bodies)

6. State or national sources of project and program funds (both private and public)

7. The museum community (i.e., directors, curators, educators, and/or professional organizations like the American Association for State and Local History and the American Association of Museums)

8. Academic communities with researchers in evaluation or leisure behavior.

Robert Stake, a leading authority in evaluation research, has noted that too many evaluation reports are written for the last sphere of report audiences listed above—those who are experts in evaluation and/or those who are academics. As a result, reports are often prepared in a passive, academic-thesis style. Stake points out that some audiences are decision-oriented, while others are conclusion-oriented.[41] In his 1972 study, mentioned early in this chapter, Donald Newgren raises the point that surveys should be action-oriented or decision-oriented.[42] As much as possible, a planned intramuseum survey should be concerned with decisions that are forthcoming. Stake advises that anyone preparing an evaluation report of any nature should try to anticipate the kinds of decisions that will need to be made, even those that are foreseen now as occurring at a more distant time in the future, and the data-gathering should be done with those anticipated decisions kept in mind.

Developing a survey focus. The first step toward creating a focus for a survey is accomplished when potential survey users are defined. Selecting a specific focus and defining the sample are interrelated, interdependent activities. Once a focus is defined (i.e., visitor description, exhibit/program evaluation, museum description, visitor subgroup assessment), it becomes necessary to plan for a sample that will yield information appropriate to the focus.

One procedure that can help focus the thrust of a survey is to prepare a table of question specifications such as those shown in Table 3.2. Itemizing the intended goals of a survey effort can help make the focus explicit. The following example illustrates how preparing a table of survey specifications can help focus a survey.

Some historical sites and local history museums are most heavily visited in the summertime, or tourist season. The institution may even operate on a reduced schedule during the rest of the year, when visitation is very low. Because of the pattern of seasonal visitation, it may be very important to attract as large a summer audience as possible, to justify institutional support. Furthermore, the museum program may need the help of the community to publicize and draw traveling visitors. In return, the museum or historical site may be able to show that, by drawing tourists to the community, it contributes economically to the local business and tax revenue. Suppose the staff of such a museum or site wants to document the tourist audience. Staff brainstorming sessions could lead to a set of survey goals such as those shown in Table 3.2.

Table 3.2 shows four goals defined for the basic specifications of the survey. Once such goals are agreed upon, it is important to determine how each potential question fits into at least one of the stated goals. This procedure of working out survey specifications not only helps to keep the effort focused, but also serves as a vehicle to stimulate staff discussion about what the survey should accomplish.

Identifying the areas people are from and pinpointing their home residence community can be basic in documenting the geographic breadth

Table 3.2
Goals and Sample Items
for a Planned Summer-Visitor Survey

Goal Number 1

Visitor Description: Identify the summer visitor with special emphasis on describing those visitors from outside the immediate community.

Sample items:

What is your home city? _____

State? _____ Country? _____

Please indicate your home area zip code _____

How many members are in your party? _____

Goal Number 2

Visitor Access: Identify the way visitors learned about the museum and the way they gained access to the setting.

Sample items:

I first heard about the museum from:

☐ Highway signs

☐ Travel brochures

☐ Friends

☐ Newspapers

☐ Magazine advertisements

☐ Other _____

Did you travel to the museum?

☐ By Route 20 from Tinyville?

☐ By Interstate 12 from Metrocity?

☐ By Route 13 from Rabbitgulch?

☐ By aircraft to the Community Airport?

☐ Other _____

While on this trip, will you visit other sites?

☐ Stonewort National Park?

☐ Deepriver Lake Resorts?

☐ Metrocity?

☐ Other _____

Goal Number 3

Visit Description: Identify features of museum visit.

Sample items:

Is this your first visit to the museum?   ☐ Yes   ☐ No

How long was your visit today?

   ☐ Less than one hour

   ☐ 1-2 hours

   ☐ 2-3 hours

   ☐ Over 3 hours

Do you plan to visit the museum again within the next three years?

   ☐ Yes   ☐ No   ☐ Maybe

Goal Number 4

Community-use description: Identify visitor use of community resources.

Sample items:

Was the museum the primary reason you stopped in Mainstreet today?

   ☐ Yes   ☐ No

Indicate which (if any) of the following you plan to do while in Mainstreet today:

   ☐ Buy gasoline

   ☐ Eat at a restaurant

   ☐ Visit curio shops

   ☐ Stay overnight at a motel

   ☐ Shop at a supermarket

   ☐ Other _____

   ☐ Will make no other stops in Mainstreet

of a museum's audience. In the event of a summer visitation institution, identification of major residence areas could aid in planning future promotional efforts at stimulating visitors. Most museums are not a trip destination point, but they can be added to trip plans as a place to visit for a break in travel or as part of an overnight stay in the community where they are located.

Tied to trip origin and planning are the types of questions that would constitute a second goal (see Table 3.2). Knowing what information sources reached—and influenced—actual visitors can be useful in deciding what promotional methods to use (although this information would not clarify what sources might reach people who *do not* attend). Being aware of popular highway routes people use could suggest locations for advertising through signs and/or pamphlet distribution. Museum visitation may also be related to travel to a major vacation point, such as a national park. Publicity and efforts at increasing traveler awareness of the museum could be linked with the major trip destination point.

A third goal would further identify visitors as first-comers or repeat visitors, provide an estimated length of visit and intention to return, all measures of visit commitment.

The fourth area of information also assesses commitment, but in this case, commitment to using resources in the community. Answers to questions related to this fourth goal would document visitor investment in goods and services. An alternate question would have visitors estimate the dollar amount they have spent or will spend during their stay in the community, although that may be a difficult question for some to answer. It should be possible to learn from different business establishments what the average amount spent per person is and extrapolate dollar amounts to the frequency-of-use data produced by a question like the example in Table 3.2. It would then be possible to estimate the economic impact of tourists traveling to the museum and also to estimate potential sales tax revenue from such visitors' presence in the community.

Obviously, there are other ways to focus a summer-visitor survey. The point is to limit any specific survey to a few goals and pursue each one in sufficient depth to provide useful information. Whatever the focus, the final scope of a survey must meet the needs of some audience who can make use of the information provided. Defining the survey focus also has implications for determining a sample.

Developing a sample focus. Deciding who will be included in a survey sample is also an important step in determining the focus of the effort.

The nature of the sample is not only a big factor in project cost, but also determines the degree to which results can be generalized. It is helpful to think of a sample focus as a point on a continuum. At one end is a small sample taken from an audience attending a gallery lecture or an oral presentation at a historical site. The sample represents people who experienced that one event, and it may even include all who attended. At the other end of the continuum would be a year-long sample of visitors attending a particular institution. This latter sample could consist of thousands (or at least hundreds) of individuals. In between these two extremes would be a one-season sample, such as a summer-visitor survey, or a limited-term sample of people attending a special exhibit.

The nature of the sample determines much of the information to be gained, and it is important that the sample focus reflect interests of the audience for the survey information. Just as the scope of questions should anticipate the interests of survey report users, the nature and extent of the sample should reflect interests people have about specific visitor groups and/or characteristics. Are staff members interested in identifying the repeat visitor? Are people wondering who comes to the museum during evening operating hours? Is there a concern with documenting the out-of-town visitors and their reactions to the museum? Each of these questions implies specific sample properties. One should be cautious about automatically assuming that an intramuseum survey means a year-long effort. Much shorter range samples can yield significant information and are often more workable in terms of resources available.

Samples need not be large to be useful, although a larger number of respondents is desirable if adequate resources are available.

In fact, one of the major determinants of the nature and size of a survey sample is cost. Keeping a survey effort going requires resources, whether they be bought services, staff time, or volunteer contributions. Cost must be included as a factor determining the focus of a survey sample.

Locating resources to cover survey costs. Perhaps the most basic advice that can be given about resources for completing a visitor survey is—let somebody else do it! That approach solves the problem of finding the expertise to plan, execute, analyze, and report a visitor survey. Unfortunately, it *does not* solve the cost problem, and the cost of having someone do a survey is often prohibitive for many institutions. Still, it may be appropriate to consider having a qualified outsider conduct a survey before launching into the project yourself.

Some possible outside sources for conducting a survey may be found at professional survey or marketing firms that undertake such projects for nonprofit institutions as a public service contribution and for tax-deduction purposes. Sometimes these firms will contribute advice (or provide staff-contributed time) if the museum staff plans to undertake their own survey.

In fairness to commercial survey firms, larger museums should price the cost of using professional services. Smaller institutions can some-times work together to contract with a single survey firm to complete a study that will serve both individual and collective needs. Audience development research is a legitimate expense, and sometimes it is best simply to pay the cost of having the work done professionally.

Colleges and universities are another source of survey expertise for museums. Professors often look for community service projects to pro-vide students with field experience. Sometimes an entire class or a sin-gle student can collect the information needed for a survey and prepare the concluding report. It may sometimes be helpful for key museum staff members to work with the student in preparing the final report.

Government-commissioned studies of visitors to public facilities are a fourth source for survey work. Some municipalities or state tourist agen-cies routinely conduct visitor surveys. It is in the best interests of museum leaders to be aware of and to participate in these undertakings, if possi-ble, so that the unique problems and needs of museums are communi-cated to government people. In return, some of these more broadly based surveys could answer questions about museum visitors.

Finally, it might be possible to persuade benefactors to contribute the cost of including museum survey questions in a metropolitan or regional marketing survey effort. These efforts in modern times represent con-tinuing surveys of potential and actual audiences for different markets, including cultural enterprises and institutions. Typically, organizations buy specific survey items of interest to them. Museums could survey the community about public perception and knowledge of museum programs by using these metropolitan survey programs. (Technically, this kind of survey is external to the museum; see fuller discussion of it in chapter 4.) If respondents are asked to declare whether they have visited a par-ticular museum, it is possible to identify characteristics of the declared visiting audience and compare them to people sampled who claim never to have visited the museum. By these means, it would be possible to col-lect and evaluate some characteristics of the visiting audience, even though an intramuseum survey is not used. The cost of individual items is usually low for this kind of community service, and all the details of writing questions, drawing a sample, and analyzing results are provided as part of the service.

If none of the alternatives for having a visitor survey done by others proves feasible, then the following list of costs and possible resources for completing a survey could be useful:

1. *Expertise.* Knowledge about surveys must be acquired, and this cost can be covered in a number of ways. Various members of your staff may have some knowledge for completing a simple museum survey. Cost would involve only the temporary release of their time from other duties. An expert in surveys could be hired for a few days at consultants' costs. The expert would advise staff members on basic tasks for completing a survey project. Occasionally, business or academic organizations might lend their expertise as a public service contribution to a nonprofit organization. Finally, checking with the museum's volunteer and member groups might provide a lead to someone with a social science or market research background who would be interested in either contributing time or working on a short-term contract.

2. *Supervision.* A key cost in museum surveying is the money to pay someone to supervise the work from start to finish. Release time for this work would have to be negotiated for any staff member serving as survey coordinator. A volunteer or museum member might also serve as a survey supervisor. The work of the survey supervisor or project coordinator is principally to insure that the project is done properly and within a reasonable time. Someone very capable must be identified for this task.

3. *Survey administration.* Help must be lined up in advance to hand out questionnaires and/or to interview visitors at sampling sessions. The cost for this becomes major if a survey is to be conducted for a fairly long time. Volunteers can be a major source of help in survey administration. Sometimes museum guards or other personnel can administer questionnaires. Other staff people, including the project supervisor, can administer a few surveys each day without serious disruption of their other duties.

4. *Publication costs.* Questionnaires, interview sheets, and final reports all require secretarial and duplication services. Sometimes these services can be supplied as routine costs from museum operations. At other times, volunteer help and/or gifts are needed to underwrite the survey. Phones are a cost item if a telephone survey is used, as is postage for a mailed survey.

5. *Data analysis.* Coding and analyzing data is a major cost to be antic-

ipated. As museums acquire their own microcomputers (or more extensive office computer facilities), it may be possible for a staff member to analyze survey results with a descriptive data program. Some universities operate a computer lab service for analyzing data, either as part of a class project or for a fee. This kind of service should be consulted at the planning stage of a survey, to facilitate setting up an appropriate data analysis.

6. *Report preparation.* More than one survey has failed because no one person was responsible for preparing and disseminating a final report. The cost of preparing the report could be borne by the survey supervisor. It may also be necessary to rewrite or, at least, to reinterpret reports prepared by individuals outside the museum.

In conclusion, most survey costs can be handled through a variety of paid and contributed resources. A visitor survey on a modest scale can also be assimilated as part of operating costs in many situations.

Task Two: Designing a Survey

Once the audience for survey information has been determined, a content and sample focus has been established, ideas have been solicited from staff members and/or gleaned from reading, and costs have been estimated, it is time to work out a plan or design for the survey. The design preparation will contain the details of the survey work and include a specific sample strategy, a selection of the kind of instruments to be used (i.e., questionnaires, phone interviews, face-to-face interviews, mail questionnaires), considerations of data analysis, and some pilot testing before putting the total survey effort into operation.

Determining a sample method. Sample methods can typically be thought of as *one-time* or single-cross-section, *successive* or repeated, and *panel* or repeated surveys on the same persons. There are many combinations and elaborations on those three basic strategies. One-time samples work best for a single event, such as a special program; successive sampling involves some decision about critical time periods to be included in the survey. Panel or repeated surveys on the same individuals can be useful for assessing whether a change has had any impact on visitors. For example, the same people could be surveyed for their evaluation of exhibit labels both before and after a new system of labeling is installed. Member surveys, discussed earlier, could also be repeated on the same people before and after a major change in member benefits or some other aspect of programming for museum members. It could also be useful to repeat a survey with the same group of visitors, conducting the first survey as they enter the museum and the second after they have completed their visit. The first survey could include expectation questions; the follow-up survey could measure the degree to which the visitor's expectations were met by the museum. Any sample strategy must fit the unique properties of museum visitation.

A museum audience consists of a continual flow of visitors. Therefore, most visitor surveys are based on some form of a successive sample. Attendance-count evaluation will almost always reveal a changing rate of visitation at various times of the day, days of the week, and seasons of the year. Ideally, survey sampling should be sensitive to attendance patterns with more visitors sampled during periods of higher visitation.

One sampling plan that takes into account the dynamic nature of museum attendance is called *stratified random proportional* plan. While such a sample sounds very technical, it is quite logical when each component is defined. *Stratified* refers to the number of levels or predetermined groupings the sample will include. For surveys in general, neighborhoods or other geographical units may be levels; or classifications of people—blue-collar versus professional, buyers versus nonbuyers—could be levels. For museum surveys, levels are usually different time periods, such as weekday visitation versus weekend visitation. *Random* refers to the fact that each specific sampling session and individual selected is done randomly within the quota of levels defined. *Proportional* refers to adjusting the rate of sampling to attendance rates. Some survey workers make surveys proportional by setting quotas for the number of respondents surveyed during any session dependent upon previous attendance on that kind of day or time of day. A more direct method is to contact every fifth visitor who comes through the front door or is about to exit. This method both makes respondent selection at random and also permits more surveys to be completed during busy periods, automatically assuring proportionality to the overall sample completed.

The stratified random sample has been used to measure the audience attending a variety of cultural institutions in Denver.[43] Investigators found it useful to stratify their sample in a year-long study by levels of month, weekdays versus weekends, and time of day (morning, afternoon, evening). This kind of sampling strategy (which used a sample size of around one thousand) not only helped insure a representative sample, but also permitted analysis of survey results by key time periods.

A somewhat simpler version of this sampling strategy was applied to a year-long sample of visitors to a single institution, the Denver Museum of Natural History. Summer and winter were defined as one level and weekends/week days the other level. The size of the summer sample as opposed to the winter sample and weekends compared to week days was determined by organizing attendance figures according to these four time periods and then calculating sample size as recommended by W. G. Cochran in his *Sampling Techniques*.[44] It was important for the investigators to be able to describe any differences in visitors throughout these different time periods. The time stratification also provided a focus to the survey, since interesting comparisons could be made between winter and summer visitors as well as between weekend and weekday visitors. Such comparisons could yield information useful to program development. Forty days in each session were picked at random and twenty interviews conducted each day. Care was taken to balance weekend and week-day sample periods for both winter and summer. Since the winter period was spread over nine months, and the summer over three, the survey encompassed a full year with a total sample of eight hundred.

An even simpler strategy was followed in another visitor study supervised by a major marketing research firm.[45] One week was picked during each of four seasons and intensively sampled, with a thousand individual surveys collected. By intentionally collecting a large sample (a total of four thousand), the investigators compensated somewhat for the more restricted time coverage, although there is always a possibility that any specific week might have had a unusual pattern of visitation. The advantage to using the four sample periods is that it is far less time-consuming and easier to administer than a continuous sample for the same total time period.

How large should a sample size be? Technically, the sample should be large enough to (1) insure adequate coverage of the sample plan and permit break-out comparisons of various subgroups of data, and (2) keep sampling error within acceptable levels. There is no magic number for a sample size! Too small or too large a sample simply wastes resources. Most survey researchers calculate the minimum size sample needed for the planned survey design and then increase the sample by some factor (depending upon resources available) to secure a margin of safety. Many good sources are available on this topic.[46] Appropriate to our discussion here are the two aspects of sample determination mentioned at the beginning of this paragraph.

Finding a focus for the sample was mentioned earlier, and it is important to determine the number of major comparisons of subgroups before-hand. A sample where seasonal comparisons is a major break-out (comparison) will normally require more visitors to be sampled than a month-long study of visitors to a temporary exhibit. More respondents are needed if the year-long survey has additional levels of day-of-week and time-of-day to be broken out in the analysis. Data comparisons are also related to the number of visitor-description questions asked and the number of response categories used in the questions. Thus, if one wants to make detailed comparisons between such variables as age, sex, income, residence, first-time visit, etc., a larger sample is called for. If several comparisons are made at once, some of the break-out categories may have very few people in them. It is best to avoid a situation with several categories consisting of only a few respondents. The lower end of the response distribution (called the *tail of the distribution*) tends to run out of respondents, and this can be a problem if a lot of different comparisons or break-outs are planned.

Sample error refers to the likelihood of a particular result happening by chance. For example, suppose that in that sample of one hundred, ninety answer that they are from out of state. That would be a decisive result, and the chances are only five in one hundred that the actual percentage difference in residence would range from 2 percent in-state to a low of 82 percent out-of-state. For a sample of four hundred, the range of sampling error would be from 86 percent to 94 percent out-of-state answers. Sampling error is dependent upon actual sample size and the margin of difference in results. Election results are often hard to predict, even for professional survey researchers, because there may be only a 2 percent separation between preferences for two candidates. Such a small difference would fall into a sampling error range, even with a fairly large sample.

In conclusion, a sample of only a few hundred can be adequate if a limited survey sample design is used and interpretation of results is confined to a few major comparisons based on the total sample and clear-cut trends occur in the results. Sample size should be increased for more elaborate sample designs and analyses of results. Convenient tables exist for estimating sample errors for samples of different sizes and ranges in response break-outs.[47]

Select survey instrument. Another major component of survey design is selection of the kind of instrument used to collect information. The easiest to use is a prewritten questionnaire that visitors can fill out. Questionnaires can be prepared in an attractive format and do not have to look academic. Hotels, airlines, and other commercial organizations are good sources for examples of attractively designed questionnaires. Interviews require more time and the ability of the survey worker to handle a more demanding encounter with visitors. Robert Wolf has developed a naturalistic, or conversational style of interview that some may find useful. A good discussion of the pros and cons of interviews versus questionnaires is found in *Research Methods in Social Relations,* edited by C. Sellitz, L. S. Wrightsman, and S. W. Cook. That volume also contains appendixes on question-writing and sample selection that are very helpful. Warwick and Lininger have detailed chapters on all the survey tasks discussed in this section, including detailed sections on questionnaire and interview development. Don A. Dillman has prepared an invaluable source on conducting telephone or mailed questionnaire surveys. Finally, a recent and more technical book on improving the form and wording of survey questions has been prepared by Howard Schuman and Stanley Presser.[48]

Determine data analysis. It is also important to determine the way results from the survey sample will be analyzed. This point underscores what has been said already about anticipating sampling error and the number of comparisons to be made with survey results. Most visitor surveys rely on a descriptive break-out (some call this a cross-tabs analysis) of results to individual items. Each question is summarized by the percentage of results to each answer category (for example, sex: 55 percent male, 45 percent female). Descriptive computer programs for summarizing survey data are common nowadays, and part of the survey design planning is to anticipate data analysis needs.

Pilot tests. A final part of the survey design task is to pilot-test questions and the planned instruments, be they questionnaires, interviews, or both. This point cannot be emphasized enough. Specific questions and entire instruments can be improved by trying them out on a small sample of visitors. It is particularly important to find out whether questions are understood by visitors in the same manner as they were intended by the question-writer. The best way to determine visitors' understanding of question intent is to talk informally with visitors in the pilot sample and solicit their advice and help. Invariably, some changes grow out of pilot tests.

Task Three: Organizing Field Work

Once questionnaires and/or interviews are pilot-tested and completed, it is time to set up the specific procedures for collecting information. Warwick and Lininger have a good summary chapter on organizing field work, including suggestions for training interviewers. Their advice is most appropriate for large-scale professional surveys, but a number of the ideas they propose can be applied to the typical visitor survey.[49]

Final forms of questionnaires and/or interviews need to be printed and made ready for distribution. If possible, have the survey printed on one side of a page only, since people are likely to miss questions printed on the reverse side. Some survey workers prefer the final survey instrument to be printed with data-coding spaces placed in the margin, for ease in keypunching. Another useful tip is to have a professional writer go over printed instructions and questions prior to the final printing, to check for readability and ease of understanding. A good writer or an English teacher can also pick up grammatical mistakes that may have escaped attention earlier.

Gene Ball, at the Buffalo Bill Historical Center, found it useful in his survey efforts to have the fieldworker note and record such basic visitor information as sex, age level, size of group, and number of children in a party, rather than to include these items on the survey form.[50] Having workers record some information directly cuts down the survey length, but it is important to train the workers to collect the right information.

Specific procedures for administering a questionnaire need to be worked out. This step includes notifying museum security about the survey project. A table or booth may be needed to serve as a work station. Interviewers should have proper identification badges to distinguish them from solicitors. Questionnaires and/or interview forms need to be available to workers when they come to the museum for a sampling session. Sometimes completed survey materials can be picked up and dropped off at a guard station, since the station would be open during museum operating hours.

This discussion of field work is a good place to consider a new development in survey administration. Future visitor surveys may make use of computers, for both administration and data analysis. Computer terminals with touch-screen response capabilities could make the collecting of visitor-information much more cost effective. Visitors would not have to use a typewriter keyboard, but could indicate their responses by touching the screen directly at the point of a preferred printed alternative. Structured questions (such as those appearing in figure 3.1) can be easily programmed for computer use. The touch-screen computer is also very easy for visitors to use. Questions can be easily modified and a wide variety of survey ingredients used. Furthermore, survey results can be analyzed by the computer in one operation and the total time commitment of doing surveys reduced considerably.

It is too early to know how well a computerized intramuseum survey will work, since some people are intimidated by computers, while others love to "play" with them. "Play behavior" by children or adults could threaten the validity of such survey projects. Computers might work best at stations staffed by attendants where visitors could be asked to participate as a means of controlling sampling. The presence of an attendant might inhibit play behavior at the terminals. In addition to collecting survey responses, computers can provide orientation information.

The various survey resource books mentioned in this chapter usually contain information on selecting and training survey workers. Most museums will find staff, volunteers, and students to be the most likely groups for recruiting survey workers. One very important recruiting tip is to pick people who like to meet the public. Approaching strangers and asking for their participation is not an easy task. Some people, however, get great personal satisfaction from working with the public, and they are the ones who would be your best recruits. A survey worker should always be thought of as an ambassador for the museum. In that connection, it is important while workers are in training to provide them with information about the museum. Invariably, some respondents will ask the survey workers for information to enrich their visit. The interaction between worker and visitor should always be approached as a positive public relations event.

Task Four: Collecting Field Data

The sampling plan selected will require specific sample periods or sessions during which a set number of surveys will be completed, if possible. This survey schedule needs to be planned with the survey workers and posted where people can verify the times that they will be working. If there are large numbers of workers and/or a sampling plan that extends over a long period of time, it is a good idea to have a system of reminders (phone calls, etc.) for survey workers. At various times throughout a working day, specified staff members can take a few minutes from regular duties to distribute questionnaires or conduct interviews. Over time, say during a summer period, a surprisingly large number of completed surveys can be collected with a small daily effort by staff personnel.

Some survey researchers prefer to have field workers code responses for key-punching and computer entry. Others leave this task until the data-analysis phase. A small-scale survey might be tabulated as the work goes along, making it easier to summarize outcomes when the last responses are collected. For small surveys, modern-day pocket calculators with cumulative entry functions can be used to analyze results on a question-by-question basis.

In professional survey work, a potential quality-control problem is falsification of results by workers. While this is not usually a major problem, from time to time a worker will make up responses rather than do the actual survey work. Good supervision is the best guard against poor quality, whether its cause be falsification or simple carelessness. Incomplete responses, missed sample sessions, and worker fatigue or boredom are typical quality-control problems. It is important not to let workers go too long without attention (and praise) from a supervisor.

Task Five: Analyzing Survey Results

Computer programs are now available that make descriptive summaries of surveys fairly routine. Help in setting up a computer analysis of data should be obtained early. A small sample of subjects participating in a short descriptive survey would not yield too much data for hand-calculated percentage breakouts to be performed. However, with the advent of small computers, even a limited survey project is best analyzed on a computer.

Simple descriptive summaries of percentage comparisons are the most common analysis of visitor surveys, and they can be conveniently summarized in a computer print-out format. More complex analyses of the way different items of information go together require greater expertise and sophistication in statistical procedures. Outside help is definitely called for if a more complete data analysis is desired. General summaries of procedures for processing, analyzing, and interpreting research data are available in social science textbooks.[51] These sources outline specific procedures that will produce a data summary suitable for use as the basis of a report.

Task Six: Reporting Survey Results

A formal survey report should contain, as a minimum, a statement of the reasons for initiating the survey, summaries of procedures used (including the sample strategy), the results, and—most important—the implications suggested by the survey results. As mentioned earlier, sometimes it is much more effective to present survey results in a brief, highly readable form for decision-makers rather than in an academic-thesis style. If a complete report is prepared, a well-written summary and implication section should be included. This abbreviated section might well be printed on paper of a color different from that used for the text or set off from the main body of the report in some other manner. *The summary is what most people will read.*

Another useful procedure in survey reporting is to organize the computer print-out summary of the survey into a permanent file that can be consulted for specific information. Instructions that will help to find specific information sought should be prepared for survey users not familiar with print-outs. Surveys often generate much more information than is of immediate interest in a report, and a permanent file of complete results can help to answer questions that may arise at a later time.

Oral presentation is an alternative approach to reporting surveys and is frequently found to be the most direct and effective way of communicating information learned about the visitor. Ideas for report preparation are summarized in several sources.[52]

Planning ways to report survey results brings the process full circle, to the point where it began—namely, the consideration of those who will use the survey information.

In planning a survey, it is well to keep in mind such major problems associated with visitor surveys as those noted by DiMaggio, Useem, and Brown in their summary mentioned early in this chapter.[53] As a survey progresses, there may be sufficient staff turnover to make the final result of little value: without staff commitment to applications of any findings produced, what began as a promising visitor survey may turn out to be an exercise in futility. Another common problem is the lack of resources to implement program changes based upon survey results. The timing of survey evaluation must be related to planned activities, so that any recommendations produced by the survey can be acted upon at an opportune time in program development.

DiMaggio, et al., also mention hostility and disinterest on the part of some staff members as factors preventing surveys from being acted upon. Some people are hostile toward any survey activity and dislike the concept of audience research. Such hostility can manifest itself as a form of prejudice that will preclude acceptance of new ideas, no matter how well a visitor survey might have been conducted. Other people may be basically disinterested in any assessment of the visiting public because they prefer to operate a museum on the basis of what DiMaggio, et al., describe as connoisseurship. According to that point of view, public interests and reactions simply are not of value in the operation of a museum, because museums should be designed and operated by professional expertise alone. Clearly, museum professionals have different opinions about the value and appropriateness of visitor evaluation.

Failure to communicate survey findings and lack of staff follow-through on results were other factors mentioned as deterrents to survey effectiveness. Often final reports are simply lost in the system or written in a manner that makes communication and follow-through difficult.

Still other factors listed by DiMaggio, et al., bear very closely on the visitor survey. Some audience surveys are not useful because of inadequate research planning, unrealistic expectations about what a survey can accomplish, poor execution, and low technical merit. The contents of some final reports were also viewed as inappropriate for issues at hand.

Good planning must precede any visitor survey effort. Interestingly, DiMaggio, Useem, and Brown reported that surveys deficient in execution and technical merit could still make a significant contribution if the museum staff maintained strong interest in the effort.

A Few Caveats about Visitor Surveys

Intramuseum visitor surveys *can* be a useful tool for evaluations. In spite of misunderstandings about surveys, it is safe to conclude that many museum professionals have obtained from them useful information, documenting accountability and providing answers to technical-assistance questions. Surveys, even if not completed to the highest of professional standards, can destroy the myth of the "typical" visitor, can help to break up stereotypes about visitors, and can answer fundamental questions about people who choose to visit museums as a leisure-time activity. A few warnings about survey evaluation:

1. Sometimes it is more important to evaluate *what people do* than *what they say*. Later chapters emphasize the *behavior* of visitors, as well as information gained in talking to them. A. C. Nielson, the founder of media research work, has emphasized that it is more useful to analyze the programs people regularly watch or listen to than to ask them questions about their attitudes or preferences in media programming. Surveys are limited to questions that people can answer, and people who participate and provide responses know that they are being measured. This knowledge makes some respondents reactive—they answer in a self-conscious manner that could influence the validity of their responses.

For example, although some people may have complaints about a museum, they may not express them on a questionnaire or to an interviewer, but are careful to express them only to people they know. Negative comments may occur less frequently than positive ones, and this lower frequency may be due, in part, to a hesitancy to complain.

2. Subtle forms of bias can occur in sample selection if care is not exercised. Sex of the respondent can sometimes be a factor in the answers given in a survey: some husbands pass the job of answering on to their wives, so that a higher rate of female responses may occur. In other groups, it is traditional for the man always to answer requests from people outside the family or the paired relationship. Since it is hard to know whether these subtle biases cross each other out across a total sample, some evaluators like to use a very deliberate method for picking respondents (such as every fifth visitor), that assures random selection. Another subtle bias is for survey workers to approach visitors who look friendly or are attractive specimens of the opposite gender. Again, a definitive system of selecting survey participants is the best safeguard against bias.

3. Workers in survey projects, whether volunteers or paid staff, tend to tire and grow bored with asking the same questions over and over. There is a factor of repetitiveness in evaluation work that is unavoidable. Good supervision, reflecting interest in the worker, utilizes rotation of assignments and recruitment of enough help to avoid overburdening a small survey staff, to prevent fatigue or burn-out. It is also important to watch for dishonest workers who fake data, rather than collect it; workers who, because they are bored, become antagonistic to visitors, or become flip and cavalier in their attitude toward the survey work.

4. It is a good practice to keep track of the refusal rate of visitors who decline to fill out a questionnaire or complete an interview. Normally, this rate of refusal should be low. If it goes beyond 25 percent or 30 percent of those asked to participate, try to find out why people are not participating. For example, people may decline at the museum exit, because they have started to leave the area and feel that they haven't time to respond. Perhaps a better location can be found for intercepting visitors to participate in a survey.

5. As a rule, it is best to keep interviews and questionnaires as short as possible to encourage participation and avoid respondent fatigue. If there is a lot of information to be gathered, it may be wise to alternate forms of a survey instrument. Some of the same questions would appear on both forms. Each form would also have different questions, enabling a longer list of survey goals to be accomplished without making the

instrument any one visitor completes too long. Normally, an alternate-forms survey administration requires a larger sample size.

It is best to limit visitor surveys to fifteen or twenty minutes in length, unless visitors are warned that more time is needed. If a half-hour or more of a visitor's time is taken, a modest courtesy gift (a copy of the museum's calender or one free admission, for instance) might be appropriate.

6. Care should be taken not to overinterpret survey results without help in analyzing research data. The descriptive summary of individual items constitutes a conservative base for interpretation. Statements about what visitor characteristics go together require more sophisticated analyses. A simple frequency or percentage breakdown summary of individual question results can be a very helpful evaluation tool.

NOTES

1. Edward S. Robinson, "Exit the Typical Visitor," *Journal of Adult Education* 3:4 (1931): 418-423.

2. David S. Abbey and Duncan Cameron, "The Museum Visitor: III—Supplementary Studies," Reports from Information Services, no. 3 (Toronto: Royal Ontario Museum, 1961), pp. 13-16.

3. "Pennsylvania Museum Classifies its Visitors," *Museum News* 7 (February 1930): 7-8.

4. Frank A. Taylor and Katherine J. Goldman, "Surveys Surveyed," in *Opportunities for Extending Museum Contributions to Pre-College Science Education*, ed. Katherine J. Goldman (Informal publication of the Smithsonian Institution, Washington, D. C., 1970), pp. 15-20.

5. Paul DiMaggio, Michael Useem, and Paula Brown, "Audience Studies of the Performing Arts and Museums: A Critical Review," Research Division Report no. 9, Washington, D.C., The National Endowment for the Arts, November 1978. This report sampled a broad range of arts audiences, and the museum-visitor data discussed in this chapter was extracted from Tables 2-7 in the report.

6. Han-Joachim Klein, "Analyse von Besucherstrukturen an ausgewahlten Museen in der Bundesrepublik Deutschland und in Berlin (West)" (Berlin: Institute fur Museumskunde, 1984, Heft 9), pp. 193-196.

7. Donald Andrew Newgren, "A Standardized Museum Survey: A Methodology for Museums to Gather Decision-Oriented Information" (Ph.D. dissertation, Syracuse University, 1972), pp. 13-16.

8. Ross J. Loomis, "Please! Not Another Visitor Survey!" *Museum News* 52 (October 1973): 21-26.

9. "The 1966 Audience of the New York State Museum: An Evaluation of the Museum's Visitors Program," unpublished report (Albany, N.Y.: State Education Department, January 1968), p. 29.

10. Ted Cramer, "Marketing the Museum," *Museum News* 57 (January/February 1979): 36-38.

11. For a discussion of the way bias can influence perceptions of other people, see David J. Schneider, Albert H. Hastorf, and Phoebe C. Ellsworth, *Person Perception*, 2nd ed. (Reading. Mass.: Addison-Wesley, 1979), pp. 224-245.

12. A. Tversky and D. Kahnemen, "Availability: A Heuristic for Judging Frequency and Probability," *Cognitive Psychology* 5 (1973): 207-232.

13. Arthur Niehoff, "Audience Reaction in the Milwaukee Public Museum: The Winter Visitor," in *The Museum Visitor*, Publications in Museology 3, ed. Stephan F. de Borhegyi and Irene A. Hanson (Milwaukee: Milwaukee Public Museum, 1968), pp. 22-31. See also Arthur Niehoff, "Characteristics of the Audience Reaction in the Milwaukee Museum," *Midwest Museums Quarterly* 13:1 (1953): 19-24.

14. Michael O'Hare, "The Audience of the Museum of Fine Arts," *Curator* 17 (June 1974): 126-158.

15. Walter S. Brown, "The Public Visitor to the Seattle Art Museum's Tutankhamen Exhibition: Demographics and Behavioral Studies," unpublished report (Seattle: Seattle Art Museum, 1979), pp. 10-16.

16. O'Hare, "Audience of the Museum of Fine Arts," p. 151.

17. Marilyn S. Cohen, "A Yale University Art Gallery Survey," unpublished report (New Haven: Yale University Department of Art History, 1972), pp. 7-9.

18. Steven A. Griggs and K. Hays-Jackson, "Visitors' Perceptions of Cultural Institutions," *Museums Journal* 2:3 (1983): 121-125.

19. "Pennsylvania Museum Classifies Visitors," p. 7.

20. O'Hare, "Audience of the Museum of Fine Arts," p. 100.

21. A number of visitor considerations for historic house museums are mentioned in Laurence Vail Coleman, *Historic House Museums* (Washington, D.C.: American Association of Museums, 1933), pp. 81-86.

22. David Johnson, "Museum Attendance in the New York Metropolitan Region," *Curator* 12 (March 1969): 201-230.

23. See Kerry D. Vandell, Thomas E. Barry, Jay D. Starling, and Philip Seib, "The Arts and the Local Economy: The Impact of 'Pompeii A.D. 79,' " *Curator* 22 (September 1979): 204.

24. Gene Ball, informal reports, Cody, Wyo., Buffalo Bill Historical Center, 1977-1981.

25. George Nash, "Art Museums as Perceived by the Public," *Curator* 18 (March 1975): 60-61.

26. For an introductory presentation of bipolar or semantic differential questions, see Robert Sommer and Barbara B. Sommer, *A Practical Guide to Behavioral Research: Tools and Techniques* (New York: Oxford, 1980), pp. 147-151. For an advanced discussion, see Robert B. Bechtel, "The Semantic Differential and Other Paper-and-Pencil Tests," in *Behavioral Research Methods in Environmental Design*, ed. William Michelson (Stroudsburg, Pa.: Hutchinson Ross, 1975), pp. 41-78.

27. Carolyn Wells, *The Smithsonian Visitor: A Survey* (Washington, D.C.: Office of Museum Programs, Smithsonian Institution, 1969), pp. 45-46.

28. O'Hare, "Audience of the Museum of Fine Arts," p. 156.

29. "1966 Audience of the New York State Museum," pp. 53.

30. Cohen, "Yale Art Gallery Survey," pp. 24-28.

31. Brown, "The Seattle Art Museum's Tutankhamen Exhibition," pp. 3-17.

32. Walter S. Brown, "Member Survey of Seattle Art Museum, Part I," unpublished report (Seattle: Seattle Art Museum, 1979), p. 34.

33. Robert T. Bower and Laure Sharp, "The Japanese Art Exhibit: A Study of its Impact in Three Cities" (Washington, D.C.: The American University, Bureau of Social Science Research, 1955).

34. Vandell, et. al., "The Arts and Local Economy," pp. 210-212; Walter S. Brown, "The Economic Impact of the Public Visitor to the Seattle Art Museum's Tutankhamen Exhibit," unpublished report (Seattle: Seattle Art Museum, 1979), pp. 11-14.

35. Leslie Buhler, "The Business of Membership," *Museum News* 59 (November/December 1980): 42-49.

36. Elliot Mittler and Walter Wallner, "A Membership Study of the Los Angeles County Museum," unpublished report (Los Angeles: UCLA Graduate School of Administration, 1967).

37. Edward P. Alexander, *Museums in Motion: An Introduction to the History and Functions of Museums* (Nashville: American Association for State and Local History, 1979), pp. 3-116. For a good bibliography of background sources on museums, see *Museums in Motion*, pp. 284-292.

38. Beverly Serrell, "Survey of Visitor Attitudes and Awareness at an Aquarium," *Curator* 20 (March 1977): 48-52; Beverly Serrell, "Looking at Visitors at Zoos and Aquariums," *Museum News* 59 (November/December 1980): 36-41.

39. Rochelle H. Prague, "The University Museum Visitor Survey Project," *Curator* 17 (September 1974): 207-212.

40. Donald P. Warwick and Charles A. Lininger, *The Sample Survey: Theory and Practice* (New York: McGraw-Hill, 1975), pp. 20-45.

41. Robert E. Stake, "Evaluation Design, Instrumentation, Data Collection, and Analysis of Data," in *Educational Evaluation* (Columbus, Ohio: State Superintendent of Public Instruction, 1969), pp. 58-71.

42. Newgren, "A Standardized Museum Survey," pp. 13-16.

43. Gordon E. Von Stroh, "Who Uses Denver Facilities?" fifth report (Denver: Denver Urban Observatory, 1981), pp. 1-3.

44. "1974 Survey of Visitors to the Denver Museum of Natural History," unpublished report (Denver: National Association of the Denver Museum of Natural History, 1975); W. G. Cochran, *Sampling Techniques*, 2nd ed. (New York: Wiley, 1963), p. 72.

45. Leo Burnett, USA, "The Art Institute Survey," part 1 (Leo Burnett Research Department, 1975).

46. See, for example, Warwick and Lininger, *The Sample Survey*, chapter 4; I. Chein, "An Introduction to Sampling," in *Research Methods in Social Relations*, ed. C. Selltiz, L. S. Wrightsman, and S. W. Cook (New York: Wiley, 1976); and W. Mendenhall, L. Ott, and R. L. Sheaffer, *Elementary Survey Sampling* (Belmont, Calif.: Wadsworth, 1971).

47. Warwick and Lininger, *The Sample Survey*, pp. 312-313.

48. Robert L. Wolf and B. L. Tymitz, "A Preliminary Guide for Conducting Naturalistic Evaluation in Studying Museum Environments" (Washington, D.C.: Office of Museum Programs, Smithsonian Institution, 1979), pp. 14-40; Sellitz, et. al., *Research Methods*, pp. 291-329; Warwick and Lininger, *The Sample Survey*, chapters 6 and 7; Don A. Dillman, *Mail and Telephone Surveys: The Total Design Method* (New York: Wiley, 1978); Howard Schuman and Stanley Presser, *Questions and Answers in Attitude Surveys: Experiments on Question Form, Wording and Context* (New York: Academic Press, 1981).

49. Warwick and Lininger, *The Sample Survey*, chapter 8.

50. Ball, informal reports, Buffalo Bill Historical Center.

51. See, for example, Selltiz, et. al., *Research Methods*, chapters 13 and 14; Warwick and Lininger, *The Sample Survey*, chapters 9, 10, 11; or E. R. Babbie, *Survey Research Methods* (Belmont Calif.; Wadsworth, 1973), pp. 187-204.. Because computer analysis of survey data is common and keeps changing with new programs and hardware, readers should consult appropriate guides such as: Norman H. Nie, et. al., *Statistical Package for the Social Sciences*, 2nd ed. (New York: McGraw-Hill, 1975) and appropriate SPSS updates as released. There are also SPSS manuals for some microcomputers. A general source for microcomputer users is: Philip A. Schrodt, *Microcomputer Methods for Social Scientists*, Sage Publication Series in Quantitative Applications in the Social Sciences, no. 40 (Beverly Hills, Calif., 1984). See also Judith Rattenbury, Paula Pelletier, and Laura Klem, *Computer Processing of Social Science Data Using OSIRIS IV* (Ann Arbor, Mich.: Institute for Social Research, 1984), 196 pp.

52. Selltiz, et. al., *Research Methods*, chapter 15; Warwick and Lininger, *The Sample Survey*, pp. 321-327.

53. DiMaggio, "Audience Studies of Arts and Museums," chapter 3.

4

The Identity of Museums: Evaluation, Marketing, and Audience Development

Dozens of essays and books have been written defining the kind of place that constitutes a museum.[1] This chapter, while discussing museums as institutions, will stress the concept of *evaluation as a means of learning about institutional identity and audience development*.

Surveys conducted in the community are one specific tool for finding out what kind of image the public has of museums. Surveys can also help museum staff members determine who is likely to be a part of the museum audience and identify specific public perceptions of the museum that may be changed through public relations programs. At a time when development of both public and private support for museums is essential, we need to know what museums are all about, know how they are perceived by others, and recognize and work with the highly social nature of both museum visitation and support. The identity of an institution is directly tied to the nature and the source of its support.

Evaluation and Marketing the Museum

Increasingly often, marketing techniques and strategies from business are being applied to museum audience development. Such strategies may seem inappropriate for cultural institutions, but in actuality, there is a growing technical-assistance area called *marketing*, for public and nonprofit organizations. Writing on that topic, C. H. Lovelock and C. B. Weinberg distinguish marketing techniques for nonprofit organizations from those for commercial organizations in two ways: planning for nonprofit groups emphasizes nonfinancial objectives, and the needs of both users (visitors) and benefactors (donors, patrons) must be anticipated.

Museums can benefit from the technology of modern marketing methods. One important step is to develop a marketing plan as a form of self-study (see chapter 1). A marketing plan establishes desired visitor-related goals and indicates specific steps for reaching those goals. Lovelock and Weinberg suggest that a useful marketing plan should answer such questions as these:

1. Where are we now, in terms of what we have to offer and specific groups of people currently being served?

2. Where do we *want* to go, in terms of increasing the commitment of existing visitors and/or developing new audiences?

3. How do we increase audience commitment and/or size? What segments and groups in the public should we try to reach?

4. What resources (time, people, money) exist for audience development?[2]

Experts in marketing nonprofit organizations can provide many possible answers for these questions; readers may want to consult some of these sources. Many appear as references here,[3] and others are listed in the bibliography.

Evaluation is an important aid in implementing a marketing plan. Assessment of attendance and surveys of visitors are essential for answering questions about marketing. Also critical is identification of those segments of the public that may be potential visitors, museum members, or patrons. Good marketing must monitor the outcome of public programs and the way users or visitors evaluate their experiences.

Measuring Public Perceptions

Effective evaluation of the images people form of museums should produce both positive and negative reactions; and positive steps to change an unfavorable image can be taken only if critical or negative assessments of museums and their institutional identity are known. In "Demise of an Institution," Martha G. Hayes emphasizes the importance of monitoring for signs of institutional decay. Low staff morale, negative press coverage, and physical deterioration of building and collection are potential signs of a declining institution. She also notes that declining attendance can suggest that the public perceives a change in a museum. A decline in attendance is also likely to be accompanied by lower levels of volunteer support. Conditions within a museum can project an image that visitors and the public in general can often sense. Hayes correctly emphasizes that tighter economic times can make it difficult for museum staff members to keep a strong, positive image before the public.[4] Reduced budgets also make it hard to provide the quality programming that helps enhance a positive image. *It is exactly during such lean times that assessment of what people think about a museum becomes very important.*

Contributions, volunteer support, allocation of public funds, attendance, and success in acquiring grant funds all have some effect on the image an institution projects. Support depends not only on projecting the institution's function or mission well in public images, but also on the general level of institutional health or strength so conveyed and perceived by the public.

Social scientists have not always been kind to museums in their assessments of the way museums relate to the public. For some observers, museums project an image of elitist separation from the majority of society. Even the architectural design of many museums intimidates the public, projecting a formal image predicated on ancient designs for temples. Ce'sar Grana suggests that museums, especially those devoted to art, often project *mixed* images to the public. He bases this suggestion on the distinction between museums as public places and museums as private sanctuaries. As mentioned earlier, museum professionals differ in their beliefs, as to whether museums should develop public education programs and be highly accessible places or cater to a limited audience that already understands the collection. Grana observed that even the kind of interpretive label installed can communicate different images. Some labels are so technical in their message that they reinforce the image of museums as very private places for those already well informed.[5] Other label content is clearly intended for a wider audience and communicates information for those who may have little personal knowledge of the museum's holdings. This distinction between the institutional roles of educational democrat or cultural aristocrat confronts many museums, and not just those devoted to art. Whatever identity the staff and governing groups of a specific museum may choose to create, that identity cannot be completely understood without an effort to know the perceptions of the institution formed by both visitor and nonvisitor.

Nelson Graburn suggests that museum evaluation has neglected this important topic of *image*.[6] Not only must evaluators understand the way people view a specific museum; they must also understand how museums are perceived relative to other cultural and leisure-time institutions.

Museums exist within a cultural context that includes a growing number of alternatives for activities pursued during time off from work. Museum professionals must understand that the public may perceive their institution very differently from the way museum workers do. This divergence in perception does not mean that museums must necessarily change what they are and the functions they perform. It may, however, be necessary to work on the way the museum communicates its purpose and mission to the public.

How may public perceptions of museums be measured? One answer to that question was provided in George Nash's survey at an art museum. Nash surveyed samples of visitors and the public in general, asking each to indicate (on a checklist) words that described their more subjective impressions of the museum.[7]

Direct questions comparing museums to other institutions also provide insights into the institutional identity of museums. As an example, Manfred Eisenbeis describes a public survey completed in West Germany in the mid-1960s that focused on a description of the ways people view museums within the broader context of society. The description was shaped from answers to such questions as frequency of visits to museums as compared to time spent at other recreational activities such as visiting theaters, zoos, and going sightseeing; the extent of habitual museum visitation; specific attitudes toward museums as informative versus entertaining outlets for leisure pursuits; and knowledge of whether museums and other cultural institutions exist in the immediate vicinity. One innovative question asked respondents to pick institutions from a list (i.e., church, school, bank) that most reminded them of museums. Not surprisingly, monuments, palaces, and libraries were among the places most frequently associated with museums. Eisenbeis points out that the image projected by a museum can raise barriers to its use by some segments of the public.[8]

Barriers to Visitation

A notable strength of external surveys is that they include and make possible consideration of reasons people give for *not* visiting museums. By surveying samples of the public at large, it is possible to gain insights into barriers to museum visitation, since the sample includes people not already in the museum audience. Hans-Joachim Klein, in Karlsruhe, West Germany, completed a good example of a public survey designed, among other things, to define barriers to visiting a museum.[9] Klein and his colleagues sampled a cross-section of households in Karlsruhe and asked people their perceptions and visit patterns for a variety of local museums. Two major barriers for nonvisitors were identified.

First, the nature of the cultural institution itself could be a barrier. Differences in income and educational levels predisposed people to different perceptions of the desirability of visiting an art museum as compared to visiting a museum of science or industry. Museums—at least, some kinds of museums—were thought of as not being very approachable. A self-imposed restricted access seemed to be working.

The second major barrier was a social one: respondents who visited museums tended to be culturally active and made use of other institutions, such as libraries and performing arts centers. Museum visitation was a social expectation, and a natural part of leisure-time planning. For many of those who reported little or no use of museums, this social factor operated as a barrier. There was no expectation for visiting museums, or any other cultural institution, for that matter. Museums were not perceived as leisure-time alternatives, and visits to them were never planned. This social barrier to visitation was reinforced by the fact that family and friends within the nonuser's social circles did not attend museums, either. Klein was able to identify more specific barriers to museum visits among nonusers. Some of these barriers reflect the tendency, mentioned earlier, to avoid some museums as places that project an image of formality or are built with a templelike facade. According to Klein, the formal image, for some nonvisitors, was definitely a barrier to going to a museum. The idea that one must be an expert to understand the museum was another image that went along with perceived formality. Some survey respondents indicated that they knew objects in museums were valuable, but they felt that they would be unable to understand the objects and their meanings. Museums were also perceived as places where understanding and effort were required to experience the setting, and it was unlikely that one would have fun or actually enjoy the setting. Another barrier to nonusers was the opinion that museums were unfamiliar and uncertain situations, where one is not sure how to behave. For some, a barrier to museum use was that museums are unchanging in their nature, while sporting events and performing concerts and presentations must be attended, or the opportunity, presented only once, will be lost.

A final barrier mentioned was the notion that, at a museum, one would not learn anything useful or relevant to everyday life. Museums were not seen as being very practical or useful. This last barrier to nonusers reflects a deeper problem of people simply not valuing the experiences cultural institutions provide. This barrier may prove very resistant to change, and it is important to emphasize that a highly pluralistic society needs many different kinds of alternatives for leisure-time activities.

It is unlikely that these perceived barriers are typical of West German or European societies only. Their identification is valuable in revealing images that relate directly to the general public's understanding of museums.

And identification of perceived barriers is not the only useful "outside" information external surveys can provide. They can also reveal the enriching influence museums can provide for visitors' values or experiences when museum visitation is part of one's leisure-time activities.

Evaluation of Visit Benefits and Values

Closely related to the way people perceive museums as places and institutions in society is the concept of benefits or values they personally associate with museums. Some writers have advanced a number of imaginative ideas about the way visiting different kinds of exhibit spaces could produce a variety of perceived benefits. For example, Nelson Graburn speaks of *reverential experience* and Sheldon Annis of *dream space* that reflects a positive aspect of museums as temples.[10] Museum visitors often sustain some sacred or higher experience transcending everyday occurrences of work and living. Benefits from museum attendance parallel those of church or synagogue, in that something majestic and of great value is experienced. People need a place to fantasize, to let their minds explore ideas beyond everyday, routine matters. Graburn and Annis also suggest that museums can have associational or pragmatic space where the museum provides opportunities for a social occasion. What is actually in the museum may not be as important, in some ways, as the shared experience of visiting, of making the excursion a family event, a gathering of friends.

This benefit of experiencing a setting with someone is the positive side to the social barrier Klein talked about in his work. It is because of social expectations that one goes to the museum and uses the public spaces as group areas devoted to shared experiences. Stephan de Borhegyi entertained a related idea, years ago, when he suggested that the design of exhibit space should anticipate different levels of social activity, from solitude to group participation.[11]

Finally, the writings of Annis and Graburn mention *educational function* or *cognitive space*. Visitors can use museum spaces to pursue rational thought. Much of this kind of space uses didactic communication and attempts to teach some kind of lesson. Graburn thinks that museums are successful in this function only so long as the space is not viewed as overdemanding or too much like a school. Recall again that Klein, in his analysis of barriers to museum visitation, mentions that, for some, museums are seen as boring places that require great effort to understand. Graburn presents the positive side of this perception of museums as educational places by noting that museums are "front stage" settings, where visitors are concerned. By this, he means that people expect the museum to be a cultural production that will teach them about the world—not by exposing them directly to some aspect of the world, but by a carefully prepared representation of history, science, art, nature.

Both on-site surveys and external surveys can define and measure benefits like those suggested by Annis and Graburn. While evaluation of benefits and values associated with museum visiting is not so advanced as work with recreation research,[12] some examples of the measurement of public perceptions and visit benefits appear below.

The Social Nature of Visitation

One finding that keeps appearing in both on-site and external surveys is that museum visitation is a highly social event. Most people visit museums as part of a group that may include a friend, a spouse, several family members, or larger collections of people, from clubs, school outings, or groups of travel companions. The social nature of visitation should be kept in mind when discussing audience development. Part of the social nature of visitation is that people are most likely to hear of a museum, or be prompted to visit one, as a result of direct communication from another person. A basic implication is that audience development should reflect the importance of social influence, both as it relates to the experience of visiting museums and as a factor in causing visitation in the first place.

A conversational suggestion to visit a museum may well constitute the museum's single most effective source of publicity and public relations. As G. Donald Adams observes, even media messages designed for and received by thousands are likely to have their ultimate impact through word-of-mouth influence.[13] This person-to-person influence is especially important for prompting such activities as museum visitation. People who visit museums frequently are probably self-motivating, because of active interest in the museum and its offerings as well as the fact that they regard museums as familiar places. In addition, frequent visitors are likely to belong to that segment of the public that is active, in general, and often are initiators of different activities. It is exactly this segment of the audience that could be an important facilitator to others to try a visit.

In contrast to frequent visitors, occasional visitors may not initiate trips to the museum, but they would be receptive to prompting or to an invitation to visit. Messages about the museum carried through the media may have their primary impact only if reinforced by face-to-face discussion. In one experience at tracing this personal influence effect, it was found that the decision to visit was made over breakfast, while reading the Sunday papers. Impetus for that decision came from a feature story in the current-events section of a local paper. The story described a special object that had been put on display. People read the story, discussed it with friends, and then decided whether or not to go to the museum to see the object written about and extend their stay to see other things.[14]

All the messages aimed at visitors and potential visitors are likely to be channeled through the personal-influence process. Donald Adams has outlined what he terms "the word-of-mouth message chain," whereby museum literature, media messages, and any other source of information is processed in word-of-mouth communication by direct person-to-person influence. That influence may not only prompt a visit, but may also set up expectations for the exhibit items the visitor sees at the museum and the kind of experiences that result. Word-of-mouth influence continues after the visit, when visitors pass on to others their evaluation of their visit experience. *This evaluation is the most significant form of museum evaluation made, where visitors are concerned.* Postvisit evaluation either influences others to visit or suggests that museum visitation may not be for them. Word-of-mouth evaluation can cover all aspects of the museum, from the quality of objects displayed to whether it was easy to find a place to park.

Examples of Audience Development
(External) Surveys

A study of specific examples of surveys of different-sized samples intended to evaluate public perceptions of museums, benefits of visiting, and the social nature of museum use can be helpful. External surveys can have a strong marketing or audience development focus, since the results can be very useful for planning. While some examples that follow will be based on national, regional, or community-based samples, meaningful work can be done with small-scale samples, as illustrated in the discussion of community surveys. As good examples of external surveys about museums are limited in number, some surveys related to other cultural institutions have been included in this section.

A National Museum Survey

In the early 1970s, Brian Dixon, A. E. Courtney, and R. H. Bailey completed a nationwide survey of the Canadian public, designed to provide accountability and technical assistance information about Canadian national museum policy.[15] Of particular interest was the government policy of encouraging democratization of museums through making museums accessible to the public. The survey contrasted visitors and non-visitors and provided institutional identity information, as well as some ideas about the way people value museum visitation. Respondents in this national sample completed an at-home interview and a follow-up, mail-in questionnaire. Obviously, a survey as extensive as this could be accomplished only with major public and/or private financial support. A number of important findings came out of this survey. More than half the citizens sampled had visited a museum, confirming the belief that Canadian museums were accessible to the public. Visitors constituted a broad cross-section of the public in general. There was a tendency for museums to be concentrated in urban settings, making it less likely that rural residents used museums. The survey also confirmed that the public viewed museums as educational resources providing current and historical perspectives about Canada and its people.

Dixon, Courtney, and Bailey focused the survey toward audience development. One of the most important conclusions from their work was that *efforts to increase attendance should be concentrated on those who already come*, rather than on that segment of the public who have no interest in museums. Increased repeat visitation from those who have visited the museum at least once and those who come at infrequent intervals would provide a strong, increased attendance to Canadian museums, since more than half the public already visited once a year. Of great significance was the finding that infrequent visitors were less put off by the outward images of museums than by the interpretation found in the exhibits. Occasional visitors did not feel that the exhibits they saw communicated very well, and this gap in communication detracted from the value of the visit. This finding concerning occasional visitors is consistent with some of the perceived barriers noted by Klein in his survey work with householders in West Germany. Specific suggestions that would encourage greater visitation included having friendlier guides, better orientation information, and labels bearing more information about the objects displayed. Also of interest was the finding that the nonvisiting sample viewed museums positively and were not intimidated by the public images of museums; the public did not really view museums as elitist and *did* expect them to serve an educational function.

The Canadian study suggested—for *that* public, at least—that visitation was influenced less by negative images than by problems of accessibility and lack of communication. Given Canada's geography, many residents found it difficult to get to a major museum. Museums, for their part, needed to increase their communication to the public, to inform people about the kinds of experiences provided. The researchers concluded that admission fees were less of a barrier than lack of information about museums and problems in gaining access. Though mentioned earlier, it bears repeating that museums would also improve communication by evaluating the interpretational needs of occasional visitors and encouraging that segment of the audience to become more frequent visitors.

A Regional Survey

External surveys can sample a geographic region or a specific network of museums or other cultural institutions. The specific example discussed here was conducted by the National Research Center for the Arts and focused on arts institutions in New York State.[16] Thus, the survey effort was aimed at both a geographic region and a limited segment of cultural programs. Residents of New York State were surveyed about their participation in the fine arts and their attendance at cultural institutions, including museums. Participation in local arts organizations was queried, as well as that in major institutions in metropolitan areas within reachable distances. Respondents were also asked about their expectations for their children's involvement with the arts. While this survey was not focused directly on museums, it provided an excellent example of the way evaluation can counter stereotypes of public perception of cultural institutions. The New York Arts survey revealed that there was far more public interest and support for arts programs and institutions than is often thought. Geographic variables (rural versus urban residence), experience with the arts as children, admission cost factors, access problems (being able to get to a performance or museum), a strong sense of community or neighborhood competition for leisure-time commitments and knowledge or awareness of arts opportunities were all important reasons New Yorkers gave for supporting or not supporting cultural institutions. A broad range of public interest existed. The challenge for managers of arts institutions was to publicize and plan programs that would capitalize on this interest, develop ways of increasing access to the museum, and create programs competitive with the myriad other leisure-time activities available. Well-done external surveys can provide crucial information for this kind of institutional planning.

A regional or geographically focused sample can be designed on a much smaller scale than an entire state or region. In *The Quadrangle Research Notes*, D. Geoffrey Hayward planned a survey program for a group of four museums.[17] The surveys were coordinated to provide sample responses from both visitors and community residents. Readers may recognize the public relations or marketing potentials of several institutions working together to gather audience information and sharing or "networking" costs and resources to develop audience support for all participants. Shared external surveys can be a good way for smaller institutions in a region to collect information about actual and potential visitors. Hayward worked with four quadrangle museums in the Springfield, Massachusetts, area and led staff members through a series of evaluation tasks that included analysis of attendance and preparation of a visitor survey to be used at each of the four museums. This survey permitted identification of meaningful visitor groups for the museums and also made audience comparisons between the four institutions possible. As an example, the art museum in the quadrangle group drew more single visitors or couples than it did family groups, which often frequented the natural history museum. Such distinctions in user groups provided a basis for public relations appeals aimed at attracting people to each of the individual museums.

The intramuseum survey set the stage for completing a community-focused sample of downtown area residents. The survey was designed to move from a broad topic focus of the way respondents viewed downtown Springfield, to estimates of their use of local cultural facilities in general, to a specific focus on the four museums. Respondents answered museum-related questions about their awareness of specific museums and gave self-reports of visits made to any of the institutions. Queries included requests for basic information about visiting hours and willingness to pay admission fees. Nonvisitors or infrequent visitors were asked to give their reasons for not visiting or suggest reasons that would cause them to consider visiting (or increasing the frequency of their visits), as well as to indicate specific program interests. Such questions as the latter reflect marketing evaluation strategy. Responses to them give insight into what attracts (or fails to attract) people to a museum, and both programming and publicity can be developed to emphasize these points of attraction. The external survey concluded with fairly detailed questions about demographics.

Results from an intramuseum survey can be compared with findings

of the external sample of the public at large. One important thing to look
for is the frequency with which groups or kinds of people in the community at large turn out to be members of groups or types that are similar to or the same as the visitors identified in the intramuseum survey.
These people and groups comprise a ready-made potential audience. It
should be possible to draw more of the type of people who already come
by aiming publicity at that part of the community with similar interests
and encouraging those who do visit to bring friends and to tell other people they know about the museum. Hayward's work with the Springfield
museum group illustrated not only that the combining of external and
internal surveys provided information for audience development or market planning, but also that such evaluation can be very efficient when
a number of institutions in a region or a community pool resources and
work together.

Community-based Surveys

The Springfield museums survey could also serve as an example of
a community-based evaluation. This sample focus can include a suburban
community, a small town, or a major city. For example, large urban
museums can afford a modest survey effort by a professional research
organization. In the early 1980s, the Denver Art Museum engaged a survey organization to do a study of residents of an urban community. The
survey was focused on public perceptions of the museum and public
demand for various features and programs the museum provided.[18] A
strong advantage to using an established research organization is that
community sample units and data analysis procedures are already worked
out and available.

Table 4.1
Survey Objectives for a Community-Based Evaluation of a Local Museum

1. Demographic comparison of visitors (users) and nonusers
2. Relative ranking of museum in comparison to other places of interest in the community
3. Assessment of the awareness, interest, and participation in specific features and programs provided by the museum
4. Measurement of perceptions of the museum; what is the museum's public image?
5. Evaluation of museum operations such as store, restaurant, and theater
6. Analysis of sources of information about the museum, such as mailings, media releases,
   word-of-mouth

Source: This general list of goals is based on a specific survey prepared for the Denver
Art Museum by Research Services, Inc., Denver, Colorado, May 1982.

Table 4.1 summarizes the objectives of this survey and is a good working example of what can be studied with this kind of evaluation procedure. Results from the survey, which included museum visitors and nonvisitors, generated some interesting ideas about the public's perception of an art museum. The museum was mentioned as one of the top three interesting places to visit in Denver, and both visitors and nonvisitors showed generally positive impressions of the institution. An example of the kinds of specific questions the researchers asked, to assess perceptions, appears in Table 4.2. A question format that asks the respondent to assess specific attributes can yield both a general impression (by looking at the overall pattern of answers) and impressions of particular features as revealed by responses to individual questions. In the Denver survey, both visitors and nonvisitors made positive, overall evaluations to questions about the museum by indicating that positive statements described the museum better than negative ones. Differences between the two groups were important for a couple of items. Nonvisitors were less inclined that visitors to perceive the museum as a place that helped them understand and learn about art and as a place to which they would like to return, time and again. Both these findings are consistent with the Canadian study by Dixon, Courtney, and Bailey in the early 1970s that disclosed a difference between occasional and frequent visitors of museums. Active visitors feel benefit from a trip to the museum and like to come often. A real key to audience development is developing something new that will persuade occasional visitors (or nonvisitors) to cross over the line into more active involvement.

Table 4.2
Examples of Specific-Attitude Questions
Intended to Measure Public Perceptions of the Denver Art Museum

1. The Denver Art Museum is a place that helps me understand and learn more about art
2. A place to take a friend
3. A place that offers prestigious cultural exposure
4. A place that lets me be myself
5. A place that is difficult to learn about
6. A place I like to return to time and time again
7. A place that is only interested in a select group of people

Source: Research Services, Inc., Denver, Colorado, May 1982.

Note: Respondents answered each question by rating how strongly individual statements described the museum. Ratings ranged from 1 (not strongly at all) to 5 (very strongly).

The Denver community survey results challenged the strong stereotype of art museum visitors as being from the higher-income, higher-education levels. To be sure, users of the art museum were "up market," or inclined to be somewhat older; they did tend to have higher incomes, and many had completed more years of formal education than those their age with lower incomes. However, the total sample of visitors included some blue-collar and lower-income individuals. The museum visitors surveyed were a more balanced group demographically than some might think likely, for an art museum.

Community-based surveys can assess the demand or market for cultural events and opportunities. In this survey focus, members of the public are asked directly to indicate their interest in different cultural events or activities, such as museum visitation, and also to estimate the likelihood of their attending such offerings. Some psychologists advocate asking specific questions that include intentions to do a specific thing, such as visit a local museum.[19] It is important to establish a time frame for the intended activity to be carried out. Marketing research uses intentions frequently, to estimate demand, by asking respondents to indicate whether they intend to buy a particular product or attend a certain event within the next month, year, or some other time period. The following question illustrates this kind of survey focus:

Do you plan, within the next month, to buy a season ticket to the cultural events held at the community performing arts center? ☐ Yes ☐ No ☐ Don't know

The question was adapted from a community marketing survey for the arts in a city of about seventy thousand.[20] The survey was commissioned to help cultural resources management assess the demand for different kinds of programs, in an area where a new community center was soon to open. While the focus was on the arts, a similar type of marketing survey could easily be adapted to museums (see Table 4.3). Basic objectives for this survey focus would include:

1. Estimates for current level of use of the museum and other cultural institutions.
2. Estimates of awareness and interest in various events and programs.
3. Perceptions of reasonable cost levels.
4. Determination of courses of information about the museums.
5. Estimations of market or audience size for museum attendance and/or different museum programs.
6. Determination of the size of the specific market, such as local university students.

Table 4.3
Sample Questions for Use
in a Community-Marketing or Consumer-Demand Survey
about Museums

1. *Past Attendance*
Estimate the number of times you have visited the following places during the time periods indicated:

Place	During the past month	During the past year (including the past month)
1. The local history museum		
2. Local movie theaters		
3. The local art museum		
4. Museums outside the community		
5. Local sports events		

2. *Awareness/Interest*
How interested are you in attending each of the following? (Check appropriate square).

	Very high	High	Low	Very low	Not aware of this choice
1. Local theater productions					
2. Local history museum					
3. Local sports events					
4. Local ballet productions					
5. Local art museum					

3. *Cost (Willingness to Pay)*
What would you be willing to pay to attend each of the following?

	Indicate dollar amount
1. A local live theater production	
2. A visit to the local art museum	
3. A first-run movie at a local theater	
4. A local ballet production	
5. A visit to the local history museum	

4. *Source of Information*
When planning personal and/or family leisure-time activities, what sources of information do you use?

Activity	Monthly schedules or newsletters	Mailed adver- tisements	Tele- vision	Radio	Papers	Friends
1. Museum events						
2. Sports events						
3. Movies						
4. Live theater						
5. Music performances						

5. *Intention to Attend*
The local history museum would like to know how likely it is that you would do any of the following during the next year.

Activity	Very likely	Likely	Unlikely	Very unlikely
1. Visit the museum galleries				
2. Attend a guided tour of the museum				
3. Attend an evening film presentation				
4. Visit a temporary exhibit				
5. Take out a museum membership				

Source: Sample questions are modified from the student survey *Marketing the Arts in Fort Collins,* by students of the College of Business, Colorado State University, Fort Collins, Colorado, May 1978.

This community arts marketing survey was cited for another reason: the work was completed by local Colorado State University students majoring in marketing and is a good example of the way a nonprofit cultural organization, without an extensive budget for marketing research, could conduct a community survey. The students, in turn, were provided with a useful learning experience.

The Colorado State survey revealed a definite market in Fort Collins for increased cultural programs; it provided guidelines for types of events that would be most frequently attended; set price levels and preferred performance times; and chose the most effective radio and newspaper sources for promoting arts programs. The study also identified types of events that would appeal to local university students.

All community surveys mentioned thus far have required considerable planning and sampling to learn about public images of museums. It is not always possible to survey a sample of a few hundred respondents, and some small sample procedures can be used to estimate community perceptions of museums.

Donald Adams, in his book on public relations for museums, calls attention to the focus group survey procedure as a way of learning how people perceive museums.[21] A small group of people—twelve or so—are given an in-depth interview and asked to discuss their answers to the questions. The exchange between group members often brings out a variety of interesting ideas. Mixing different types of people in the group can lead to insights about differences between community groups. An example is a survey of the Witte Memorial Museum in San Antonio, Texas, for which a local research firm—EGC Associates, Inc. —conducted community focus group interviews. In one instance, a focus group of mothers were interviewed together, at a shopping center setting, about their use of such local institutions as the zoo and the natural history museum. The mothers did not know the interview was commissioned by the local natural history museum. As the museum director, Mark Lane, put it, listening to people discuss your museum in comparison to other places they visit is like overhearing your best friends talk about you. The experience can be painful, but it does provide insight. A focus interview generates the opportunity to gain insights quickly. Some mothers sampled in the case in point noted that the exhibit of festival gowns (part of an annual celebration in San Antonio) interested them and enhanced a visit to the museum. This interest was revealed at a time when museum staff people were seriously considering dropping the annual exhibit— and the outcome of the interview was renewed staff interest in the exhibit.

The interviews also revealed that children were often the first in the family to know about new things in the community, such as the opening of a dinosaur exhibit at the museum. While children would learn first about things of interest, parents made the decision to visit. The Girl Scout organization in San Antonio was identified as an especially effective source of information about events that would interest children and families.

Overall, the series of San Antonio focus group interviews provided information about optimal operating hours, images the public had about the museum, the need for more interpretation, and varied interests in different exhibits. Group visits were heavily influenced by children, and this finding was consistent with the perception of the museum as an educational institution. However, the appeal of providing children with an educational experience must be combined with the perception that museums can also provide an enjoyable group experience. In other words, *to attract a broader cross-section of people, museums need to be seen as both educational and fun.* Furthermore, the focus group surveys in San Antonio promoted the idea that museum attendance is less a matter of demographics (i.e., level of education, income) than of life styles. People who are active, who like to do things and go places, are good candidates for museum visitation.

Another small sample strategy is to ask a carefully selected group of people to visit the museum or other setting and then have them complete some kind of evaluation exercise. As a case in point, the staff at the Ashton Villa Historic House Museum in Galveston, Texas, asked a cross-section of local residents to visit the house and complete a post-visit questionnaire.[22] The only common denominator in the sample was that all the respondents had an interest in historical preservation. Obviously, different kinds of samples could be invited to the museum. The questionnaire used was quite complete and asked for evaluation on a variety of topics (see figure 4.1).

This procedure of inviting a small, selected group of people to evaluate something is a variation of a consumer-panel method, where products are rated by small groups of actual or potential users. Information can be collected rather quickly; and often, important reactions become apparent. However, the limitation of a small and possibly biased sample must be kept in mind. Ideally, results from small sample surveys should be replicated with a larger sample effort. An invitation to visit aimed at a sample of nonvisitors can also be combined with a focus interview that follows completion of the visit.

Comparison of Visitors and Nonvisitors

Some of the external surveys discussed thus far have included both visitor and nonvisitor samples. This sample strategy provides for a very important comparison and can be the primary focus of a survey. The sample can be based on actual visitors and an equal number of people from the community who have not visited. On the other hand, the total sample can be drawn from the community, with respondents divided into those who indicate visits and those who do not. Obviously, this is not a foolproof separation, since some people may not accurately indicate their visitation history. On the average, however, people will provide a fairly accurate statement and can remember and report basic information about themselves.

One use of such a comparison-focused external survey is to contrast very detailed profiles of museum users and nonusers, as illustrated in a study of library patrons and nonpatrons by Michael Madden. Madden completed a follow-up study to a national survey of life styles conducted by the Leo Burnett advertising agency of Chicago.[23] The survey had asked respondents to indicate how often they used a library. The follow-up analysis was performed for the Schaumburg Public Library in Illinois, on existing data, to estimate profiles for library nonusers, moderate users (one to eleven visits a year), and heavy users (twelve or more annual visits) among residents in a medium-sized community. Madden's report is a good example of taking advantage of a larger, completed project to learn something about a nonprofit organization's audience. Such opportunities can be found and can help compensate for the absence of major funds for evaluation.

Because the original Chicago survey was designed to assess life styles in the United States, a lot of interesting information could be compared by level of library use. Results indicated that life styles in general could suggest appeals or needs related to library programs. For example, women who were already nonusers of libraries were unlikely prospects for outreach efforts, since their life styles were very home-oriented and restricted to few outside interests. This finding is not much different from that of other surveys already reviewed that suggested nonusers would be the hardest segment of the public to recruit for a cultural institution. In contrast, Madden found that the high-use library visitor is very active in pursuing a variety of other interests outside the home and makes demands that local libraries have difficulty meeting without networking with other institutions to provide resources for high-use patrons. Consistent with findings from other external surveys, moderate users are the best prospects for audience growth through encouragement of increased repeat visits.

The key finding, consistent with museum visitor research, was that heavy users of libraries are active people in general and are likely to use a wide variety of community resources. Museum publicity and programming efforts must intervene or be capable of breaking into that pattern of activity. At the same time, this segment of the public consists of people who feel confident about using resources and they are people who will make commitments. They also are likely to be a part of groups frequented by other active people, who are prime candidates as new visi-

FIRST IMPRESSIONS	"GRADE"	COMMENTS/SUGGESTIONS
A "welcome" feeling	————	
Landscaping	————	
Signage	————	
Is it clear how to enter?	————	
Staff greeting	————	
Information on tours	————	
Waiting period	————	
Comfort while waiting	————	
Cleanliness/maintenance	————	
Parking	————	

Opportunities for improvement:

THE TOUR ITSELF

Information value	————	
Interesting, not boring	————	
Enjoyable	————	
Length—too short/too long	————	
Knowledgeable staff/guide	————	
Helpful staff/guide	————	

Opportunities for improvement:

COLLECTIONS/FURNISHINGS

Interest/uniqueness	————	
Appropriateness	————	
Quantity—too much/too little	————	
Method of display	————	
Quality of items on display	————	

Opportunities for improvement:

VISITOR COMFORT	"GRADE"	COMMENTS/SUGGESTIONS
Seating	_____	
Temperature control	_____	
Refreshments/drinks	_____	
Lighting	_____	
Noise level	_____	

Opportunities for improvement:

AUDIO-VISUALS

Image quality	_____	
Sound quality	_____	
Content	_____	
Viewer comfort	_____	
Surroundings	_____	
Information value	_____	

Opportunities for improvement:

SUPPORTING MATERIAL

Pamphlets/brochures	_____	
Gift shop merchandise	_____	
Maps and directions	_____	
Info on GHF (Galveston Historical Foundation)	_____	

Opportunities for improvement:

Fig. 4.1. *Items from a questionnaire handed out to community respondents invited to a setting administered by the Galveston Historical Foundation. Respondents were asked to assign a grade, ranging from A (for excellent) through F (for failure), for each survey item listed.—Adapted, by permission of the Galveston Historical Foundation.*

tors, new members, and exponents of a new outlook. Audience development cannot be thought about independently from leisure-time life styles and the benefits that museum visitation provides for those life styles. The survey analysis also suggested that it could be useful to think in terms of three types of people: nonusers of museums, occasional users, and heavy users.

That three-way distinction of the public's behavior toward a cultural institution proved very important in a survey completed by Marilyn Hood for the Toledo (Ohio) Art Museum.[24] Five hundred randomly selected residents of Toledo were surveyed. Hood focused the survey on the topic of why people *do not* go to museums. She also integrated into her assessments the leisure-time preferences of the survey respondents. Her work for the Toledo Art Museum is a good example of the way a well-planned survey can accomplish a number of objectives. As mentioned, Hood found it important to keep a three-way distinction of visitor types in mind when talking about the public's perception of the Toledo Art Museum. Heavy users of the museum (those averaging as many as forty possible visits per year) understood the "museum code" or the institutional expectations of the way for visitors to act and derived great satisfaction from being in the museum. While the heavy-users constituted only about 14 percent of the residents in Toledo, they made up 40 to 50 percent of the museum's annual visitation, because of their high repeat visitation rates. Clearly, these people do not perceive the museum as having barriers to their use of that setting. Because Hood had survey respondents indicate what kinds of psychological criteria they used to judge the value of leisure-time experiences, it was possible to prepare contrasts between the three user/nonuser groups. The criteria were developed from a review of materials in museum studies, leisure science, and consumer research. Hood used six major visitor-benefit criteria in her survey:

1. The value of being with people, engaging in social interactions, and sharing an occasion.
2. The value of feeling that you are doing something worthwhile.
3. The value of feeling comfortable and relaxed in one's environment.
4. The value of being challenged by new activities.
5. The value of having an opportunity to learn.
6. The value of being an active participant.

The Toledo survey helps to fill the void in information about the reasons people decide to *visit* a museum (or *not* to visit) as part of their nonworking-time options. Hood found important distinctions in the perceived benefits of museum visitation between the three levels of use. Heavy users valued all six of the criteria listed above, and—most important—judged all of them to be a part of museum visitation. Furthermore, frequent visitors valued more than others did the benefits of having an opportunity to learn, being challenged by new experiences, and feeling that a museum visit was doing something worthwhile with one's leisure time. The frequent visitor is that segment of the audience that will respond to the challenge and opportunity of new programs and changing exhibits. They are also good prospects for high-quality programming that provides new learning and different kinds of challenges.

In strong contrast to the attitudes of frequent visitors were the benefits perceived by nonusers as being most important. Nonusers valued opportunities for social interaction (being with people), active participation in leisure-time events, and feeling comfortable in their surroundings. In addition, nonusers did not see these leisure-time features or benefits as being present in museums. Furthermore, these people did not visit museums as children. Hood cautions against assuming a stereotyped idea that people who do not visit museums are apathetical or disinterested in museums. Rather, the apathy or disinterest of many of these individuals is caused by their having already established leisure-time activity choices that compete with visiting museums. The community survey about the Denver Art Museum cited above (see note 18) revealed that lack of interest in art was not sufficient to explain why some people had not visited the museum. Nonusers also listed being very busy or simply never thinking about the museum as important reasons for nonattendance. The challenge is to get this nonuser segment of the public to try a museum visit. Part of the challenge is also realizing that people who do not visit museums also do not know the museum code of expected behavior and are likely to feel uncomfortable if they do visit. As noted above, nonusers are also people who value being at ease in their surroundings.

Given the Toledo survey information about nonusers, it is not surprising that the authors of the Canadian National survey cited above recommended developing audiences through encouraging infrequent visitors to make repeat visitations. It is difficult to get people to try a *new* experience, especially if they think they may not feel comfortable with that experience. As Hood notes, museums have typically catered to the *frequent* user and developed settings that that kind of person feels comfortable with. Attracting nonvisitors and then providing a satisfying experience for these individuals can require altering the museum to meet different criteria for leisure-time experience. It is also possible that non-visitors who start coming to museums will begin to change their expectations for leisure-time activities.

Results of the Toledo survey also caution against stereotyping the *occasional* visitor. It is tempting to think of people who visit museums infrequently as being the same as frequent visitors. People who visited the Toledo Art Museum once or twice a year were more like nonvisitors than visitors. As children, the occasional visitors were socialized into leisure-time events that emphasized active participation, social interactions, and entertainment. Their participation with museums is likely to be an activity acquired in adulthood and one that they are not completely comfortable with. They do not feel at home in a museum, and they are likely to visit museums in groups as a way of dealing with the feeling of being ill at ease. Hood's research helps clarify the Canadian National survey finding that infrequent visitors are more critical of interpretation found in museums than frequent visitors are. The Toledo Museum findings are also consistent with Klein's work on perceived barriers to visitation. Museums must not only interpret for the less-knowledgeable visitor, but must create orientation experiences that make infrequent users more at ease with the museum environment. That is, *they must do these things if they want to produce greater involvement within a larger segment of the population.*

Hood's work demonstrates that a well-planned external survey can produce a great deal of information about visitors and nonvisitors. In particular, it serves to emphasize that audience development must be based on a clear understanding of the reasons people go or *do not go* to museums.

It is also possible to separate the audience into different levels of use with on-site surveys, and that produces results similar to the external surveys discussed. Writing on museum marketing, J. E. Robbins and S. S. Robbins surveyed an audience at a major exhibit in a metropolitan art museum.[25] Though not an external survey as such, the study was able to distinguish between visitors of high, moderate, and low attendance to cultural events (museums, ballet, concerts, etc.) by using questions about frequency of actual attendance and desire to attend such events. The Robbins and Robbins survey results support the basic idea that frequent visitors constitute the central audience for cultural programs, while moderate users represent the best potential for expanding the audience. Infrequent visitors (such as the nonusers identified in external surveys) represent a resistant potential audience that could be won over only with a major effort at public relations aimed at changing attitudes. The investigators concluded that low-frequency users should be recruited only after the other two audience types have been fully developed.

Assessing Life Styles and Audience Development

Some researchers in fine arts audience development have concluded that life styles and leisure-time preference provide better information about potential museum visitors than such demographics as place of residence or occupation.[26] Life style surveys combine many of the features of marketing and public-perception studies and attempt to define the way different values and needs combine to determine social trends such as the kind of leisure-time activities people will seek and participate in.

Surveys that emphasize life styles ask questions about a wide variety of daily activities, including media use, kinds of pets kept, products bought, and preferences in recreational activities. From this large pool of background data, a set or typology of specific life styles is distilled to describe a limited number of ways in which people might react to modern society. In one example, the typology summarizes nine life styles that characterize American society in the late twentieth century.[27] According to this study, Americans can be typed according to the degree to which they are driven by basic needs (as in the case of those who are poor, or living on the edge of poverty), directed toward personal or inner goals, and directed toward belonging or achieving goals based on society's values and expectations. Adapting this values-and-life styles (VALS) typology to demand and interest in performing arts provides an interesting variation to a marketing survey.[28] Likely preferences and participation are linked to broader life style patterns. For example, people who emphasize achievement and meeting social needs are likely to attend cultural events because they view attendance as good for business and/or social advancement. Others who are more inner-directed in their choices of activities attend to gain experiential or more personal satisfactions from exposure to performing arts. The VALS approach to surveying the public is good for identifying the range of motives that prompt people to attend performing arts events and appears to yield information consistent with Marilyn Hood's analysis (mentioned above) of the reasons that people attend art museums. Such surveys can be no stronger than the basic life style typology they are based on, but they can produce some interesting information for identifying the kinds of people who might respond favorably to appeals about visitor programs.

Preparing for an Audience-Development Survey

An understanding of the perceptions held of museums by different groups among the general public, as measured by external surveys, is acquired knowledge that can be used in a number of ways. One specific use is publicity and audience development. Publicity about programs or the existence of the museum itself can be aimed at people most likely to respond. This is exactly the way professional marketing firms help clients develop buyers or consumers for different products or services. People are identified who are more likely to need or at least to be interested in a given product, and messages are prepared that are thought to address those people appropriately. The messages may contain new information of interest to those already commited to the product—think of all the television commercials that contain the word *new* associated with a well-known, long-established brand name. This *newness* is intended to attract people who already know the product and encourage them to keep on using it, especially now that it is *new* and, of course, *improved*. Sometimes the product really *is* new, and the message is intended to appeal to established buyers and encourage them to try the new product, especially if it is associated with an established company brand name. Audience development, in this case, consists of keeping those already loyal and possibly increasing the rate of their involvement, even if it means using a new product, but one that is safely in the fold of the parent company.

Museums engage in this kind of audience development when they appeal to existing visitors, or at least, to people who are very similar to existing visitors. Museums also have the problem of finding ways to present a product that is familiar. In fact, a major challenge for museums is dealing with the image that museums are unchanging. Frequent visitors of museums may visit often because they have learned to use museums through independent study and self-directed activities. But special programming, memberships, previews, and changing exhibits are ways in which museums offer something *new* to their established audiences. Too much change, or newness, can upset some established visitors, since it can mean the loss of a valued feature. Established audiences are retained with a combination of changing features and retention of "landmarks"—that is, well-established exhibits or programs that the visitor is known to value.

Sometimes information in publicity is directed toward those who are somewhat uncertain about a choice and may be open to buying a different product, or, as in the case of museums, to trying a new or less familiar experience. Occasional visitors may be the best target for this kind of message. Consistent with the profile of perceived benefits discussed earlier, occasional users of museums are likely to be more interested in active events that provide social interaction. They may perceive the museum as a place they will not find comfortable, one that will be of little interest. Information that emphasizes sharing of experiences, the active nature of participation, the possibility of interactive occurrences, and the museum as a setting they *can* be a part of and comfortable with stands the best chance of encouraging occasional visitors or nonvisitors to try a museum appearance. Occasional users are likely to have a degree of uncertainty in their minds about museums and can be reached with messages that provide positive information about the potentials of museums. Messages should be active in voice and positive in appeal to one's interest in doing things as well as merely getting out of the house and undergoing new experiences. It is the occasional visitor's uncertainty, combined with the fact that people in this group already *know* about the museums, that makes infrequent visitors likely targets for museum audience expansion.

It is much more difficult to attract first-time visitors from that segment of the public showing little interest, with no personal social history of contact with museums. It is precisely *this* segment of the public that provides a caution against naive assumptions about making museums appeal to everyone. The United States is a very pluralistic society, and there is room for many opportunities to coexist. Museums are appropriate for clearly defined segments of the general public, and efforts to build visitation should concentrate on these segments of active visitors and occasional visitors.

This does not mean that *new* audience groups cannot be brought into the museum community. It *does* mean that recruiting first-time visitors will be difficult and may require special programs and efforts. A special section at the end of this chapter discusses the challenge of recruiting first-time visitors.

The majority of a museum's audience is something like a series of expanding circles. Staff, volunteers, major financial-support patrons, and high-frequency visitors are at the center of the circles, with medium-use visitors next, and occasional users further out from center. At the outer circles are the nonusers, with those who have no interest in the content of the museum being furthest from the center. In general, success with audience development will diminish as groups stretch further from the center of these circles of support. This community of support can cut across income, education, neighborhood, and other characteristics of the public at large. What is of importance is *a shared interest in the museum*. Results of external surveys bear out this point about shared interest cutting across background factors. Most surveys reveal that there is a breadth of interest among visitors that can include wide segments of the public.

It is a mistake to tie museum visitation too closely to socio-economic variables. A museum's audience, both realized and potential, is attracted by the museum's type and emphasis, its collection, location, information program, resources for visitor programming, and quality of interpretation, especially for infrequent visitors. If it is a mistake to stereotype the potential audience as being any and every individual in the general public, it is also important not to assume that only a limited segment of people will visit. The specific circle of influence or community of support for a particular museum must be determined in a verifiable way. Realized and potential audiences will both be very different at different kinds of museums.

Finding a Focus for an External Survey

As with a visitor survey conducted on-site, it is important to focus the mission of a specific external survey. The following five categories of information summarize many of the topics found in external surveys.

1. *Demographics*. Knowing such demographic connotations as age, sex, occupation, and area of residence for the individuals in an audience can be of practical help. Neighborhoods or communities that contain high levels of potential visitors can be identified and publicity and/or outreach programs can be concentrated toward these areas. Identifying sectors of a city where museum visitors or potential visitors are few in number might suggest opening a branch museum in such areas. Sometimes the best way to involve new audiences is to locate a branch museum in a community and plan that branch so that it is easily accessible to people in that community. This immediate, community accessibility can be especially important for neighborhoods at some distance from temple-like main museums situated in exclusive locations not frequented by a wide sector of the public. Demographic information can also help guide planning for a museum's mobile unit, or other traveling exhibit programs.

2. *Comparisons of leisure-time preferences*. Modern advertising and marketing research has gone beyond surveys comprised solely of demographic information—now it is important to match products and mes-

sages to types of people or profiles of life style interests. As discussed here, frequent visitors to museums differ in their interests and in perceived visitation benefits from nonvisitors or even occasional visitors. Publicity messages, new programs, special exhibits, and certainly museum interpretation should all be developed *with the interest of each different group deemed important.* For example, a new exhibit or a temporary show could be planned to include opportunities for family interaction and the social nature of visits emphasized in publicity. These two features should help draw the less-frequently-visiting museum public to the exhibit. Interest or life style profiles can help suggest where a local museum fits into the opportunities for leisure-time activities and what specific niche it might fill.

3. *Assessment of perceptions and images of the museum.* The importance of a museum's public image cannot be overstressed. Tied to assessment of image is the public's perception of barriers to visitation, especially among infrequent visitors or nonvisitors. Publicity can be aimed at groups that might feel uneasy about visiting a museum because they feel that they might not fit in. Photographs displaying visitors in casual attire (very casual, in the case of tourist visitors) and/or family groups with small children can be a subtle way of emphasizing accessibility and a relaxed atmosphere. Interpretation aimed at the more general public can be developed to encourage first-time visitors or infrequent users to discover a more meaningful aspect of visitation. Programs that appeal to family or other group attendance and group interactive exhibit features can be included in new exhibit planning. The important point is that the nature of these public images must be assessed.

Closely tied to assessment of image are surveys of the consumer demand or need for the experiences and programs offered by museums. Demand for specific programs or experiences can be a means of drawing to a finer focus general leisure-time preferences. One set of questions may deal with both general leisure interests and estimates of specific intentions associated with each interest. Questions of this kind might be somewhat modified versions of those in Table 4.3—something like the following.

1. Do you plan to engage in an outdoor recreational activity within the next three months?
   ☐ No
   ☐ Yes (If *yes*, check the activity or activities you would most likely engage in during the next three months)
      ☐ Local river fishing

☐ Picnicking in local parks
☐ Overnight camping at local sites
☐ Backpacking in local forest areas
☐ General hiking on local trails
☐ Other:

2. Do you plan to attend a community performing arts event during the next three months?
   ☐ No
   ☐ Yes (If *yes*, check any of the following you plan to attend during the next three months.)
       ☐ Local ballet performance
       ☐ Performance of the local symphony orchestra
       ☐ Community theater performance
       ☐ Other:

3. Do you plan a visit to the local history museum during the next three months?
   ☐ No
   ☐ Yes (If *yes*, check any of the following you would attend during the next three months.)
       ☐ A visit to see the galleries and exhibits
       ☐ A visit to hear a presentation
       ☐ Participation in the museum's weekly Thursday night film program
       ☐ Participation in the museum's monthly history walk tour
       ☐ Other:

The question format illustrated above can be modified in many different ways. Instead of intention, the focus can be on interest in different leisure-time activities, both general and specific, that are available in the community. The time frame for activities can also be modified.

People may acquiesce in or go along with queries on surveys and provide data that are questionable. Care should be taken to verify external survey findings. Sometimes a focus interview or more of an in-depth discussion with a few individuals can help validate whether or not estimates of interest or likely use are realistic. It may also be helpful not to identify the museum as the sponsor of the survey, as some people might feel inclined to present a good image by showing that they support the museum even though their actual interest is not great. On the average, however, most people try to give an honest estimation of their interests and intentions, provided that they understand the questions and have knowledge about different alternatives.

Knowing the images formed of the museum by different sections of the public and something about the public's demand for different experiences and programs may suggest possibilities for combining efforts with other institutions and organizations. Some communities have a voucher or paid-admission pass that can be used at more than one institution within a specified time period. Because frequent visitors of one cultural institution are likely to be active people, in general, they make good prospects as users of other cultural opportunities. A museum can host a series of musical concerts as a means of introducing music audiences to the music setting. A local theater production could be staged at the museum in conjunction with a special exhibit or new installation. One common way to networking or pooling institutional efforts to reach audiences is through local tourist agencies or commissions. Shared advertising and cross-listings in publicity materials can often result from cooperative efforts. Visiting a museum can be part of an appeal to tourists to stop in a community and use a number of the local services and institutions available.

4. *Assessment of museum-related benefits.* It is important to understand the key amenity values or perceived benefits people derive when they interact with museums. Equally important is to contrast the perceived benefits of nonvisitors with high-use groups. Programs can be developed to broaden the range of benefits so as to encourage greater visitation and involvement. Benefits are closely related to perceived images, and one caution to observe is not to project images that *suggest* benefits that cannot be realized through participation with a museum. Both external and on-site visitor surveys can help define visit-related benefits.

5. *Evaluation of sources of information.* A common practice in external surveys is to evaluate the way different segments of the public learn about leisure-time resources and events in their community. It can be very important to identify an information source that might reach new audience groups. For example, one museum tried billboards in highly visible locations, to prompt visits among the general public.[29] This mode of publicity was not typical for the museum, but it seemed to be effective. Knowing information sources used by those heavily involved with the museum is important also. These people are good candidates for messages about special shows, changing exhibits, new programs, and events tied to the holidays or other seasons of the year. A continuing problem is getting information out to people who are likely to respond. One survey was able to define not only the most effective local sources of information (i.e., specific radio stations and newspapers) but also the timing of messages to stimulate planning and decision-making that lead to participation.[30]

The five possibilities for a focus in external surveys can all be used to compare frequent visitors, occasional visitors, and nonvisitors. Other groups or ways of identifying different public groups can be compared for interests, perceived barriers to visitation, etc. For example, exhibits and programs could be reviewed with an eye to their effectiveness in fitting the needs of different age groups. On-site surveys can determine the existing distribution of age groups in the audience. External surveys can determine, along with existing census data, the age levels within a community. Programming can be altered to appeal to a specific age group, and publicity can be undertaken to encourage that segment of the public to attend. Another focus could be on special-interest groups that relate to the purpose of the museum. A local history museum might concentrate on history-related groups within a community and find out what the members of these groups perceive as benefits related to the museum. Local historical societies, history enthusiasts, academics, and students not only provide a source of visitors, but volunteers, research expertise, and financial support. Having a clear profile of these people and knowing the ways they view the museum is very important.

Some Caveats about Conducting an External Survey

A more cautious position should be taken in having an external survey conducted. Sometimes on-site visitor surveys are recommended even at the risk of some loss of validity; such a loss could be minimized by following recommended procedures, and the risk of invalid findings is sometimes worth taking, to gain needed information.

External surveys require more professional assistance than on-site surveys, and most museums prefer to get outside help for them. The logistics of external surveys require professional advice in selecting and completing a sample, preparing questions, and analyzing results.

A proper external sample requires careful planning and execution. Existing community marketing research firms are likely to have a strong sampling plan already set up. Local business colleges and social scientists also know the sample requirements for their areas. Typically, external surveys are based on either a random (probability) sampling plan or a quota strategy. Random samples can be drawn by picking every tenth person from a list or interviewing an agreed-upon number of people in a shopping center or some other public location. Probability sampling can also be applied to a geographic area with a set number of residents picked at random. Quota sampling uses existing census tract data and builds a sample that reflects the demographic profile of a community, or at least mirrors selected groups within a community. Respondents may be selected at random within a category, but the ultimate goal is to complete quotas for the number of categories or types of people called for in the sampling plan. In practice, a professional survey researcher may use a combination of sampling strategies and have a sample procedure and trained workers to collect the sample. Most museums would be best advised to get professional help. That help could also determine the way the sample should be completed. Choices include a phone survey, house-to-house interviews, return-mail questionnaires, or location sampling at shopping malls, downtown areas, etc.

Question construction also requires expert help. Marketing-oriented questions about intentions, interests, pricing, and basic consumer-type information are best prepared by people who understand that line of work. Likewise, questions intended to elicit information about perceptions of the museum and attitude assessment in general require some expertise in writing and analysis. Questions prepared to assess perceived benefits and amenity values work best when used as parts of larger scales that combine items.

The use of more sophisticated questions also requires more complex procedures to analyze results. Even well-funded surveys have sometimes failed in this task.[31] Analysis must move beyond descriptive summaries and use information combined in ways that require expert knowledge. Survey data can be misleading unless properly interpreted. External surveys, as a rule, will require more elaborate interpretation than descriptive surveys done with the visiting audience.

While seeking expert help is strongly advised for external surveys, it should be remembered that such surveys can be done in cooperation with other institutions. Umbrella organizations like cultural-resource agencies, chamber of commerce groups, and tourist-related organizations may commission public surveys that include local museums.

Finally, preparation of an external survey can be done in collaboration with college personnel and students, and/or local marketing or survey research firms. Different resources within a community can be identified and called upon to help with an external survey. For museums that can afford it, contracting with a marketing research firm to do an audience development study can be a worthwhile aid to self-study and long-range planning.

An External Survey Planning Checklist

1. Has a marketing plan been developed for future exhibits and programs?
   ☐ Yes   ☐ No

2. Is there information available about public perceptions of the museum?
    ☐ Yes   ☐ No

3. What kinds of barriers to visitation exist?
    A. A poor public image?   ☐ Yes ☐ No ☐ Uncertain
    B. A poor physical location?   ☐ Yes ☐ No ☐ Uncertain
    C. Lack of interpretation or public programming?
       ☐ Yes ☐ No ☐ Uncertain
    D. Little public awareness of the museum?
       ☐ Yes ☐ No ☐ Uncertain

4. Has the museum been included in a community or regional survey of potential audiences for cultural events and opportunities?   ☐ Yes   ☐ No

    A. Have specific groups or public segments been identified to target for program development and publicity?

       ☐ Yes   ☐ No

    B. What are major competing opportunities?

    List: _____

    _____

    _____

    _____

5. What are potential benefits the museum can provide its visitors?

    List: _____

    _____

    _____

    _____

6. What scale of external survey is possible?
    ☐ Local community
    ☐ Metro area
    ☐ State
    ☐ Regional
    ☐ National
    ☐ Other: _____

7. What resources exist for completing an external survey?
       ☐   Within-house staff/volunteer resources for doing a phone or mail survey

  ☐ Potential for a cooperative effort with other institutions in the area

  ☐ Potential for contributed help from local academic, research, or business organizations

  ☐ Potential for contracting with a marketing research firm to do the survey

8. Has any planning for external surveys been coordinated with information about existing visiting groups?

  ☐ Yes ☐ No

Recruiting the First-Time Visitor

It has been noted several times that significant differences can exist between frequent visitors to museums and both occasional visitors and nonvisitors. To draw people to the museum for the first time requires some special efforts. One effort needed is to get information into the word-of-mouth chain of the circle of friends. The problem there is that nonvisitors are likely to socialize with other nonvisitors. One strategy has been to recruit people who are likely to be opinion leaders from groups not necessarily active with museums. The idea is to involve a few people who will influence others, and a facilitation effect would begin.[32] This selection of opinion leaders is not always easy to accomplish. Outreach programs can sometimes get this process started.

At other times, a new audience develops because the museum makes a deliberate effort to involve people not in the audience. For example, one natural history museum created a Native American Advisory Council as part of the planning for a new hall about different Indian cultures and artifacts.[33] The advisory group provided advice on Native American reactions to plans and an opportunity for the museum staff to learn about sensitivities, customs, and perceptions of the Native American community. The influence was not just one-way, because as Native Americans became involved with the museum, word spread among that community that the museum was doing something of interest. Furthermore, when the museum hired some members of the community for staff assignments, a facilitating effect occurred through word-of-mouth communication, and members of the community began to visit the museum on their own right. The result was a greater participation by a minority group within the larger community—and a new audience group for the museum. Where barriers had existed before, the museum was now seen to be more approachable, at least for some members of the subcommunity.

This example of drawing in participation from those not previously involved with the museum stands in sharp contrast to tokenism as an effort to attract new groups of visitors. Tokenism can be illustrated by a museum putting on a specific exhibit about a group's heritage or on some other topic thought to be of interest. While the specific exhibit may be well-intended, it may fail to involve the targeted group because all of the barriers to visitation are still there. That is, if people feel uncomfortable with a museum and do not see it as of value to them, they may not come even for the special exhibit. Furthermore, even if they do come, they may not find the experience rewarding.

Involving a new segment of a community is a major public relations task and must include more than tokenism. Trying to build a new group into the audience requires not only evaluation of the museum's overall goals, but a look at the way the museum deals with its public. It may be necessary to change orientation, visiting hours, interpretation, and other features of the museum to make the setting more approachable to different people. At the same time, a sincere effort to create a continuing relationship with a specific segment of the public is required. This involvement could include asking leaders and influential members of the community group to become active in the museum. It might entail special events, such as festival days or community recognition activities. Some museums maintain an annual calendar of special events or seasons designed to draw various groups into closer involvement with the museum. The idea is to use the events as a basis for shared goals and interaction between the museum and a community group or subculture.

A shared goal is a very important tool for bringing people together. It can be a means of integrating people who have doubts, concerns, or even prejudices toward each other. Identifying and emphasizing shared goals, such as planning a community festival at the museum, are but one thing that can be done to establish improved intergroup relations.[34]

It is also important that members of each community feel they have status in the eyes of the other. Ideally, this perceived status should be equal. A problem for museums is that they may be considered intimidating surroundings by those not familiar with them, and that possibility may make it difficult to create a sense of shared status. The Native American Council example cited earlier was also interesting because some veto-power status was given to the Native American group over planning for the Indian exhibit. Letting an outside group have a decision-influencing role was a major commitment for staff members to make, but the commitment was viewed as necessary in light of strained relations between some Native American groups and some museums at the time. Having members of the community group participate actively with staff members can help build both common goals and a sense of shared status, although good leadership is also needed. However, the way specific museums may beneficially interact with community groups has to be left up to the individual institutions and their specific situations.

Two other factors that can help facilitate intergroup relations are the avoidance of strong stereotypes about group differences and the communication of the value or importance of good relations and interactions between groups. On the first point, it is important that when a museum tries to encourage visits by people who are infrequent visitors or nonvisitors, things that convey impressions to visitors should not reflect stereotypes of elitism or exclusiveness. That is, attendants, signs, labels, orientation aids, and the general ambience of an institution can convey different messages about the "openness" or "exclusiveness" of a place. An overpowering sense of formality is one of the problems that the templelike architecture of some museum entrances can present. To a part of the public, the architecture reinforces an exclusive atmosphere. It is interesting that some museums with formal facades have used colorful banners and signs, bright lighting, and friendly greeters to create warmth in a setting that otherwise may seem cold.

As to the second point, it is important to communicate that it is of value for groups to interact. A museum may communicate the importance of good intergroup relations by sponsoring annual festivals or events that reflect the importance of a group within the community and the museum's association with that group. By the same token, a business company can communicate its relationship to a museum not only by making public gifts, but through programs designed to encourage employees to visit and use the museum. The message communicated is that there is a common bond between two groups or organizations and that that bond or relationship is an important one to keep.

Sharing a common goal, avoiding large differences in perceived status, avoiding strong stereotypes that emphasize group differences, and emphasizing the importance of interaction and a positive relationship between groups are conditions that are not easy to create. When they are created, there is a good chance that a positive bond will start to grow between groups. The last condition of integration or establishing a new relationship is that participants come to have a natural liking for each other and a sense of rapport. This positive bond is exactly what exists between frequent visitors as a specific subgroup and the museum. Ultimately, the nonvisitor must come to feel positively toward the museum

and consider visiting there a natural and desirable activity. As challenging as these conditions of successful integration are, they represent tasks
necessary to involve people in the outer circles of the museum community mentioned earlier in the chapter.

NOTES

1. For a bibliography of books about museums, see Edward P. Alexander, *Museums in Motion: An Introduction to the History and Functions of Museums* (Nashville: Ameri-can Association for State and Local History, 1979), pp. 284-292.

2. C. H. Lovelock and C. B. Weinberg, *Marketing for Public and Nonprofit Managers* (New York: Wiley, 1984).

3. A summary article on marketing for museums is provided by Claire L. Fronville, "Marketing for Museums: For-Profit Techniques in the Non-Profit World," *Curator* 28 (March 1985): 169-182. General sources on nonprofit marketing in addition to the Lovelock and Weinberg book include Philip Kotler, *Marketing for Nonprofit Organizations*, 2nd ed. (Engle-wood Cliffs, N. J.: Prentice-Hall, 1982); David L. Rados, *Marketing for Nonprofit Organiza-tions* (Boston: Auburn House, 1981); and a source of collected readings about marketing for arts organizations, *Marketing the Arts*, ed. Michael P. Mokwa, William M. Dawson, and E. Arthur Prieve (New York: Praeger, 1980).

4. Martha G. Hayes, "Demise of an Institution," *History News* 38 (April 1983): 14-16.

5. Ce'sar Grana, "The Private Lives of Public Museums," *Trans-action* 4:5 (1967): 20-25.

6. Nelson H. H. Graburn, "The Museum and the Visitor Experience," in *The Visitor and the Museum*, ed. Linda Draper (Berkeley, Calif.: The Lowie Museum of Anthropol-ogy, 1977), pp. 5-26.

7. George Nash, "Art Museums as Perceived by the Public," *Curator* 18 (March 1975): 55-67.

8. Manfred Eisenbeis, "Elements for a Sociology of Museums," *Museum: A Quarterly Review* 24:2 (1971): 110-119.

9. Hans-Joachim Klein, *Barrieren Des Zugangs zu Offentlichen Kulturellen Einrichtun-gen*, unpublished report (Karlsruhe, West Germany, 1978).

10. Graburn, "Museum and Visitor Experience," pp. 13-14; Sheldon Annis, "The Museum as Symbolic Experience," unpublished paper (Chicago: University of Chicago, Department of Geography, 1980), pp. 4-5.

11. Stephan F. de Borhegyi, "Space Problems and Solutions," *Museum News* 42 (Nov. 1963): 18-22.

12. An extensive bibliography on recreation research from 1961-1982 appears in *1961-1982 Recreation Research Publications*, by Hubert E. Echelberger, Donna Gilroy, and George Moeller (Washington, D. C.: United States Department of Agriculture, Forest Service, 1983), 94 pp.

13. G. Donald Adams, *Museum Public Relations* (Nashville: American Association for State and Local History, 1983).

14. Ross J. Loomis and Carl F. Hummel, "Observations and Recommendations on Visi-tor Utilization Problems and Potentials of the Denver Museum of Natural History," (Work-

ing Paper no. 1, Denver Museum of Natural History, Denver, Colorado, 1975), pp. 12-13.

15. Brian Dixon, A. E. Courtney, and R. H. Bailey, *The Museum and the Canadian Public* (Toronto: Culturcan Publications, 1974), pp. 1-5, 244-247.

16. National Research Center for the Arts, *Arts and the People: A Survey of Public Attitudes and Participation in the Arts and Culture in New York State* (New York: Publishing Center for Cultural Resources, American Council for Arts in Education, 1973), chapters 1, 4, 6.

17. D. Geoffrey Hayward, *The Quadrangle Research Notes: Springfield Library and Museums Association*, unpublished reports nos. 3-8 (Northampton, Mass.: People, Places, and Design Research, 1982).

18. *Images of Denver's Civic and Cultural Institutions* (Denver, Colo.: Research Services, 1982), pp. 1-28.

19. Icek Ajzen and Martin Fishbein, *Understanding Attitudes and Predicting Social Behavior* (Englewood Cliffs, N. J.: Prentice-Hall, 1980), pp. 5-52.

20. "Marketing the Arts in Fort Collins," unpublished report (Fort Collins, Colo.: Colorado State University, College of Business, 1978), pp. 11-30. See also notes 26, 27, 29 for additional examples of fine arts marketing surveys.

21. Adams, *Museum Public Relations*, pp. 32-25. See also *Focus Group Interviews: A Reader*, ed. James B. Higgenbotham and Keith K. Cox (Chicago: American Marketing Association, 1979), 129 pp.

22. This example and the questionnaire shown in Figure 4.1 were provided by Keva Hoffman, of Ashton Villa, in Galveston, Texas.

23. Michael Madden,"Marketing Survey Spinoff: Library User/Nonuser Lifestyles," *American Libraries* (1979): 78-81.

24. Marilyn Hood, "Staying Away," *Museum News* 61 (April 1983): 50-57. For a more detailed account of this survey, see Marilyn Hood, "Adult Attitudes toward Leisure Choice in Relation to Museum Participation" (Ph.D. dissertation, University of Toledo, 1981).

25. J. E. Robbins and S. S. Robbins, "Museum Marketing: Identification of High-, Moderate-, and Low-Attendee Segments," *Journal of the Academy of Marketing Science* 9:1 (1981): 66-76.

26. See A. R. Andreasen and R. W. Belk, "Predictors of Attendance at the Performing Arts," *Journal of Consumer Research* 1 (1980): 119.

27. See Arnold Mitchell, *The Nine American Lifestyles* (New York: Warner Books, 1983), 302 pp.

28. Two volumes summarize an extensive survey effort of audiences for professional performing arts, using the VALS typology. Volume 1 describes the estimated 40 percent of the public most likely to be involved with performing arts; volume 2, the 60 percent less likely to participate in the arts programs. See Arnold Mitchell, *The Professional Performing Arts: Attending Patterns, Preferences, and Motives*, vol. 1 (Madison, Wis.: Association of College, University, and Community Arts Administrators, 1984). Volume 2 has the same author and title and was published in 1985.

29. Personal communication from Mark Lane, director of the Witte Memorial Museum, San Antonio, Texas, 1985.

30. "Marketing the Arts in Fort Collins," pp. 11-15.

31. See Howard Wainer, "Museums USA: A Type III Error," *Museum News* 53 (Dec. 1974): 42-44.

32. Some original work on audience development including the use of existing community groups was done in the Netherlands: G. J. Van Der Hoek, "Bozoekers Bekeken,"

Mededilingen, Gemeenttmuseum van den Haag 2/2 (1956) [English abstract]; and G. J. Van Der Hoek and Thea Van Eijnsbergen, "Audience Research in the Netherlands," *Museum's Annual* 2 (1970): 15-16.

33. Personal communication from Arminta Neal, former Assistant Director for Exhibits, Planning and Program Development, Denver Museum of Natural History.

34. For a complete discussion of ways to integrate groups or individuals into a shared experience, see S. W. Cook, "Motives in a Conceptual Analysis of Attitude Related Behavior," in *Nebraska Symposium on Motivation* 1969, ed. W. J. Arnold and D. Levine, (Lincoln, Neb.: University of Nebraska Press, 1970), pp. 179-231. For an account of using an advisory council and survey evaluation to increase teenager involvement with art museums, see Kathryne Andrews and Caroli Asia, "Teenager's Attitudes about Art Museums," *Curator* 23 (March 1979): 224-232.

5

Welcome to the Museum:
Evaluating Visitor Orientation

. . . .There is no question about it; a few outlines, given a certain direction by a few skillfully scattered dots, permit of much greater freedom than the yearned-for absolute freedom, for this absolute freedom is at the mercy of the imagination of the individual who, as we all know, has no ideas at all, none whatever, and in whom a blank sheet of paper can provoke just as much despair as the empty hour when the television set is out of order.[1]

Heinrich Boll's above observation, from his book *Absent Without Leave* is an appropriate starting point for a discussion of museum visitor orientation. Freedom to explore the environment of museums is *not* simply a matter of absence of structure. Boll suggests that the mind needs some structure from the environment in order to bring about the possibility of free choice between alternatives. This idea of structure relating to freedom is the start of a psychological concept that underscores much of what is said about visitor orientation.

What Is Orientation?

Visitor orientation, in the most general sense, consists of providing specific information to help people understand the environment they are visiting. Good orientation information should increase the visitor's freedom to choose from alternative experiences available in the environment and suggest ways of completing a visit with the accomplishment of desired experiences and/or the discovery of unanticipated opportunities.

As used here, *visitor orientation* will include the concepts or ideas that visitors have about the museum environment, their successful exploration of the museum in terms of finding areas they want to visit, and considerations of visitor comfort and safety. This chapter emphasizes orientation to the museum as a whole, and the topic will appear again in chapter 6, as part of exhibit evaluation.

Evaluation of the way visitors understand and use the museum environment is particularly important in helping first-time or infrequent visitors feel more comfortable with their visits. We mentioned earlier that infrequent or nonuser segments of the public tend to see museums as forbidding, uncomfortable places; effective orientation helps visitors understand and effectively use the museum and thereby reduces some of this perception of discomfort. For that reason, much of the discussion that follows is especially relevant to first-time or occasional museum visitors.

Freedom and Orientation

The museum environment is often thought of as an open, "free" setting, compared to such places as classrooms, lecture halls, or theaters. Museum visitors do not sit in assigned seats and wait for a show, lecture, or performance to begin. They do not have to direct and hold their attention to a sequentially prepared presentation. Visitors are free to move about the exhibit environment independently of others, looking at whatever catches their attention, and reading written materials, such as exhibit labels, if they so wish. Visitors are also free to impose structure on their visit, if that pleases them. They can join a formal tour and let the docent organize the museum visit for them. They may opt to use a written gallery guide or simply let a member of their group act as a leader. In a very real sense, every visitor can experience a unique tour, especially in a large museum that offers many galleries and specific exhibits.

Visitors may bring structure with them by having preconceived ideas about what they want to see and how long they will visit. Or visitors may give very little thought to the way they will organize their visit. This latter condition is much closer to the psychological state suggested by Boll. What appears to be absolute freedom is actually quite limiting. To a psychologist, this limitation could involve unpleasant emotions, such as confusion, or the despair Boll describes.

Psychologists have suspected that freedom of choice between environmental opportunities may not be independent of structure or form. Harold Proshansky, William Ittelson, and Leanne Rivlin believe that individuals try to organize the physical environment to maximize freedom of choice.[2] People find satisfactions and gratify personal needs by using different alternatives provided in specific features of a physical setting. A museum visitor, for example, may want to get away from other people and enjoy solitude as part of a visit. Or a visitor might seek the *presence* of other people and find a museum visit a highly social experience that breaks the isolation of living alone. A "free" environment should provide both of these social alternatives of either being alone or being with other people. Visitors will choose alternatives in the physical environment to fit their needs and moods, if alternatives are provided. The same visitor may change his or her interests during the course of a visit. At one point, the visitor might simply want to enjoy the beauty and aesthetics of an exhibit, a historic site, garden, or park. At a different time in the visit, the same person could decide to study the available information in more depth and carefully read labels or listen to a docent explanation. An ideal exhibit setting should provide both alternatives. The setting should have enough structure or organization contained within it to suggest alternatives.

A visitor entering the museum for the first time will perceptually organize the setting in terms of individual needs and expectations. Freedom, for the visitor, is not just the absence of physical constraints, but also the "suggestion of an outline" of potentials to be realized in that setting. Architects, designers, curators, and educators have all planned for different visitor experiences in the way they have created the physical design and interpretive programs of museums. Visitors must select from the alternative experiences available, as well as adding some of their own creation, such as the visitor who uses a museum visit as an opportunity to meet someone. It is very important for visitors to know what kinds of experiences are available. Finding out about the environment is at the heart of visitor orientation.

Visitors will vary in the amount of dependence they place on information from the environment. Psychologists have known for some time that some individuals are more field- or environment-dependent than others.[3] Field-dependent personalities may rely on environmental stimuli in general, may be somewhat passive and inclined not to assert their own organization into a setting. To the extent that this idea of field dependency helps to explain the way individuals relate to a physical setting, it is useful in suggesting that some visitors will be much more inclined than others to use guided tours, maps, signs, and other sources of information about the environment they are visiting. Other visitors will pay little attention to such guidance and may even resent the amount of organizing imposed upon them. In fact, there is an idea of behavioral reactance used by some psychologists to account for resistance shown to environmental barriers or restraints.[4] Some individuals find constraints or perceived environmental control over their freedom so bothersome that they rebel, often by undertaking the prohibited behavior. "Do Not Touch" signs will stimulate some people, who might not otherwise do so, to touch objects, as an act of defiance. Rope or cord barriers stimulate some others, who will try to see whether they can trespass into the forbidden area.

From a psychological perspective, orientation involves meeting the visitor's needs for some pattern in the environment, without that pattern's appearing overbearing. Visitors need some logical organization to provide them with information about environmental alternatives. Some will rely on this information about the environment more than others. Psychologists are also learning about ways people make basic decisions that guide their behavior and about the kinds of bias people show in decision-making, including overconfidence, or having a false sense of control in instances where control is lacking. A bias of overconfidence may help to explain why some people ignore orientation information when its observance would be helpful to them.[5]

Evaluating Visitor Orientation Needs and Problems

Identifying Visitor Orientation Needs

Entering a new environment for the first time is a demanding experience. One must assemble and sort out a considerable amount of information about the new surroundings, whether the setting be village, airport, resort area, or shopping center. The individual new to the place must answer a number of questions about the setting:

- Where am I?
- Where do I go next?
- Can I find what I am looking for?
- Is this place similar to other places I have been?

Steven Kaplan, an environmental psychologist, emphasizes that the human ability to answer such questions about the environment is central to adaptation and survival in all the many places humans inhabit.[6] Museum visitors must not only answer basic questions about finding their way through a three-dimensional environment, but must also study the setting carefully to gain personal experiences and benefits. For the visitor, the exhibit environment *is* the primary medium of communication. For that communication process to begin, the visitor must make some decisions about where to go next; and then must find a way to get there.

Wayfinding. Obviously, visitors need help in finding their way about in a large museum with many galleries and different floor levels. Entering a single gallery or a one-room local history museum also requires decisions about movement. Does one go to the left, to the right, or straight ahead? A longstanding observation, at least in the United States, is the marked tendency for people to turn to the right when entering an open or unstructured area. A right-hand-turn bias was noted by Edward Robinson and Arthur Melton in their research on the behavior of museum visitors (see note 33, chap. 1). Joseph G. Yoshika also studied the right-turn bias in an early direction-orientation study.[7] In the museum, visitors' wayfinding results in specific circulation patterns or routes most often used to tour the museum. These visitor routes are established by the particular decisions made at different points in the museum environment, especially points that serve as transitions or changes in the setting (i.e., the entrance to a gallery, the end of a room or hall, stairways to another level of a building).

How does a visitor make these wayfinding decisions? A great deal of research is currently underway to increase understanding of the way individuals process information about the environment. Gary W. Evans's "Environmental Cognition" provides a technical and thought-provoking review.[8] A somewhat oversimplified distinction can be made between internal and external cues. A very significant internal cue is the kind of mental map a visitor has of a setting.[9] This mental or cognitive map may be based on past memories of the actual setting, as in the case of a repeat visit. Or the map in the mind may be more general, based on a prototype of what a particular kind of place is like. Museum visitors probably have the prototype or generic maps about museum settings and draw upon that general knowledge when visiting a specific museum for the first time.

External cues are specific features of the environment that suggest or prompt a particular choice of movement. A worn path in a forest or field is a classical example of an external cue that guides movement. In a museum, a strong dramatic object prominently displayed can catch attention and draw the visitor toward it, thereby influencing wayfinding behavior. The shape of an exhibit gallery and the placement of display cases in that gallery can both influence wayfinding by suggesting a particular circulation pattern. Even the location and number of exits from an exhibit area can prompt different wayfinding decisions.[10] Researchers who draw heavily on the idea of external cues or features being paramount to wayfinding have been influenced by the perceptual learning studies of psychologists J. J. Gibson and E. J. Gibson.[11] They suggest that essential information the perceiver needs to understand the surrounding environment is contained in the actual stimuli of the setting and not in mental representations. H. Heft reflects this emphasis on external cues by suggesting that people find their way by picking up information over time as they move through a particular space.[12] Wayfinding results in being able to recognize significant features or transition points that aid in making a wayfinding decision.

Geographer Roger Downs continues this line of thinking by defining specific procedures that individuals must go through to find their way successfully. First, people must know where they *are* (or that they are lost!) and have some idea of the spatial environment around them. Second, they must be able to decide on a route that will take them to a destination; and third, they must be able to keep on the right track to use the route. Finally, they must be able to recognize that they have arrived at the intended destination. Downs's list of wayfinding tasks is particularly important for the usual situation of trying to find a specific destination point in a city, shopping center, or neighborhood.[13]

Museums, however, present a somewhat unique wayfinding situation, since a museum visitor may not be searching for a specific destination. He or she may be quite content to browse along, considering this or that object of particular interest. Coming to a destination point may be more of a matter of determining whether one has seen everything and whether the tour of the museum is complete. Of course, some visitors do engage in a more typical wayfinding pattern by looking for a specific exhibit or gallery. And many visitors may initiate fairly intense wayfinding behavior when they realize they are lost in a large museum and haven't the faintest idea where the exit is located. Most visitor movement through exhibits is closer to what Downs termed a "random walk process," where visitors move about without a clear pattern of progress toward any specific destination. Thus, wayfinding orientation in a museum provides a real challenge to designers and architects. Downs also is critical of designers of public spaces like libraries and museums because they leave wayfinding entirely up to users and do not anticipate orientation needs. Signs, maps, titles, and other aids can be stategically installed and designed to help both the visitor searching for a specific feature and the person who just wants to muse; but at some point, even if only to find the exit, most first-time visitors will need some wayfinding orientation.

Conceptual. While wayfinding is an important orientation need and process, museums present a specific kind of orientation challenge. People want to know what the museum is all about, what it is that they are going to see. Visitors need help in *conceptually* organizing their visits. This need is especially strong in larger museums, where the visitor must select a limited number of galleries to visit. Sometimes the tension associated with trying to establish conceptual orientation can be observed by watching visitors as they enter the lobby of a large museum. People look about, often with puzzled expressions on their faces; sometimes they come to a standing halt in the middle of the lobby area, as they try to figure out which way to go, and occasionally they engage in arguments with others in their party about what to see and how to get there. Entrance areas are prime spaces for providing conceptual orientation about the museum and its exhibits.

Conceptual orientation is also needed for specific galleries, and often the name of the gallery is one of the main aids for orientation. Consider, however, the common practice of naming galleries after benefactors and the confusion experienced by visitors who must learn, for example, that the gallery of modern art is called the "Smith Gallery" in a particular museum. It is really important to provide conceptual information for visitor orientation as underscored in a study by Robert Wolf at the Metropolitan Museum of Art. Wolf and his co-workers asked visitors to talk about their orientation needs. While wayfinding was mentioned, conceptual orientation was much more frequently brought up as a need. People wanted to know what kinds of exhibits were available and the contents of specific galleries. Visitors needed conceptual orientation about the kinds of objects in the museum in order to plan their visit.[14] Effective conceptual orientation can give the visitor a sense of control and organization over the vast array of information contained in a museum—large or small.

Needs for wayfinding and conceptual orientation obviously can vary among visitors. As mentioned earlier, some individuals are more field-dependent than others and need more structured information from the environment. Field-dependency needs might explain why some visitors ask for wayfinding and conceptual orientation, even though they have looked at signs, maps, and other sources of information. They may need to confirm or verify their orientation to the environment with more than one source of information. Other visitors may pay small attention to orientation aids and use them as little as possible. Certainly, visitors who know the museum "like the palm of their hand" can find their way with a very direct pattern of movement to a quickly recognized destination. The same is true for conceptual orientation. Some visitors know the contents of a gallery and have personal knowledge of the collection. Others need orientation information in order to select which galleries to visit in a large museum and/or the nature of a collection in a specific gallery.

Comfort and safety. Years ago, Gordon Reekie published a paper entitled *Toward Well-Being for Museum Visitors*, in which he called attention to a number of issues related to visitor comfort.[15] Comfort is a part of orientation because it is involved with individual levels of adaptation to an environment. Museums require physical locomotion and acts of physical exertion, such as climbing stairs. A museum visit also requires time, and this means that basic human needs must be cared for. Restrooms, lounges, telephones, food service, and drinking fountains are all specific amenities related to visitor comfort. The location and accessibility of a coat-check room is another example of a simple, but basic, comfort-related feature.

Reekie emphasized that visitor comfort was usually put very low on the priority list by museum planners. This low priority is unfortunate, since a number of simple considerations can add measurably to visitor well-being. Availability and comfort of seating in galleries, room temperature, and location of water fountains and restrooms should all be included as part of a master plan that anticipates human needs from the time visitors enter the museum until they leave. Reekie also realized that wayfinding and conceptual orientation were closely related to visitor well-being.

A central reason for considering physical comfort is to minimize fatigue. The mere physical nature of museum visitation makes fatigue inevitable, but anticipation of visitor comfort and other orientation needs can help delay the onset of fatigue and perhaps limit the amount of exhaustion one feels from a museum visit. Such amelioration of fatigue can be especially important for the very young, the elderly, and the handicapped. But in fact, reduction in fatigue is important to even the strongest visitor who plans a full day of museum visitation.

Another insight Reekie had into visitor comfort needs was that orientation information should be available throughout the museum and in more than one form. Only by anticipating visitor orientation needs at every critical juncture in the museum setting can orientation really be effective and visitor comfort maximized. What is needed is a system of orientation that coordinates several sources and kinds of information to meet visitor needs. Reekie put it this way:

Most people find maps and plans hard to follow, and museum visitors are no exception. In all "areas of decision" in a museum, such as foyers, landings, and corridor junctions, large floor plans and exhibit listings should be installed. They should duplicate those pictured in the giveaway folder provided for the visitor, but should be marked with a prominent *You-Are-Here* indicator. The exhibit listings should, of course, be keyed to the halls on the floor plans.[16]

Maps may be more useful than Reekie thought, and evaluation has shown some ways for making You-Are-Here maps more effective. Reekie's insight of providing information in "areas of decision" is at the heart of a modern museum orientation system. Such a system is also consistent with the earlier discussion of people processing information at transition points as they move through a setting.

General Orientation: Finding the Museum

People will not visit a museum or a historic site they cannot find or do not know even exists. Orientation begins with the images and messages that inform the public of the existence and location of a particular museum. Next, specific wayfinding information aids visitors in finding their way to the museum. Visitor surveys can be used to tap both the general public's knowledge and that of actual visitors about a museum and ways to find it. The way people view the accessibility of a museum includes a wide variety of orientation information: Is parking available? Is there an admission fee? Is the museum open today? What are visiting hours? Are there new exhibits to see? Which streets (routes) do I take to get to the museum?

Surveys can provide information about what kinds of general orientation questions and needs exist. However, there is one much more direct and simple way of evaluating potential visitor orientation: conduct a series of simulated activities for the visitor or potential visitor. One can go through a role-playing exercise of driving to the museum from major access highways or routes. Are there signs that provide wayfinding information? Do local hotels, restaurants, and the Chamber of Commerce provide visitors with information about the museum and do personnel in these places know how to guide people to the museum? What kind of listing is in the telephone directory? Does it give adequate information for getting to the museum?

One general orientation aid to finding a museum is the use of road signs—including billboards, if they are available and in place. Such signs both prompt the idea of making a visit and provide wayfinding information about a successful destination route. Darrel Ullman completed a formal evaluation of road signs installed along an interstate highway in Nebraska, some years ago, for the state's department of roads and economic development.[17] The signs announced local museums and also provided wayfinding information for driving to each museum. The evaluation provided evidence that signs did make a difference in travelers' decisions to take a rest stop at a museum. Evaluation is also needed to make sure that additional road signs are placed at critical points along the route to the museum. Keep in mind that wayfinding includes decision-making at significant transition points in the environment. People familiar with the location of a museum can afford to ignore wayfinding signs—they have learned other cues in the environment that direct them to the correct destination. Tourists and first-time visitors need signs to help them find the museum.

In addition to being placed at important wayfinding points, the signs will produce maximum effect if a distinctive color easy for the eye to see is used and if they display an attractive logo or symbol that helps visitors verify that they are on the correct route to the museum. A useful logo may be a silhouette or an outline of the museum building, or the image of a prominent feature of the building exterior that provides information enabling visitors to recognize their destination. Maps distributed by tourist organizations or other sources can augment route signs.

It can be worth the effort to ask government agencies, such as a state highway department, to install signs on major public routes. Attendance evaluation data (see chapter 2) may be needed to provide support for sign installation. Survey data that underscore wayfinding problems and a demonstration "trip" to the museum that points out difficulties in finding the building can also be evaluation tools useful for documenting the need for highway signs.

Orientation within the Museum

Orientation at the museum includes meeting needs for information at the point of entrance, a specific orientation center or exhibit, and coordination of a number of aids throughout the public areas of the museum. Orientation to specific exhibits and their content is also part of the intramuseum orientation.

Entrance orientation. Every museum, no matter the kind, location, or size, should provide orientation information at the visitor entrance. As Daniel Dailey and Roger Mandle note in their article "Welcome to the Museum," "The orientation center is a preamble for learning, a preconditioning for the physical and psychological ambience of the entire museum experience." Their advice applies equally well to entrance as well as orientation center areas.[18] First impressions are formed as visitors pass through the doors and begin to organize their visit (see fig. 5.1).

Each setting, no matter how small or large, communicates its unique ambience to incoming visitors. Visitors, on entering any new setting, are at a critical point of needing information as they start a visit. Some kind of visit pattern is required, if nothing more than as an aid in deciding to turn right or left. In large museums, wayfinding orientation may require planning a specific route that will include certain galleries and exclude others in order to keep a visit within a prescribed time limit. Evaluation of entrance orientation should address topics of wayfinding, conceptual, and comfort needs. For example, the entrance to a local history museum can provide visitors with a number of alternatives (see fig.5.1).

Effective entrance orientation evaluation should provide information for answering the following specific questions:

• Where do visitors go, on first entering the museum? What is the first stop they make in their visit?
• What questions do visitors have about the museum?
• How many visitor needs does the entrance area serve?
• What changes (experiments) can be made to improve entrance orientation?

The first question deals with wayfinding and can be answered with simple observation. One hundred visitors can be unobtrusively observed and their first stop recorded. It is important to observe unobtrusively so as to avoid influencing visitors to move in one direction or the other. Ideally, observations should be spread out over different time periods, to sample periods of both high use and low use and changes in circulation that occur on specific days or other time periods. In museums with slow rates of visitation, it may take longer to get a sample of one hundred visitors, and it might be prudent to have an attendant or a volunteer keep a log over several days until the sample is completed.

Figure 5.2 displays a hypothetical outcome for one hundred observations at the entrance of a museum like the one pictured in the earlier figure. Note that both the direction of turn and the point of first stop were recorded in the observations. This simple procedure of collecting a set of observations can identify problems with orientation and can be refined by keeping notes on specific incidents that suggest people are having difficulty knowing where to go in the museum. For example, a summary of entrance circulation like that shown in figure 5.2 might reveal that people stop first in the middle of the entrance and look around or ask orientation questions of others in their group. Careful observation can also detect unintended circulation patterns suggesting that people are not

Fig. 5.1-A

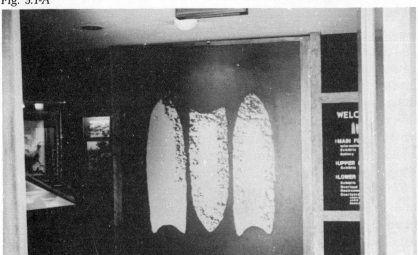

Fig. 5.1-B

Figs. 5.1-A and 5.1-B. Orientation aids for visitors can add to the appeal of the typical local history museum even in the entrance area (fig. 5.1-A). Visitors to the museum shown here pass through a welcoming introductory area (fig. 5.1-B), from which they can see the beginning of divergent exhibit spaces to be reached by making either a right or a left turn.

Fig. 5.1-C

Fig. 5.1-D

Figs. 5.1-C and 5.1-D. Here, a right turn (fig. 5.1-C) takes viewers past the introductory area and the reception desk toward a view of the main exhibit area. A left turn (fig. 5.1-D) takes the visitor into a background or orientation exhibit. Visitor evaluation can help with the design and placement of signs and maps to aid museum-goers choose a route throughout a museum's exhibit areas.—-Photographs by the author.

looking at the museum but are trying to find their way. Quick movements in and out of an exhibit without stopping to look at objects displayed and/or facial expressions of puzzlement or uncertainty can indicate orientation problems. It is important to note on the observation form when and where these specific types of behavior occur. Sometimes the observer must use a bit of intuition to anticipate or detect visitor-orientation problems.

Intuitive impressions can lead to a refined observation procedure. Qualitative observations can suggest new observation categories. For illustration, assume that while making first-stop and direction-of-entrance-movement evaluations, the observer notes that several visitors ask each other whether they are going in the right direction to find exhibits and that these inquiries always occur at the same location point in the entrance lobby. Visitors appear uncertain about their destination, and some transition-point information is needed at that location. An observation category for recording the number of visitors asking each other for information could be added to the observation form.

In large entrance areas, it may be useful to do a sequential analysis of stops—that is, note the number and sequence of stops visitors make before entering a gallery. Do they stop first at the cashier's desk (if the first step should involve paying for admission)? Do visitors ask for information from the volunteer host/hostess at the reception desk—or from the museum guard, because the guard station is located nearest to the front door? Sequential-stop analyses can reveal any confusion that exists about where to go upon entering the museum and/or unnecessary movement in the entrance area that can add to confusion.

There is a distinction that grows out of research on entrance circulation patterns that is well to keep in mind. Ervin Zube, Joseph Crystal, and James Palmer studied a sample of National Park Service Visitor Centers and concluded that the design of the centers usually produced one of two basic circulation patterns: (1) open or radial circulation, in which visitors fan out in several different directions toward one or more exhibits—signs often can provide orientation in such open situations; and (2) sequential circulation, which occurs in entrances with physical restrictions or barriers.[19] For instance, visitors can be funneled in controlled pathways to a reception area or cashier, if admission tickets must be purchased, and then moved to an orientation area that provides information about the museum. From that point of circulation, visitors would select the specific galleries they want to visit. Orientation aids, like maps or pamphlets, can be handed out at the cashier's station or the reception desk. The guard station, coat room, and other amenities can also be included in a sequential circulation plan. Museums with large entrance areas, and/or heavy visitor circulation flow periods, may find a controlled circulation pattern useful in preventing confusion and unnecessary movement in the entrance lobby area.

Whether or not a museum has an open (radial) or sequential entrance, circulation pattern depends heavily on the architecture of the building. Architecture, however, can be modified with features like wall partitions, rope barriers, signs, lighting, and placement of desks and counters. Modification of features provides flexibility in preparing improved orientation for visitors. A major choice to consider is whether or not to guide visitors to some central conceptual orientation area. An orientation area might include special exhibits, an amphitheater and/or attendants who give an introduction to the museum and answer specific questions on wayfinding information.

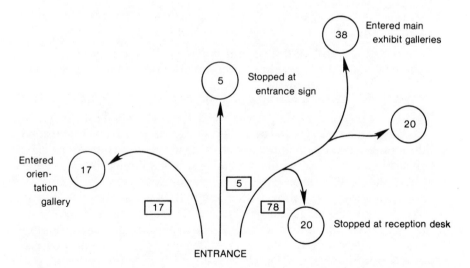

Fig. 5.2. *Hypothetical outcome of one hundred observations of first stops (numbers in circles) and direction of first turns (numbers in squares) for visitors entering a museum like that shown in fig. 5.1.*

Once circulation patterns are identified and it is known where visitors move and stop upon entering the museum, on-the-spot short interviews can identify various orientation needs and problems. Visitors can be asked why they stopped where they did and what specific orientation information they require. If visitors have difficulty suggesting orientation needs or problems, a checklist question may help. For example:

Check the following three items that describe features of the museum you are most interested in as you enter the building (other than the exhibits themselves):
☐ A place to hang your coat
☐ A drinking fountain
☐ An attendant who can answer questions
☐ Restrooms
☐ A map of the museum
☐ Snack bar (or vending machines)
☐ A place to rest
☐ Signs or pamphlets that explain how to visit the museum
☐ Information about the history and purpose of the museum

Examples of open-ended questions that could be asked include:

• What could the museum do to improve the quality of your visit?
• What questions do you have about the museum?
• How could we make your visit more enjoyable?
• Were you able to find exhibits you wanted to see?

Such questions work best near museum exits. People may mention the need for more signs or a guide pamphlet or the need for specific orientation information about the museum.

Interview questions can also inquire about specific problems identified in the observations. If visitors are observed to be wandering or appear lost, they can be interviewed at that point of observation and asked about information needs. This intervention-style of interviewing can be effective at identifying orientation problems in the entrance area as well as at important transition points within the museum.

Augmenting observation with a few interviews should also include talking to volunteers, guards, attendants, and any other staff people stationed near the museum entrance. A good question for these people is to ask for a description of the questions most frequently asked by visitors entering the museum. People who regularly meet the museum's public often have very definite opinions about orientation needs, since they have to answer the same visitor questions over and over again. In fact, it could be argued that evaluation of entrance orientation should begin by systematically interviewing the staff people who work with the public. There is an advantage, however, to performing observations and interviews without too many preconceived ideas and then validate the outcomes of these measures against staff and/or volunteer observation.

Acquiring a set of observations, a sample of spot interviews, and reactions from staff and/or volunteers who interact with visitors will provide the basis for some working conclusions about strengths and weaknesses of entrance orientation. One more evaluation procedure can be of help at this point: a planned change can be introduced in the entrance area and assessments made before, during, and after the change. A change might be the moving of a reception desk to a more prominent entrance location, or emphasizing its presence with additional lighting and installing more vivid signs to attract attention. Emphasizing the reception desk could be a desirable change if admissions must be purchased there and if newcomers receive major visitor orientation at the desk through distribution of pamphlets or spoken greetings and comments by attendants who deal with the public. Creating a mock-up for a new orientation lobby sign and museum map is another example of a temporary change that could be evaluated. The temporary sign and map could be tried in more than one location to determine which placement draws the most use. Frequently, the difference between an effective or an ineffective orientation sign depends on placement. Comparing sets of observations made at different placements can determine where an orientation sign works best.

Before, during, and after observations, provide tangible evidence that a change does (or does not) make a difference. So often, changes are planned and completed with no real knowledge of whether the modification really will be useful or effective. Suppose, for the sake of illustration, that a reception desk in a quite corner of the entrance area was relocated to a place directly in front of the entrance doors. The desk would be prominently displayed as visitors come into the museum. Suppose further that the relocated desk had forty-three first stops and the rate of stops dropped back to twenty-one after the desk was returned to the original position. A change of twenty or greater in one hundred observations is not likely to be caused by chance,[20] but suggests that the location change of the reception desk is influencing the choice of a first stop. Furthermore, a change back to the earlier rate of first stops provides additional evidence that the desk location *does* relate to the frequency of first stops.

The example of the relocated reception desk is hypothetical, and a series of *before, during,* and *after* observations might have shown very little difference in the rate of first stops at that point in the entrance. In a real situation, it could be argued that it is too costly and/or too time-consuming to make a change back and forth and complete the observations. For some permanent changes, a cost problem would be a limiting factor. Other changes could be made on a temporary basis or a low-cost mock-up or simulation of the change tried before the permanent modification is installed. Considering the length of time a given arrangement of entrance lobby features may serve a museum and the number of people that will be served by that arrangement, spending some time and resources to make visitor entrance orientation the best possible is a wise investment.

Whether or not the third procedure of planned change is used, the basic evaluation strategy of combining observations with a few on-the-spot interviews and staff or volunteer reports of orientation questions frequently asked by visitors will yield useful information about visitor orientation. In fact, that basic strategy can be useful for evaluating orientation at other points in the museum. The strategy can be summarized in the following outline:

A Three-Step Outline for
Evaluating Entrance Orientation

Step One: Systematic Observation

A. Observe one hundred visitors at random as they enter the museum and note (1) direction in which they move, the pathway they use, and (2) the point of their first stop.
B. If needed, note second and third stop locations (or however many sequential stops are of interest).
C. Make qualitative observational notes of any indications of visitors looking confused, lost, or disoriented. Note signs of unintended wandering or unnecessary movement because of disorientation.
D. Summarize the one hundred observations as percentages of routes taken and stops made. Determine whether the observations suggest any orientation problems.

Step Two: On-the-Spot Interviews

A. Stop a small sample of visitors (twenty-five or so) in the entrance area and ask them about information they need for their visit. Observations from Step One might suggest ideas for specific interview questions.
B. Interviews can be taken as people either enter or leave the museum. It can also be useful to interview visitors briefly as they enter and then complete the interview at the time they leave.
C. Interview volunteers and/or staff for their perceptions of orientation problems and commonly asked information questions from visitors. Try to validate observation and interview findings against staff perceptions.
D. Summarize results of observations, interviews, and staff and volunteer reactions to see whether specific orientation problems can be identified.

Step Three: Planned Changes

A. Results from the first two steps may suggest specific changes that would improve orientation. For example:
1. Relocating entrance furniture (reception desk, etc.)
2. Adding signs for directing wayfinding.
3. Relocating signs and/or maps.
4. Adding an orientation exhibit.
B. Whenever possible, use mock-ups of temporary formats to test their effectiveness and control costs.
C. Collect one hundred observations and/or a small sample of interviews *before, during,* and *after* the change.
D. Look for different rates or outcomes in the evaluation measures across the three samples (before, during, after) to verify that change is having the intended impact.
E. If the results are positive, make permanent modification.

One conclusion that may be drawn from evaluation of the entrance area is that an orientation exhibit or center is needed. It may be desirable to include, at one location in the museum, signs and information on exhibit content providing conceptual information about the history, purpose, and nature of the museum and collections. Wayfinding information may also be included. Museum designers and planners have experimented with a wide variety of orientation centers. Evaluation can help improve the effectiveness of such centers and exhibits.

Orientation centers and exhibits. In her book *Help! For the Small Museum,* Arminta Neal describes a good example of an entrance area orientation sign (see fig. 5.3).[21] Visitors are greeted by a prominently displayed sign informing them of all the areas of the museum, with directions for finding each area and the basic concept of the collections contained in the different areas. Thus, one sign succinctly presents both wayfinding and conceptual orientation information. A map of the museum and/or a brochure for visitors could be included as part of a major orientation sign, or as supplements to it. An entrance-lobby sign is one stratagem for orientation; and for many museums, that may be as much of a center or orientation exhibit as is needed.

Other museum settings may require more extensive orientation of visitors. To meet that need, a specific area of the museum may be equipped and staffed to provide visitor wayfinding, comfort, and conceptual information needs. Different design alternatives for orientation exhibits and/or centers can be identified.[22]

The first alternative, described above, emphasizes orientation in

IN OUR SMALL MUSEUM YOU MAY SEE THE STORY OF OUR LOCAL HISTORY. On this floor there are three main display rooms:

> *The Natural History Background and the Earliest Inhabitants—the Indians* (to the left of the main corridor)
>
> *Early Explorers and Travelers* (in the room straight ahead at the end of the corridor)
>
> *Permanent Settlements:* Development of towns with industries, agriculture, transportation, and communication (to the right of the main corridor)

Second floor exhibits show the development of our community since the transition from Territory to present-day State.

The Museum also owns extensive study collections of historical objects, photographs, and manuscripts, which are available to scholars and students upon application.

WE HOPE YOU ENJOY YOUR VISIT

Fig. 5.3. Example of a main-entrance visitor-orientation sign providing both conceptual and wayfinding information.—Used, with permission, from Help! For the Small Museum, by Arminta Neal, pp. 15-16. Copyright 1969 by Arminta Neal.

entrance lobbies. Admission cashier booths, a reception desk, and signs are arranged in a manner to emphasize and provide orientation. Restrooms, public telephones, and a coatroom may be conveniently located at or near the entrance, or signs giving clear directions for finding them should be prominently displayed. For many museums, using the entrance area as an orientation center is quite adequate. The evaluation of a lobby orientation strategy has been discussed and a combination of observations, interviews/questionnaires, and planned changes can yield information for improving visitor orientation. The lobby may be the most practical location for visitor orientation in settings such as historic houses or small local history museums where space is at a premium.

A second alternative for visitor orientation is use of some sort of prepared commentary—a film or a slide show production or an oral presentation by a volunteer or staff member. At some historic locations or living history sites, it is important to orient visitors conceptually to the time period of the setting and also to provide information for taking a tour around the site. Films can present a re-creation of a historical event as a way of orienting the visitor to the buildings and artifacts involved. Large museums may also use a slide presentation or movie to help the visitor realize the variety of exhibits available and the need to make choices of specific areas to visit.

Orientation presentations may be given to *all* visitors, through use of a sequential circulation pattern that includes an amphitheater or a controlled-access route into a room or reception area; or the choice of listening to such a presentation may be left up to the visitor, and the area where it is presented may be located off a main circulation route. In this latter situation, a major evaluation task would be to observe and estimate the percentage of visitors using the presentation and to interview a sample of those who did *not* take in the presentation, to find out whether the omission was intentional or an oversight. Sometimes visitors may be unaware that orientation presentations are available.

In general, formal orientation presentations can be evaluated by a combined observation, spot interview, and planned change procedure described earlier. In the case of formal presentations, questions asked by visitors at the conclusion of a talk or program would be a source of evaluation information. Observations could include noting the number of visitors who stop for the presentation and recording the percentage of that audience who stay for the complete program. If slide, videotape, and movie presentations are too long in duration, people sometimes become bored and leave. Evaluation can reveal how well the presentation holds attention.

If the orientation presentation is given orally by a staff member or volunteer, that same individual can collect evaluation data. In fact, a report sheet can be used to collect such information as:

1. Number of people attending presentation
2. Estimate (in percentage) of audience staying for complete presentation
3. Orientation-related questions asked by audience

The presenter could also distribute questionnaires and/or conduct spot-interviews with people to gain specific information or visitors' comments about the museum's orientation information prepared for them.

The orientation presentation itself can be evaluated to discover whether or not concepts and information are being presented clearly and comprehensibly, as intended. It is possible to evaluate visitor information presentations, as a way of developing their quality and value to visitors. Marilyn Cohen, in her review of orientation strategies used by museums, parks, and historic settings, cautions that it is important to evaluate the presentation for comprehension.[23] Films and other materials should be pretested, if possible, to insure that they communicate the messages intended. Evaluation can also reveal problems with the message format itself; and Cohen mentions one museum in her review that found multi-image presentation to be more confusing to visitors than single-image sources of orientation information.

A third alternative is to set aside space for an exhibit designed to orient visitors to the museum with both conceptual and wayfinding information. Sometimes an introductory exhibit area also serves as an orientation center. The purpose of the center is to provide background about the museum and help visitors plan their visit. Exhibits may include interactive displays or even a microcomputer that asks visitors to feed statements on their interests into the machine and then prints out a personalized guide to the museum for the visitor.

In her "state of the art" review, Cohen describes the components of an orientation center installed at the Boston Museum of Fine Arts.[24] Wayfinding information was provided through color-coded floor plans for each major area of the museum. Above each floor plan, a changing slide show displayed objects that could be found in the area described in the graphic. Slides and sound tapes also informed visitors of special exhibits in the museum. Programs and events were announced on a large memo board that permitted posting events by the month, week, or day. Finally, a few small objects were exhibited in display cases, to give visitors a preview of the collection.

An orientation center should be placed where visitors can see it and plan a visit accordingly. This visit-planning function becomes very important in large museums where visitors are best advised to develop some kind of plan for touring both the building and the collections. One important goal of evaluation for a center like the one just described is to discover whether visitors gain an overview of the museum adequate for them to use in completing some kind of planning activity.

The center described by Cohen at the Boston Museum of Fine Arts was evaluated, and the results of that study raised a number of questions about orientation centers.[25] Only 13 percent of the visiting audience used the center, with weekday patrons being more likely to visit the center than those who came on weekends. Because the museum had a fairly high attendance rate overall, 13 percent of the total audience translated out to some twenty-seven hundred visitors served by the center each week. One basic question that should be determined early about orientation centers is the audience for their use. Should all visitors pass through the center? If reaching the total audience is the goal for an orientation center, it would be best to locate the center on a sequential-circulation-flow pathway near the entrance. A limitation to directing all visitors though an orientation area is that many will be familiar with the museum already and really do not need orientation, since they know where they want to go and what they plan to see. For this reason, there is an advantage to making the orientation center optional, taking care to publicize its presence with effective signs. Thus, while the Boston Museum's center-use rate was low, that 13 percent may represent the portion of the audience most in need of the information supplied by the center's exhibits. Authors of the evaluation study also concluded that the atmosphere of the pilot orientation center was not inviting, a factor that may have contributed to a low-use rate.

The importance of deciding who should use the center is underscored by a general finding from the study of National Park visitor centers (cited earlier—see note 19) by Ervin Zube, Joseph Crystal, and James Palmer. With three exceptions, first stops by visitors entering park centers were at exhibits, rather than information desks. The first exception was for a center located high in the Rocky Mountains, at a midway point on a highway through the park. First-stop preference at *that* center were the restrooms! The other two exceptions were buildings with circulation patterns that started visitors in orientation/information areas away from exhibits. People are interested in exhibits when they enter a museum or similar facility. Slowing them down from that pursuit to become better oriented to the environment requires some careful planning and decisions made about exactly how much orientation information is needed.

A second question that emerged from the Boston study was how well the center helped visitor wayfinding. In general, the center did not help much in visit-planning. It was concluded that more use of pictorial maps would help wayfinding; and a more direct communication of the purpose of the center as a place where one could identify exhibits and plan a visit would increase visit-planning.

The evaluation revealed that, in spite of shortcomings, visitors who used the Boston center liked it and supported the concept. They also liked having some educational exhibits that informed visitors about the museum and its collections. A major outcome of the study was a refined list that itemized orientation-center features and included:

1. *A profile display* that provides background of the museum's historical and current status as an institution.

2. *A museum calendar* easy to keep up-to-date, to inform visitors of current events. Ideally, this calendar would also be displayed at key transition points throughout the museum.

3. *A pictorial directory* of collections that would make it possible for visitors to identify specific works of art or entire collections they would like to see. Interview evaluation of questions visitors ask about the collection could provide information for organizing this element of the center.

4. *Pictorial maps* would have route designations indicated by lights activated when visitors pressed buttons next to names of galleries and exhibits. Pictures would be used as much as possible to make the maps useful to people who have difficulty reading English. Handout versions of the maps could also be available for use in the museum proper. Ideally, maps used would be drawn in three dimensions and indicate easily identified landmark features of the building.

5. *Racks or machines* would dispense maps, calendars, self-guide brochures, and other information publications about the museum. Some museums might want to experiment with the trail-guide system used in some parks. Visitors can use the guide free if they return it to the distribution rack, or keep the guide for personal use by paying a small fee.

6. *Educational exhibits* provide visitors with objects to look at, which may capitalize on their natural tendency to want to look at exhibits as soon as they enter the museum. The purpose of these exhibits in the orientation center, however, is to inform visitors about features of the museum that will enrich their overall visit. Educational exhibits can be changed to emphasize special themes and/or occasions.

7. *Ideally, an orientation center* should be designed to function with or without attendants present. Many visitors prefer to find information on their own, but others seek someone to speak to. Attendants may be especially helpful during periods of peak visitation such as holiday or tourist seasons.

The evaluation of the Boston Museum Visitor Center used variations of evaluation procedures mentioned above. Observation was used to find out how long people stayed at the center and the patterns of use for different features (i.e., maps, objects exhibited). Observation was also used to establish the rate of visitor use through head counts broken down by different directions of access to the area. It should be mentioned that if observers are not available to make this kind of evaluation, guards can hand to visitors slips of paper with gallery-entrance time marked on them and then collect the slips as visitors leave, taking care to note the time of exit. This simple procedure will provide an estimate of time spent in the gallery. Interviews were used in a number of ways. Specific features, like the maps, were tested by asking visitors to find particular exhibits. A more comprehensive exit interview was conducted with balanced samples of users and nonusers of the center. The interview was focused on information needs. The investigators also role-played as visitors and asked visitors for specific information about exhibit locations. This variation of interviewing can be especially helpful in identifying orientation needs at various locations around the museum.

Orientation centers also lend themselves to the planned-change experimentation evaluation described earlier. Different types of maps could be displayed and evaluated. Or a major feature, such as an exhibit locator, could be tested for a short time, to determine the value of its inclusion in the center. Variations on observation and interview techniques, combined with limited experimentation, can provide visitor center evaluation just as these same techniques help understand orientation at the museum entrance. The Boston study also pointed out the importance of sampling across different time periods to collect a balanced set of visitor reactions.

Orientation throughout the museum. Another lesson learned from the Boston study was that orientation centers work best if effective aids such as signs and maps are present throughout the museum. Guards and other staff people who regularly meet the public need to be briefed on orientation problems, current exhibits, and special programs that visitors are likely to inquire about. The importance of having orientation information available throughout the museum cannot be overstressed.

Two research studies have provided useful insights into the overall orientation of visitors. Geoffrey Hayward and Mary Brydon-Miller evaluated visitor orientation at an outdoor history museum at Sturbridge Village and used entrance and exit interviews.[26] The interviews were designed to assess overall evaluation of the setting, the visitors' knowledge of the village, understanding of interpretive themes, and specific evaluation of orientation aids. Several orientation experiences were available through maps, exhibits, information panels, oral presentations, films of a visitor center theater, and from staff people stationed at a membership desk. Both wayfinding and conceptual orientation were emphasized through the various aids. First-time visitors constituted the study sample.

Results from the Sturbridge Village evaluation confirmed the need for visitor orientation. First-time visitors had little background information about the setting and needed assistance in planning their visit. Hand-carried visitor maps and films were reported to be the most useful aids, both in terms of actual rate of use and visitor feedback that the information was of value. An important conclusion of the study was that orientation information needs to be keyed to the time available for visitors to the village. Brief and to-the-point information is needed for those planning a short stay. More in-depth orientation programming should be provided for those who have a longer visit in mind. One of the most basic purposes of visitor orientation could be to suggest time-based strategies for seeing the museum. Outlines of visits of different lengths could be included in a visitor brochure with a map for those who would welcome a time-based suggestion for planning their visit.

The evaluation at Sturbridge Village was not alone in suggesting that orientation aids differ in their relative effectiveness. Marilyn Cohen and co-authors Gary Winkel, Richard Olsen, and Fred Wheeler completed an extensive study of visitor orientation in a large museum of history and technology.[27] The evaluation made good use of planned experiments based on different strategies of placing signs and a variety of map designs. Some general ideas from the evaluation findings were that any aid must relate directly to the properties of the physical environment; and aids must take into account limitations in human memory. No matter how sophisticated or how attractively designed orientation sign, films, etc., may be, the central message must be *easily understood information about the building and alternative choices of exhibits to visit.* Images used to describe the building or setting must be well-matched to the actual physical layout. It should be anticipated that visitors will forget orientation information during their visit, especially in a large and complex setting. Redundancy of orientation information should be provided by repeating significant information from time to time through signs and maps. A hand-carried brochure map displays a continual source of information, provided that the map is well designed for visitor use. Walk-through interviews, spot interviews at major transition points in the museum, and role-playing as a visitor seeking information can all help identify locations where orientation information should be repeated.

A strength of the Cohen, et al., study was the experimental separation of maps, signs, and a control condition with neither maps or signs present. Samples of visitors were interviewed about their use of exhibits under the different conditions of orientation. Overall, maps helped visitors to understand the layout of floors or wings of buildings and to locate exhibits they wanted to visit. Maps also helped visitors determine whether they had seen all of a given area of a building. Signs were particularly useful in helping visitors find entrances to exhibits they wanted to see. Use of signs and maps together was preferred to use of a single aid alone since each of the two served a somewhat different purpose. Attendants on duty seemed to answer even different types of questions and thereby furnished information distinct from that obtained in signs or maps. Ideally, all sources of orientation should be coordinated to meet the most common visitor orientation needs.

Cohen and her colleagues also demonstrated that effective use of information can help visitors avoid disorientation, a term used to describe ineffective wayfinding behavior that results in fatigue, increased boredom, frustration, and missed opportunities. Gallery direction signs and floor maps helped reduce such disorientation problems as missing a specific exhibit one wanted to see, entering an exhibit from the rear rather than front access, and unnecessary backtracking over areas already seen.

In addition to the research just described, a good summary of visitor orientation appears in *Communicating with the Museum Visitor*, a Royal Ontario Museum publication.[28] Not only is the summary consistent with points already raised—it also mentions some additional features. One such, very useful to visitors, is any vivid, easily recognized architectural property of a building that serves as a landmark. A great hall, entrance lobby, atrium, piece of statuary, or similar feature can serve as a landmark. Such landmarks become familiar points of reference that visitors can use in their wayfinding. Recall that the idea of a landmark was used in reference to people finding their way to the museum and a prominent orientation feature works just as well for the interior of a building. Maps, signs, and attendant wayfinding instructions to visitors can make excellent use of landmark features.

The Royal Ontario summary also suggests using color to prompt visitors about orientation information. Colors can be used to help visitors recognize different floors or exhibit areas. Some designers prefer to use a multicolor scheme, with different colors meaning different things. Researcher Dorothy Pollet cautions, however—in "You Can Get There From Here"—[29] that different colors can confuse people; she has found that a single orientation color can work well. One color of a hue easily seen by the eye can signal visitors that orientation information is displayed at a particular point. Wall maps, directional signs, signs for such amenities as drinking fountains and restrooms, and the visitor pamphlet can all make use of a key color. This suggestion about color is consistent with the earlier suggestion that color can be used as an orientation cue on signs outside the museum and in association with carefully thought-out logos and symbols.

Other advice from the Royal Ontario Museum publication includes thinking of all orientation information as an organized system. Each sign, map, or attendants' station should be seen in the context of all other sources of information provided for visitor wayfinding, conceptual, and comfort orientation. No one source of information should be designed to overpower the others or become too much of a focus for attention. Visitor centers, in particular, should not be overdesigned so that they compete with exhibits. The purpose of orientation is to help the visitor realize maximum benefit from the museum environment; orientation must not become an end in itself.

Logical sequencing of halls or grouping of exhibits that go together in a manner easily understood is a final feature that can be drawn from the Ontario summary. While this kind of conceptual orientation is not always possible, it should be incorporated into the orientation system when feasible. Visitors are likely to have a conceptual system in mind for organizing the different kinds of objects and content found in a particular museum. As a personal example, I asked a sample of college students to group pictures of exhibits from a natural history museum into subgroups of items that seemed to go together.[30] In addition, names were assigned to each grouping of pictures that best described the idea or concept the student had in mind for putting selected pictures into a group. The students, none of whom had been to the museum, organized many of the specific exhibits into groupings that were similar to the actual installation at the museum, using such logical cues as rocks and minerals that go together and the fact that human culture artifacts are distinct from exhibits about animal habitats. Having some idea of the way people tend to group the different areas and content of the museum in their minds can help plan orientation information. It may also reveal that people have some misunderstandings about the way exhibits are arranged in a building. It should be emphasized, however, that ideas or symbols describing a setting work best when combined with words.

Below are examples of the way orientation throughout the museum can be improved by attention to the details of each orientation aid. Signs carry more impact if they are kept simple and produced with effective graphics. A number of good reference sources on effective graphics are available.[31] Signs should contain simple, direct statements that are easy to read. Some visitor observations may be needed to make certain that signs are placed where they draw attention most readily and are most frequently used by visitors. The correct location for an important orientation message may take some trial-and-error placement, followed by simple observation of the number of people using the sign at different sites.

Maps also require careful preparation to be effective and avoid unintentional disorientation. Marvin Levine has studied "You-Are-Here" maps and has a number of useful tips for improving these orientation devices.[32] One of the most common problems of maps is that they may not be oriented properly to the environment as seen by the map user. Directions of right or left, up or down, should be consistent between the map and the actual environment. Levine suggests placing a map flat and parallel to the ground with the features and pathways depicted on the map lined up with their actual counterparts in the setting. Most maps are mounted vertically on a wall, and Levine believes that people make a natural transition of "Forward" to "Up," so that pathways and features of a setting that are in front of the viewer are shown at the top of the map. One idea that grows out of Levine's advice on orienting the map to the setting is that museum entrance or orientation center areas should have a table-top map that displays the museum floor plan with correct directional alignment. Vertical wall-mounted maps should then be located at transition points in the museum, with forward-direction features displayed at the top of the map.

In addition, Levine offers some useful tips for specific features of "You-Are-Here" maps. It helps if parts of the environment are labeled. Room numbers are a basic kind of label; but in museums, gallery names can convey information about a specific area pictured in the map. Viewers can match labels on the map to areas or features in the setting. It is also helpful to use asymmetry of building features to establish direction in the setting. That is, changes in the level of a building, outcroppings of walls, or other salient architectural features can serve as cues for locating where one is. "You-Are-Here" maps should be positioned near these points of architectural asymmetry. The "You-Are-Here" symbol used on this type of map can be more informative if it is used to indicate on the map the point where the viewer is standing, with an arrow leading from that point to an outline of the panel in the area map that shows where the viewer is standing in relation to the actual setting. This kind of artic-ulated "You-Are-Here" symbol provides a specific reference point that lets the viewers orient to their exact location in the setting. Finally, Levine encourages redundancy of information throughout the setting. Crucial wayfinding information should be repeated throughout the museum.

Pictorial representation maps are another technique that could improve map information. In his paper on visitor needs at Longwood Gardens, Colvin Randall mentions the nineteenth-century German tech-nique of *Vogelschaukarten*, or bird's-eye-view map designs.[33] This tech-nique presents the drawn outline of topographical features (i.e., trees, roads, hills, buildings) so that map readers gain an overall view or pic-ture of the setting. A *vogelschaukarten*-based visitor map would be very useful for historic sites or for any setting that has extended grounds or a campus. A "You-Are-Here" symbol could also be incorporated with a pictorial map.

Effective "You-Are-Here" maps are one small feature that can increase the amenity benefits of a museum visit by improving orientation. A good orientation pamphlet is another feature that can help the visitor under-stand the museum environment. But what constitutes a "good" brochure? There is one easy evaluation task that can help determine how good a pamphlet is as an orientation aid. If pamphlets are being handed out to visitors entering a museum, the pamphlets' effectiveness can be assessed by observing how often visitors are seen using the guides. In a museum with an effective brochure, visitors can be seen consulting the aid at var-ious transition points. Another test for an effective pamphlet is to count the visitors walking about with the brochure *open* and in hand, ready for immediate viewing. Interviews are required to get a more in-depth assessment of how well specific items in the pamphlet work.

Some details that help an orientation pamphlet include:

1. A clear, simple, easy-to-read map with routes and galleries marked.

2. Brief descriptions of gallery content to provide the visitor with con-ceptual orientation.

3. Suggested visit sequences can provide structure and can be based on different time lengths (i.e., for a one-hour stay, visit the following areas . . . ; for a two-hour stay, the following sequence is suggested . . .).

4. Running times for audiovisual or live presentations can be indi-cated in the pamphlet, so that visitors can decide whether they have time to take in the presentation.

Distinctions must be made and kept clear between what constitutes a visitor-orientation pamphlet and public relations brochures or gallery interpretation guides. Orientation aids should constantly refer to way-finding and conceptual information needs and avoid extraneous material. The orientation brochure should be designed as an integral part of the complete orientation system. The same gallery names that appear on signs should be in the pamphlet. Consistencies should exist between the pamphlet information and information found in signs, maps, and any orientation information.

For many small museums, overall orientation may be of limited importance, since the setting is small in size and easy to understand. However, more complex historic settings, zoos, parks, nature settings, and large museums can present visitors with an overwhelming task of planning their visit and making decisions about what to see. More is being learned about orientation, and there is increasing evidence that highly effective orientation aids can be developed. Overall visitor orientation—even to a very large setting, such as the backcountry areas of Yellowstone National Park—can be improved with effective aids, as shown in the work of Edwin Krumpe.[34] In a study of park backcountry users, Krumpe was able to show that trail-head orientation in the form of printed handouts combined with effective maps did result in redistribution of trail use for more desirable park resource management and a better match between hiker expectations and different park features. Visitors can be helped with good orientation that enables wise decisions to be made throughout a visit.

Anticipating Visitor Comfort and Safety Needs

Conceptual and wayfinding orientation needs are involved with planning for entrances, exhibit galleries, and transition points throughout the museum. This must also be done for comfort needs. Anyone who has devoted a day's time to museum-looking or has tried to complete a productive museum visit with a group of children has an intuitive sense of what is commonly called *museum fatigue*. Any aid or idea that can help reduce, or at least delay, fatigue provides an invaluable contribution to the quality of a visit experience.

Multiple causes of museum fatigue. There are different causes of museum fatigue. Four categories of possible origins of fatigue include physical effort, ambient environmental conditions, specific task demands placed on visitors, and psychological factors. One of the very first papers published about the museum visitor—Benjamin Gilman's work, mentioned in chapter 1—discussed physical fatigue caused by visitors stretching and bending to see objects placed in exhibit cases designed with little thought for the viewer's comfort.[35] Standing for long periods, walking long distances, and sometimes positioning the body to see around people or into different exhibits all can build up physical fatigue. Unnecessary walking or climbing stairs can add more fatigue. It follows that anything that reduces physical exertion will prevent some fatigue. Elevators or escalators can take the place of stairs, and benches can be conveniently located to encourage brief rests from standing and walking. Arminta Neal observes that visitors will often use parts of the exhibit environment to take "mini-rests" or short breaks to ease muscle fatigue that builds up during a museum visit (see fig. 5.4).[36] Leaning against cases, resting against table tops, or simply shifting body weight while looking at exhibits are examples of mini-rests that provide relief from physical fatigue. It follows that exhibit case design could encourage viewers to rest by providing railings or other areas that people could lean against.

As M. Lehmbruck suggests, in his work on perception and behavior, planning a continuous circulation pattern from museum entrance to exit that avoids backtracking can reduce unnecessary movement.[37] Lehmbruck also presents an interesting idea by suggesting that some patterns of movement may be more comfortable or more natural than others. He speculates that human movement should sometimes change direction and proceed with irregularities, rather than marching stiffly in machinelike circulation or repeated sequences that are the same for everyone. Naturalness of circulation-pattern movement is an interesting idea worthy of research to see whether it is valid. Physical fatigue, then, can be reduced by designing cases that make objects easy to see without the viewer's needing to stretch or bend. Reducing physical exertion by providing aids such as elevators, designing clear circulation patterns that avoid backtracking, and the use of mini-rests are all ways of reducing fatigue.

Background factors like temperature, humidity, and noise can also produce fatigue and discomfort. Ambient environmental conditions need to be controlled, not only for visitor comfort, but for protection of the collection on exhibit. Extreme levels of either heat or cold can distract visitors from attending to exhibits and hasten their departure from a gallery. Prolonged heat contributes to fatigue and can leave one disinterested in the environment and concerned only with finding a more comfortable setting. Noise, if intense, erratic, or unexpected, can also have a stressful effect on people.[38] Noise may also impair concentration on mental tasks. Background music can help mask annoying noise, but exhibit music and other sounds can spill over into galleries and create a background of sounds that is annoying. Directional speakers that confine

Fig. 5.4. Three illustrations of the way visitors seek mini-rests during a museum visit—by leaning or bracing themselves against exhibit furnishings to reduce museum fatigue.—From Exhibits for the Small Museum, by Arminta Neal, pp. 140-141. Copyright 1976 by the American Association for State and Local History.

sound to a limited area and good acoustical design to limit distracting noise in the galleries are two ways of controlling undesirable sounds. Lighting is another ambient environment factor that can detract from comfort. Light levels that are too low contribute to eyestrain and make viewing and reading difficult. Overbright conditions produce glare. Visiting several galleries in a sequence that have poor lighting conditions can be very tiring.

A third source of fatigue is the nature of tasks required of visitors. For one thing, visitors are expected to be vigilant during their visit. That is, they are to be attentive and actively explore a three-dimensional environment. Vigilance requires effort, as anyone knows who has tried to stay awake during a typical college lecture class! Focusing one's attention on objects in exhibits over a one- or two-hour museum visit is a long exercise in attentive observance. Reading is also a task that requires effort, and a prolonged period of reading can leave the visitor very fatigued. One reason that people are often seen *not* reading display labels is that they have grown tired of reading. Changes of pace, mini-rests, and sources of interpretation besides the printed word are some ways of providing rest from sustained mental concentration.

Finally, psychological factors can add to fatigue. Early museum evaluation research clearly suggested that museum fatigue was more than physical exertion.[39] Visitors can become bored looking at a succession of similar objects; variety or a change of pace helps to keep curiosity aroused. This psychological boredom factor would be more significant for the general audience than for visitors with high intrinsic interests in a specific collection. But even the strongly motivated visitor can lose interest in exhibits that do not provide some variety or discontinuity in context.

Another psychological fatigue factor is disorientation. Disorientation is defined as confusion and a generally aversive condition that results from feeling lost or unable to manage the environment successfully. Disorientation can contribute to fatigue through unsuccessful efforts at decision-making and through physical exertion resulting from backtracking and other unnecessary movement. Visitors are likely to challenge themselves to see the whole museum, which—in a large institution—can be a very unrealistic goal. Good entrance orientation can help visitors plan a more effective strategy and avoid much of the fatigue associated with disorientation.

Crowding can also be a source of fatigue. However, crowding is more of a psychological state than just a matter of large numbers of people present. Environmental psychologists have observed that it is specific conditions that lead to people's feeling crowded.[40] In fact, the excitement of a crowd can be a positive experience and create a festive atmosphere. Having other people around may start to be stressful, however, and thereby may contribute to fatigue, if there is a sense that privacy is lost, if there is interference with what one is trying to do, or if the noise and activity associated with a number of people starts to be irritating. Visitors will tolerate crowds, even enjoy them, if they can see exhibits they want to see, participate in activities such as interactive exhibits, perceive that they have some privacy for their group, and do not have a sense of being overloaded by the noise and activity of other people. Crowding can be controlled, not only with good circulation patterns that discourage too many people's collecting in one area, but also by providing displays that make it possible for many visitors to look and read while they wait to move to another area. Crowding may be a subtle influence on reading orientation texts at the entrances of galleries. Crowding can influence this behavior, and visitors can often be seen reading label copy while they wait for a crowd to thin out. That same label copy would go unread at other times. Some museums provide extra programming in the form of films or docent presentations during peak attendance periods. Sometimes an extra gallery can be opened or temporary exhibits added to existing spaces when crowds are anticipated. The important point is that if visitors are intent on things other than the number and press of people around them, they are less likely to feel crowded and fatigued because of the presence of others.

Evaluating visitor comfort aids. The tools of interviews, questionnaires, and observation can help assess comfort and fatigue problems. Exit questionnaires or interviews can ask visitors to evaluate the museum in terms of how well facilities met their comfort needs. People can also be asked to rate such specific conditions as heat, noise, and crowding. Observation combined with staff or volunteer comments about comfort problems can identify specific needs within the museum. For example, restrooms may be hard to find in one area or level of the museum, and the guards may be the only staff people aware of this problem because they are frequently asked for directions. Observation may also reveal that benches go unused in one area and would be put to better use somewhere else.

A walk-through review and checklist can be a helpful evaluation tool for assessing physical features of a museum. Technical information can supplement a checklist review. Sources exist that can provide specific information on lighting, sound, and temperature conditions best for human needs.[41] For example, a great amount of information exists nowadays on engineering requirements for adequate sound conditions. Some writers have prepared articles specifically for museums—Robert Newman's "I Wonder Who's Hearing It Now" is a case in point.[42] Newman, an expert in acoustical engineering, states that museum exhibit areas must have auditory properties different from theaters or auditoriums. Too many galleries are designed with hard-surfaced floors, and with ceilings that amplify even low-level sounds such as human conversation. As Newman put it, without good acoustical engineering, "every little sound in such a space becomes a major episode." Sound-absorptive materials can be used to control unintended transmission of noises around a gallery. With good acoustical design, gallery space can include movement of people, sound equipment presentations, docent talks, and visitor conversation without the background sound becoming aversive and tiring. Newman also states that modern methods of sound control still permit ceilings and walls fabricated in ways that are aesthetically pleasing.

Some exhibit-design books also have information useful for evaluating visitor-comfort features of a gallery. As an illustration, Arminta Neal encourages exhibit-label placement that anticipates older visitors who wear bifocals, with labels positioned at a height that makes reading through bifocals possible and doesn't force the wearer to take his or her glasses off.[43]

Vandalism as a Problem in Visitor Orientation

Imagine the following situation. A family group is touring an exhibition and decides to have their picture taken alongside one of the displays. The father of the group encourages the family to stand in the display area, and the combined weight of their bodies causes a portion of the exhibit to collapse. This situation actually happened—and points out another aspect of visitor orientation. People need psychological organization in the form of rules or understandings about the proper behavior for a given setting. The family members above, who caused partial collapse of that exhibit, were not vandals, and yet the consequences of their actions damaged the exhibit. What prompted the family to step into an exhibit area and make contact with exhibit materials? One answer is that the setting had been designed to create an informal and more interactive mood. Ironically, the damage caused by the family occurred because the exhibit communicated an intended informality. Other visitors were observed to be also taking liberties, such as touching exhibit components, that they probably would not have done in more traditional, more formal museum settings. People pick up cues from the environment that orient them to what they interpret to be appropriate behaviors. Those cues can come from the setting itself as well as from signs that explain rules of conduct.

People have varied expectations about visitor conduct in museums. An advice column in a newspaper discusses conversation in museum galleries, because a letter-writer had stated that it was inappropriate to talk when visiting a museum. A popular, family-oriented cartoon strip shows a small child standing in front of an exhibit with his hands behind his back. Signs in the exhibit explain that it is a "Please Touch" display, and his mother is telling him that it is all right to go ahead and touch. However, the boy is resolute in keeping his hands behind his back because, after all, a museum is a place where you must not touch things. These two examples illustrate expectations about a museum. Orientation at the museum either reinforces these expectations or starts to create new ones.

Fortunately, there is a growing body of research on vandalism and changing attitudes about it that emphasize positive action rather than passive acceptance.[44] There is more than one kind of vandalism and not all damage is done because of hostility or anger.[45] Vandalism based on aggression is best dealt with through museum security—that should include design features that make it hard to damage materials, as well as effective surveillance that discourages isolation. Some damage, however, appears to result from a poor match between visitor expectations or understanding of what one may do in a setting and the design of the setting. If visitor interaction and participation is sought in a setting, the components of exhibits must be designed to withstand wear and constant manipulation. Visitors may feel free to move into restricted areas if there is no clear differentiation evident between the public domain and private space. Design ambience of a setting can influence mood and suggest different behaviors.

Orientation aids help establish rules of conduct that can prevent some forms of damage. Signs are really a kind of psychological cue card that, first, spells out the house rules, and then reminds visitors about them. There is a psychology of environmental prompting.[46] Among other things, such promptings have helped control littering behavior, and signs can help reduce other forms of damaging behavior. For example, one national park conducted a successful experiment in discouraging visitors from walking out onto a meadow, damaging the vegetation, and frightening wildlife away. A system of signs was worked out, not only discouraging undesirable behavior, but directing visitor behavior in ways that would encourage wildlife to migrate back into the setting. Visitors were discouraged not only from moving onto the meadow, but also from parking their cars in animal-crossing areas. In addition to signs, an interpretation kiosk was located at a point safely removed from animal activity. The kiosk served to attract visitors interested in looking for animal life in the meadow.

The signs used in the example above not only stated a prohibition, but explained a contingency: if visitors cooperated, the chances of viewing wildlife increased. Putting a reason or incentive into a prompting can often increase its effectiveness. Overnegative messages should be avoided. People have experimented with a variety of messages, including some that employ humor (see fig. 5.5) to orient visitors to important rules.

In summary, some types of behavior that lead to vandalism can be reduced with effective orientation. If damage at a specific location remains continuous, it would be well to examine the setting for causes other than aggressive acts. Are unintended messages being communicated to visitors? Changing visitors' behavior may take some trial-and-error evaluation. Different prompts can be tried and the location of signs evaluated. A sign that is not vivid enough to be seen, or one that is located in a spot seldom looked at, will do little good.

Getting Started On Evaluation
of Visitor Orientation

None of the ideas expressed here will have real value unless they are put into practice. Small things improve the quality of a visitor's experience. A lot of small things well done add up to a rich and fulfilling museum visit. Good orientation helps to provide a pattern or plan for visitors who want it. That plan helps the visitor choose meaningful resources from the alternatives provided by the museum. Good orientation can help minimize such negative experiences as confusion or fatigue that detract from enjoyment and can even spoil an otherwise satisfying visit.

Two suggestions for evaluating a museum's success in meeting visi-

in the museum…please…
LOOK   TO~~U~~CH LEARN
SM~~O~~KE RELAX LIT~~T~~ER
ENJOY   E~~X~~T   TALK

en el museo…favor de…
MIRAR   TO~~C~~AR   APRENDER
FU~~M~~AR   DESCANSAR ENS~~U~~CIAR
DISFRUTAR CO~~M~~ER   HABLAR

BIRDS ONLY
Beyond
This
Sign

Fig. 5.5. Different formats for signs can help orient visitors to museum rules designed to guide behavior. Several museums have experimented with the kind of museum rules shown in the sign at upper left, communicating appropriate and inappropriate behavior. This format avoids a list of negative statements. Sometimes a measure of humor or novelty in a sign such as that at lower right can attract attention and put the visitor into a more positive—and more compliant—mood.

tor orientation would be to create a checklist for orientation features and problems. The checklist should be used as the basis for a diagnostic walk-through review. Actually, the walk-through review might begin outside the setting, or even away from the museum, in order to assess signs and other aids that direct people to the place.

Organizing an Orientation Checklist

The various topics discussed above might serve as suggestions for a checklist to be used in identifying orientation problems in a specific museum or other kind of visitor setting. The example that follows has been organized around the orientation needs already discussed here: conceptual, wayfinding, and comfort. A key element of any checklist is the kind of evaluative response made to each entry on the list. Three categories appear in the list below: *Not applicable* (NA) means the particular feature listed is not appropriate for the setting being evaluated; *satisfactory* (S) indicates a feature or aid that seems effective; *Needs evaluation* (NE) indicates that some evaluative work should be completed before deciding whether things are satisfactory or unsatisfactory.

Visitor Orientation Checklist

Conceptual Orientation

1.	Outside signs, brochures, etc., provide enough conceptual orientation to define what the museum is about.	NA	S	NE
2.	Entrance signs explain purpose of museum.	NA	S	NE
3.	Orientation center has conceptual information available.	NA	S	NE
4.	Visitor brochure has conceptual information for organizing visits and identifying key areas or galleries.	NA	S	NE
5.	Galleries/areas are identified with words that are familiar and meaningful.	NA	S	NE
6.	Each gallery has an effective means of communicating conceptual information about the contents of that area.	NA	S	NE

Wayfinding Orientation

1.	Phone-book listings, airport displays, tourist pamphlets, and other community-based information about the museum contains adequate details for getting to the museum.	NA	S	NE

2. Appropriate bus routes are publicized for getting to the   NA   S   NE
    museum.

3. Direction signs are posted on major auto routes to the   NA   S   NE
    museum.

4. Entrance orientation signs and displays include wayfinding   NA   S   NE
    information for getting to the various areas of the museum.

5. Reception desk is well located to attract incoming visitors.   NA   S   NE

6. Entrance attendants at cashier desk, guard station, reception   NA   S   NE
    desk, etc., are trained to answer wayfinding questions.

7. Orientation center contains wayfinding information.   NA   S   NE

8. Visitor brochure contains a readable map.   NA   S   NE

9. Signs and/or effective "You-Are-Here" maps are located   NA   S   NE
    throughout the museum at major transition points.

10. Gallery attendants/guards are trained to answer orientation   NA   S   NE
    questions and give wayfinding direction.

Comfort Needs

1. Museum entrance area contains the following amenities (or   NA   S   NE
    signs that inform visitors where such amenities can be
    found).

Clock with current time	Yes	No
Coat and parcel storage area	Yes	No
Drinking fountain	Yes	No
Phone	Yes	No
Restrooms	Yes	No
Area to attend infants	Yes	No
Stroller and wheelchair checkouts	Yes	No

2. Locations of restrooms and other amenities within the   NA   S   NE
    museum are clearly shown on maps and marked with effec-
    tive signs.

3. Orientation information provides help for planning visits,   NA   S   NE
    establishing time limits, and minimizing disorientation.

4. Museum rules are clearly stated and repeated within the   NA   S   NE
    museum.

5. Circulation patterns minimize wasted motion and confusion.   NA   S   NE

6. Periodic checks are made on gallery temperature, noise, and   NA   S   NE
    lighting conditions.

7. Provisions are made for needs of handicapped visitors.   NA   S   NE

8. Museum security procedures include specific plans for han-   NA   S   NE
    dling such visitor-related health problems as illness or heart
    attacks.

9. Mini-rest opportunities are provided through benches, etc.   NA   S   NE

Visitor Orientation Checklist

The visitor orientation checklist provided here is merely an example. Each setting is different from any other, and the orientation checklist should always be tailored to a specific place.

Completing a Walk-Through Interview

Once a working checklist is prepared, a walk-through evaluation exercise should be planned. In a small museum, the entire staff might complete the walk-through. It would be helpful to ask an architect-designer to accompany the group on the review. For some of the items on the checklist, the review actually begins with a simulation of getting to the museum and discovering the kinds of information available about the museum in the community. The review within the museum should include all areas used by visitors. If the most common circulation patterns used in visiting the museum are known, it would be well to walk through in the same sequence used by visitors.

Taking a tape recorder along is useful in capturing your own on-site impressions about a setting and making notes about possible problems. It is easier to speak into the recorder than it is to write down comments. The checklist exercise is meant to help provide an outline for visitors that will enhance their visit. Once oriented to the museum environment, quality of experience will depend upon what happens in the specific exhibit settings.

NOTES

1. Heinrich Boll, *Absent Without Leave* (New York: McGraw-Hill, 1965), p. 13.

2. Harold M. Proshansky, William H. Ittelson, and Leanne G. Rivlin, "Freedom of Choice and Behavior in a Physical Setting," in *Environmental Psychology: People and Their Physical Settings*, 2nd. ed., ed. Harold M. Proshansky, William H. Ittelson, and Leanne G. Rivlin (New York: Holt, Rinehart and Winston, 1976), pp. 170-180.

3. Herman A. Witkin, Helen B. Lewis, Karen Machover, P. B. Meissner, and Seymour Wapner, *Personality through Perception* (New York: Harper, 1954).

4. S. S. Brehm and J. W. Brehm, *Psychological Reactance: A Theory of Freedom and Control* (New York: Academic Press, 1981).

5. See P. Slovic, Baruch Fischoff, and Sarah Lichtenstein, "Behavioral Decision Theory," in *Annual Review of Psychology* 28, ed. M. R. Rosenzweig and L. W. Porter (Palo Alto, Calif.: Annual Review Inc., 1977): 1-39.

6. Steven Kaplan, "The Challenge of Environmental Psychology: A Proposal for a New Functionalism," *American Psychologist* 27 (1972): 140-143.

7. Joseph G. Yoshika, "A Direction-Orientation Study with Visitors at the New York World's Fair," *The Journal of General Psychology* 27 (1942): 6-9.

8. Gary W. Evans, "Environmental Cognition," *Psychological Bulletin* 88 (1980): 259-287.

9. R. M. Downs and D. Stea, *Maps in Minds: Reflections on Cognitive Mapping* (New York: Harper and Row, 1977).

10. Yoshika, "A Direction-Orientation Study," pp. 9-21.

11. J. J. Gibson and E. J. Gibson, "Perceptual Learning: Differentiation or Enrichment?" *Psychological Review* 62 (1955): 32-41.

12. H. Heft, "The Role of Environmental Features in Route-Learning: Two Exploratory Studies of Wayfinding," *Environmental Psychology and Nonverbal Behavior* 3 (1979): 172-185.

13. Roger Downs, 'Mazes, Minds and Maps," in *Sign Systems for Libraries*, ed. Dorothy Pollet and Peter C. Haskell (New York: Bowker, 1979), chapter 2.

14. Robert L. Wolf, "Visitor Orientation at the Metropolitan Museum of Art: A Conceptual Analysis," unpublished report, 1982.

15. Gordon Reekie, "Toward Well-Being for Museum Visitors," *Curator* 1 (March 1958): 91-94.

16. Reekie, "Toward Well-Being for Visitors," p. 93.

17. Darrel A. Ullmann, *Attraction Sign Survey* (Lincoln, Nebr.: Nebraska Department of Roads and Nebraska Department of Economic Development, 1972), pp. 1-23.

18. Daniel Dailey and Roger Mandle, "Welcome to the Museum," *Museum News* 53 (January/February 1974): 45.

19. Ervin H. Zube, Joseph H. Crystal, and James F. Palmer, *Visitor Center Design Evaluation*, report no. R-76-5 (Amherst, Mass.: University of Massachusetts, Institute for Man and Environment, 1976) pp. 15-20.

20. Basic texts in statistics discuss the probability of different outcomes in a sample of events and rules for determining beyond-chance outcomes. A good presentation is in William Mendenhall's *Introduction to Statistics* (Belmont, Calif.: Wadsworth, 1964), chapter 7.

21. Arminta Neal, *Help! For the Small Museum* (Boulder, Colo.: Pruett Press, 1969), pp. 15-16.

22. Marilyn S. Cohen, "The State of the Art of Museum Visitor Orientation: A Survey of Selected Institutions," unpublished paper (Washington, D.C.: Smithsonian Institution, Office of Museum Programs, 1974).

23. Cohen, "Museum Visitor Orientation," pp.1-4.

24. Cohen, "Museum Visitor Orientation," pp. 6-7.

25. Southworth and Southworth Architecture and Planning, *Lost in Art: Evaluation of the Visitor Information Center, Boston Museum of Fine Arts* (Boston, Mass.: Southworth and Southworth Architecture and Planning, 1974), 80 pp.

26. D. Geoffrey Hayward and Mary L. Bryon-Miller, "Evaluating the Effectiveness of Orientation Experiences at an Outdoor History Museum," unpublished paper, no date.

27. Marilyn S. Cohen, Gary H. Winkel, Richard Olsen, and Fred Wheeler, "Orientation in a Museum: An Experimental Study," *Curator* 20 (June 1977): 85-97.

28. *Communicating with the Museum Visitor: Guidelines for Planning* (Toronto, Canada: The Royal Ontario Museum, 1976), pp. 25-36.

29. Dorothy Pollet, "You Can Get There From Here," *Wilson Library Bulletin* (1976): 456-462.

30. Ross J. Loomis, "The Visitor and the Collection: The Immediate Visual Experience of the Museum," *Mountain-Plains Museum Conference Proceedings* 7 (1976): 1-8.

31. See, for example, Dorothy Pollet and Peter C. Haskell, eds., *Sign Systems for Libraries* (New York: Bowker, 1979), chapters 4-10.

32. Marvin Levine, "You-Are-Here Maps: Psychological Considerations," *Environment and Behavior* 14:2 (1982): 221-237.

33. Colvin Randall, "Visitor Enhancement at Longwood Gardens," unpublished paper (Newark, Del.: Longwood Program, 1975), pp. 18-21.

34. Edwin E. Krumpe, "Redistributing Backcountry Use by a Behaviorally Based Communications Device" (Ph.D. diss., Colorado State University, 1979), pp. 73-114.

35. Benjamin I. Gilman, "Museum Fatigue," *The Scientific Monthly* 12 (1916): 62-74.

36. Arminta Neal, *Exhibits for the Small Museum: A Handbook* (Nashville: American Association for State and Local History, 1976), pp. 139-146.

37. M. Lehmbruck, "Psychology: Perception and Behavior," *Museum* 26:3 (1974): 191-203.

38. For a discussion of the psychology of noise, see Jeffrey D. Fisher, Paul A. Bell, and Andrew Baum, *Environmental Psychology*, 2nd ed. (New York: Holt, Rinehart and Winston, 1984), pp. 97-115.

39. Edward S. Robinson, *The Behavior of the Museum Visitor*, no. 5, New Series (Washington, D.C.: American Association of Museums, 1928), pp. 31-42.

40. Fisher, Bell, and Baum, *Environmental Psychology*, pp. 211-223.

41. See, for example, Ernst J. McCormick and Mark S. Sanders, *Human Factors in Engineering and Design*, 5th ed. (New York: McGraw-Hill, 1982), pp. 369-394; 124-141; 395-418.

42. Robert B. Newman, "I Wonder Who's Hearing It Now," *Museum News* 51 (September 1972): 20-22.

43. Neal, *Help! For the Small Museum*, pp. 32-36.

44. Sam S. Alfano and Arthur W. Magill, eds., *Vandalism and Outdoor Recreation: Symposium Proceedings*, USDA Forest Service, General Technical Report no. PSW-17 (Washington, D.C.: 1976), 72 pp.

45. For an integrated model describing vandalism, see J. D. Fisher and R. M. Baron, "An Equity-Based Model of Vandalism," *Population and Environment* 5/3 (1982): 182-200.

46. Fisher, Bell, and Baum, *Environmental Psychology*, pp. 350-355.

6

Exhibit Evaluation: Making Things Work

Somewhere in the heart of everyone who has worked with museum exhibits and what they communicate to visitors there has to be the hope that the following kind of interaction between visitor and exhibit will take place:

I was transfixed. As I now recall it, there was only one sensation in my head: pure elation mixed with amazement at such perfection. Swept off my feet, I floated from one side to the other, swiveling my brain, staring astounded at the beavers, then at the otters. I could hear shouts across my corpus callosum, from one hemisphere to the other. I remember thinking, with what was left in charge of my consciousness, that I wanted no part of the science of beavers and otters; I wanted never to know how they performed their marvels; I wished for no news about the physiology of their breathing, the coordination of their muscles, their vision, their endocrine systems, their digestive tracts. I hoped never to have to think of them as collections of cells. All I asked for was the full hairy complexity, then in front of my eyes, of whole, intact beavers and otters in motion.[1]

Lewis Thomas is speaking, in *The Medusa and the Snail*—describing his reaction to a zoo exhibit that permitted the visitor to view otters and beavers simultaneously in their respective habitats. Thomas interprets his experience at the Tucson Zoo as a temporary escape from the twentieth-century tendency to reduce everything to component parts, with a resulting failure to see the totality of an object or an event. Thomas's observation is important. Exhibits, of any kind, have the potential of giving one a Gestalt, a holistic view of what is around us, be it in science, art, or natural history. Books and lectures invariably dissect, itemize, and draw one into an elaborate maze of complexity. Exhibits, with their reliance on objects and settings, provide the individual with an experience

201

of "visiting," experiencing more directly, as it were, a culture or a period of history, art, or science. To be sure, visitors can also learn specific points of information during their time in a gallery and use it like a textbook. In fact, the purpose of exhibit evaluation is to find out how visitors are reacting to objects and exhibit features and thereby determine whether an exhibit is working the way it was planned.

It is important to keep in mind just who is visiting an exhibit and what kinds of expectations these individuals may have. It is important not to stereotype all visitors, to remember that they will vary in their commitment to an exhibit, their knowledge about topics, their curiosity and interest, and the degree to which they feel at home in an exhibit setting. They will also vary in their dependency on orientation aids to help them understand and explore a specific exhibit.

Good exhibit evaluation must begin with clarification of goals for an exhibit in terms that relate objects, interpretation features, and the physical design of space to visitors. Once exhibit goals are well understood, it is necessary to determine what specific evaluation studies will shed light on whether or not those goals are working out.

Exhibit Goals and Evaluation Goals

In this writer's experience, most exhibits have some goals or intentions stated for what the exhibit is to be about and how it is to work. With existing exhibits, it may be necessary to rummage through old files and records to find statements about what was planned for them; but once reclaimed, goals will probably be part of the planning documents. Often, the basic problem is that goals may not be stated in terms that relate well to people and the way they fit into all the curatorial, educational, and design expectations for the exhibit. Expectations for what visitors will gain from an exhibit are sometimes expressed in very general terms (i.e., "visitors will learn about Colonial America") that make it difficult to know precisely how the exhibit is to carry out that goal. Sometimes more concrete and detailed objectives that would spell out the way the exhibit is to produce visitor enjoyment, learning, etc., are not part of the planning statements.

Exhibit planners are not alone in sometimes failing to make visitor-related goals concrete and thereby more effective in creating desired experiences. In recent years, there has been increased emphasis on the "people aspects" of places and the integration of planning and design with evaluation of how well a setting fits the needs and expectations of people. A growing literature now describes what is being learned from

evaluations of a wide range of places. The entire December 1980 issue
of *Environment and Behavior,* for one instance, was devoted to post-
occupancy evaluation of environments and includes examples from office
parks, housing, and correctional institutions.

Are Exhibit Goals Related to Visitors?

C. G. Screven has long recognized the importance of relating exhibit
goals to evaluation, as reflected in his paper "Exhibit Evaluation: a Goal-
Referenced Approach."[2] A careful reading of this paper is useful both for
thinking about the way exhibit goals must relate to visitors and for planning evaluation studies to insure that those goals will be realized. While
Screven is concerned with exhibits as being effective educational settings,
his goal-referenced approach is important for planning any desired outcome for visiting an exhibit. Exhibit goals must be expressed in terms
or objectives that are measurable, and evaluation is the process used to
test and determine whether the goals (and specific exhibit features) are
working out as planned. For Screven, three questions are at the heart of
integrating exhibit goals and evaluation: What impact should the exhibit
have on visitors, how will the desired goals be achieved, and how can
it be known if the exhibit goals and objectives have the desired impact
on the intended audience? Discussion of each question follows, below.

What impact should the exhibit have on visitors? This question pertains to goals, but must be answered in concrete terms that can be tested.
If, for illustration, a goal is to provoke visitor interest through exposure
to museum objects, then the specific kinds of interests and objects should
be thought out in a planning exercise.

How will the desired goals be achieved? Objectives, which are usually
more specific planning statements than goals, need to identify ways in
which individual exhibit parts will help accomplish goals. These
individual considerations will not only include how many and what
kinds of objects will be used and dictate their placement in the gallery
spaces; it will also include various interpretative aids such as labels,
exhibit case designs, intended circulation patterns, and decisions about
whether displays will encourage visitor participation. It can be helpful
to think of basic design elements in terms of visitor-related goals and
specific design alternatives as ways of reaching those goals. Some specific
examples of linking general design elements to goals and more detailed
design alternatives are shown in Table 6.1.

Exhibit designers also realize the importance of linking exhibit goals to specific design alternatives that reflect visitor needs. For example, Lothar Witteborg, in his exhibit planning guide, devoted thirteen of thirty-three items to topics directly related to visitors.[3] His visitor-related topics ranged from such broad considerations as the effectiveness of an exhibit as a communications medium to such specific design considerations as planning circulation patterns and labels (see Table 6.1).

Table 6.1
Examples of Exhibit Design Elements, Visitor-Related Goals,
and Design Alternatives

Design Element	*Visitor-Related Goals*	*Design Alternatives*
How will the entrance area be designed to best introduce visitors to the exhibit?	What conceptual orientation information is needed by visitors? Is wayfinding orientation information needed? Should visitors be prompted to turn right, left, or proceed straight ahead?	1. Use large orientation labels. 2. Present a gallery wall map. 3. Exhibit prominent objects typical of exhibit content. 4. Use barriers, lighting, etc., to suggest direction of movement. 5. Plan an entrance orientation area with special labels, audio-visuals, etc.
How large should the exhibit be?	Will a complete tour leave visitors fatigued? Will the average visitor be bored with too much of the same thing? How much time can visitors commit to the exhibit?	1. Use a parallel gallery concept with some general interest exhibits and study or open storage spaces also available.
What circulation patterns are desired?	Will visitors become confused about wayfinding? Will visitors miss major portion of the gallery? Should visitors see exhibits in a linear time sequence? Is a random viewing sequence acceptable?	1. Use open spaces. 2. Use a critical path or tunnel-circulation pattern. 3. Design cul-de-sac areas for sequential viewing. 4. Use rope barriers, maps, signs, lighting effects, to suggest (but not require) specific movement sequences.

What perma- nent interpreta- tion aids should be included?	How will visitors identify objects? What learning is planned for beyond object identification?	1.	Use object labels(?); general labels(?); labels with grouped information(?)
		2.	Plan a limited number of cases with additional interpretation developed around: •Theme title. •Low density use of objects. •Main explanatory text. •Expanded object identification.
		3.	Use additional media such as video disks, slides, film projectors.
		4.	Provide interactive opportunities through question/answer labels, feedback exhibits, or microcomputers.
		5.	Include a special area for live interpretation.
		6.	Include a study gallery or special interaction exhibit area for more intensified study.

Source: Suggested by Lothar P. Witteborg, "Exhibit Planning," *History News* 38 (June 1983): 21-24.

Defining Evaluation Goals

Just as exhibit goals must be clarified and related to visitors, some goals and objectives must be defined for any evaluation study undertaken.

How can it be known whether the exhibit goals and objectives have the desired impact on the intended audience? This question refers directly to an evaluation component in exhibit planning. Only through evaluation can information be objectively collected to determine whether goals are being realized. All too often, exhibits fail to have the planners' envisioned effect on visitors. Some kinds of evaluation studies can guide the development of exhibits to minimize failure, which raises the distinction between summative and formative evaluation.

Summative and formative evaluation. As C. G. Screven notes, in "Exhibit Evaluation,"[4] summative evaluation is completed on existing exhibits. Typically, *summative evaluation* methodology is fairly formal and is based on large samples of visitors. Summative evaluation documents the final product in terms of "good" and/or "bad" outcomes. Often this kind of evaluation is a one-time study (a major limitation), but nevertheless it is important in determining exhibits as perceived and used by visitors.

Formative evaluation occurs during the planning and development of an exhibit and is usually less formal in methodology. The paramount value of formative evaluation is that it can provide feedback at a time when changes to an exhibit can still be made. For situations requiring specific interpretation or learning objectives that can get very complex—such as science demonstrations or history narratives—formative evaluation can help increase to the maximum visitor comprehension of the message, as well as increasing the number of visitors who heed the message. To a limited degree, some formative evaluation can be done at the final installation stage of an exhibit, but time constraints and cost factors mitigate against making extensive changes. Evaluation information at this point is limited to identifying serious errors that *must* be corrected or fine-tuning with small changes such as relocating signs or revising a major label or text panel. It is not hard to see why experienced evaluators like Screven encourage formative evaluation, since it can suggest alternatives for making exhibits more effective that can be put into operation before the exhibit opens.

A recent article by S. A. Griggs relates the summative/formative distinction to exhibit planning at the British Museum (Natural History) and considers the two forms of evaluation as ultimately complementary. Formative evaluation helps in planning an exhibit, while summative evaluation can determine whether the installed exhibit is successful. Readers interested in this distinction about evaluation will find other papers helpful in exhibit planning and preparation.[5]

Deciding on goals for a particular evaluation effort is based, in part, on determining whether or not an existing exhibit is to be evaluated or whether some formative evaluation tasks should be done to guide the planning of a new exhibit. This writer has found that many situations call for a combination of summative and formative evaluation goals. Examples include:

Summative Evaluation

Goals	*Objectives*
1. Identify the kinds of visitors to an existing exhibit.	Complete a visitor description survey.
2. Discover what visitors learn in an existing exhibit.	Complete a pre-test and post-test survey of knowledge of exhibit topics and objects.
3. Find out the route or circulation pattern most visitors use in touring an existing exhibit.	Complete an observation study of a sample of visitors.

Formative Evaluation

Goals	*Objectives*
1. Determine whether a new format and placement strategy for labels attracts visitor attention.	Complete a pilot study of temporary labels using the new format and placement before the permanent installation of the labels.
2. Determine whether new interpretive materials communicate a conceptual story-line to visitors.	Prepare a mock-up that simulates the way the new exhibit will appear and conduct a survey of visitors shown the mock-up.

It should be noted that the two formative evaluation goals given above as examples could include objectives to add summative evaluation of existing exhibits, thereby providing a useful comparison. Such a comparison cannot always be done, but this writer has found that if comparable exhibit content exists, it is helpful to test planned new features against old ones. Results of such comparisons can suggest what features of older displays should be kept, and what new ideas are worthy of permanent installation.

Evaluation of an entire exhibit would require a number of goals and several evaluation tasks or studies to carry out all objectives. By contrast, exhibit evaluation could focus on one goal and a much more limited study would be called for.

How does one decide what the evaluation goals should be? First, and most obvious, goals for any evaluation study will be suggested by exhibit goals and objectives. To illustrate, much of the evaluation work undertaken at the British Museum (Natural History) in recent years has assessed the effectiveness of story-line interpretation or visitor learning based upon acquiring concepts about exhibit content as compared to factual information. The evaluation efforts reflect a decision to emphasize thematic or conceptual interpretation as an exhibit-planning goal for new installations.[6] As another illustration, suppose a gallery is planned to include displays that invite visitor participation; then, evaluation goals could include assessing whether or not visitors use such exhibits, what they think about them, and perhaps how they compare them to nonparticipative displays.

As a second step in deciding about evaluation goals, one can review criteria that other people think are important as found in research conducted to reveal significant criteria for exhibits. Such criteria can suggest both exhibit and evaluation goals.

Third, an exploratory study can be conducted on an existing gallery to discover some visitor reactions that might lead to ideas for new or renovated exhibit designs and also suggest topics that should be evaluated in greater depth.

Finally, one can review exhibit evaluation studies, to learn about topics and visitor considerations others think are of value.

Discovering important exhibit criteria. Research can help determine important criteria for designing exhibits. Harris Shettel, some time ago, reviewed literature describing criteria for well-designed exhibits and prepared a feature-rating questionnaire for exhibits, to assess existing galleries.[7] When the questionnaire was put to actual use, Shettel found that people had difficulty agreeing on how well a particular exhibit met different criteria. This finding underscores the recognized variability of individual judgments about exhibits. Shettel's list of criteria are useful in deciding exhibit goals and thereby suggesting potential summative or formative evaluation goals (see fig. 6.1).

M. B. Alt and K. M. Shaw pursued an interesting variation of a criteria identification project by asking visitors to identify what they thought were characteristics of an *ideal* exhibit.[8] Working at the British Museum (Natural History), these authors first had visitors provide lists of characteristics the visitors would use to describe and discriminate among different museum exhibits. Other visitors were asked to select from these characteristics those they thought described ideal exhibits as well as a sample of actual exhibits in the museum. Among the findings from this study were that an ideal exhibit could be described by criteria such as the following:

1. It makes the subject come to life.
2. It gets the message across quickly.

Exhibit Criteria Reviewed by Shettel
and Written as Potential Exhibit Evaluation Goal Statements

1. Is the exhibit attractive to visitors?

2. Is the exhibit easily comprehended by visitors?

3. Will visitors perceive the exhibit as a unified concept or setting? Is there a focus of attention?

4. Do exhibit components attract attention?

5. Do exhibit components hold attention?

6. Is the exhibit presentation viewed as appropriate for the content involved?

7. Do visitors think exhibit information presented is accurate? (Is the information in fact accurate?)

8. How well does the exhibit handle crowd flow?

9. Does the exhibit match visitor characteristics?

10. How well do communication (interpretive) materials work? (I.e., labels, sound, motion, demonstrations, charts, films, models, participative exhibits.)

11. How do visitors perceive the exhibit relating to surrounding areas or other exhibits?

12. How do visitors evaluate the basic design components? (I.e., size of space, physical layout, use of color and light.)

13. How do visitors react to the choices of exhibit objects in terms of quantity, attractiveness, appropriateness, etc.?

Fig. 6.1. Examples of criteria for exhibit planning based on design considerations and expressed as exhibit evaluation goal statements.—Adapted form Harris Shettel's "An Evaluation of Existing Criteria for Judging the Quality of Science Exhibits," Curator 11:2 (1968): 137-153.

3. You can understand the point(s) it is making quickly.
4. There is something in it for all ages.
5. You can't help noticing it.

A somewhat controversial conclusion drawn from the Alt and Shaw study was that visitors defined ideal exhibits by criteria different from those emphasized in participatory exhibits where the visitor must be actively involved. Perhaps this study based on visitor-generated criteria is parallel, in some important ways, to Shettel's work with designer-originated criteria, in that features of good design—such as clarity, good organization, attractiveness—are always important goals for an exhibit that will prove effective with visitors. They are also criteria worthy of evaluation.

Integrating exhibit preparation and evaluation. More and more, people are seeing the need to build evaluation into the process of preparing exhibits.[9] Only through this integrating of evaluation and development of an exhibit can goals related to visitors be met without expensive post-installation modifications. This integration is advocated, not only for the design and preparation of exhibits, but increasingly for all planned environments. Screven's goal-referenced approach cited earlier calls for this integration (see fig. 6.2), whether a new exhibit or an existing one is under consideration. The flow of exhibit preparation activities should include defining visitor-related goals, planning a new exhibit or changes in an existing one, and then completing some evaluation tasks to see how well visitor reactions match planning goals for the exhibit. In the case of existing exhibits, evaluation would be summative in nature (although planned changes could be pretested with formative evaluation), while new exhibits can be tested with formative evaluation tasks. Evaluation results from existing exhibits can provide a choice point where it can be decided to accept the exhibit as it is, or plan for changes. Formative evaluation of new exhibits provides decision points as the plans and initial preparations evolve. Two essential properties of a goal-referenced approach, as summarized in figure 6.2 include (1) distinct decision or *choice points* at which one determines how well goals and visitor reactions match, and (2) feedback provided by evaluation for the adjustment of exhibit components to accomplish desired outcomes. Whether existing exhibits or new ones are involved, Screven emphasizes that three tasks must be incorporated into the evaluation:

1. Define the intended audience.
2. Define the visitor-related goals (including educational goals and objectives).

3. Develop dependable measures of visitor reactions, such as knowledge or attitudes to determine whether goals (objectives) are being met.

The success of any evaluation requires planning and defining clearly the kind of information asked for and specifying who will use that information. Exhibits that provide rich experiences for visitors will not happen by accident, but must be planned by carefully defining goals that relate visitors to specific design features. Evaluation should be part of determining those goals and, most important, determining how well the goals are being met. In addition, goals for a specific evaluation effort need to be developed to make sure the research is responsive to important questions decision-makers have in mind. Summative evaluation can determine how well an existing exhibit is working, while formative evaluation can guide the design process of new exhibits. If one is uncertain about what visitor-related exhibit goals should be, research on exhibit criteria, exploratory studies, or previous evaluation research can be consulted to suggest goals.

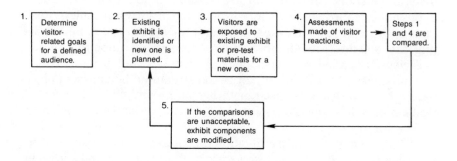

Fig. 6.2. Flow chart summary of a goal-referenced process of exhibit evaluation.— Adapted from C. G. Screven's "Exhibit Evaluation: A Goal-Referenced Approach," Curator 19:4 (1976): 271-290.

Exploratory Evaluation

An exhibit can be studied to reveal what visitors think about it and what their reaction is to different features of the exhibit environment. Such an exploratory study can be conducted without either firm exhibit or evaluation goals in mind. Such studies can be planned to yield rich descriptive information that can suggest all sorts of exhibit-planning possibilities.

In recent times, some researchers have advocated detailed descriptive studies of people in a setting of interest as a planning tool for improving the design of the setting. In fact, R. G. Barker and his disciples stress that it can be a mistake to separate behavior from the setting it occurs in.[10] Using the concept of behavior setting, Barker argued that each place is a unique combination of physical milieu and the social expectations that people hold about the way they should behave. Museums present a physical milieu of objects, exhibit cases, mazelike halls, and booklike texts printed on labels mounted in cases or on walls. Visitors enter a museum with different expectations. Some feel that a museum is a place where you do not talk out loud, do not touch anything, and plan to look at as many things as you can until you get very tired. Barker would argue that only by treating the museum exhibit and the visitor as a unit or a very interdependent system can one really understand the visitation experience.

Robert Wolf has emphasized naturalistic evaluation, in which he tries, through interviews and observation, to collect *in situ* information about the way an exhibit is functioning and the way those functions relate to plans and visitors. For Wolf, exhibit evaluation should be as unobtrusive as possible, capturing the visitor's experience in a natural context. Reactions to the visit as a total experience and the exhibit as a complete setting are sought through observations (preferably unobtrusive) and interviews intended to reveal general attitudes and experiences. A naturalistic evaluation should not be too structured by prestated objectives for it is possible to discover things no one might have expected. Wolf's approach is consistent with many of the tenets of Barker's behavior-setting approach.[11]

The flavor of descriptive evaluation is captured in the following three steps that comprise the overall strategy for performing a naturalistic evaluation according to Wolf and Barbara Tymitz:[12]

Step One: Get a flavor for the setting as a whole. Exhibit situations do not exist in a vacuum, and it is important to understand a particular exhibit in the context of the complete system or experience of visiting a museum.

Step Two: Identify the parts of problems in an exhibit system or unit that appear to have the greatest influence on the visitor.

Step Three: Select those parts or problems that appear most important in controlling what happens in the exhibit. That is, narrow the list of things identified in the second step to those that should be worked with in more depth.

Wolf outlines five sources of data or information that would implement his three steps of evaluation and accomplish a behavior-setting analysis. Collecting these sources of data depends heavily on careful observation and a conversational style of interviewing that emphasizes listening skills.

The first data source is to record general descriptive information about the physical and institutional setting. The observer must play detective— be a Sherlock Holmes, carefully noting details of the setting and distinguishing between fact and impression.

To a careful description of the physical and institutional setting is added a second source of information in the form of *action* and *behavior* descriptions: What are the people doing in the setting? What actions stand out? What behavior occurs over and over and seems to be a crucial part of the behavior setting? Common behavior patterns seem so natural to a location that it is easy to overlook them. When observing for the first time, sometimes the observer's role is that of "a stranger from another planet," observing everything seen as a novel experience.

Next, Wolf adds quotable quotes—that is, key words in a stream of thought that provide clues to visitor reactions. It is very important to record overheard comments objectively and not to try to interpret them.

Finally, two kinds of physical indicators round out the sources of descriptive information. Observers should look for traces of past behavior. Such traces can include dingy, soiled areas on the wall near a very popular interactive exhibit—evidence that many people have leaned up against the wall while waiting their turn to examine the display. Written records in files or archives can also be a source of trace measures and reveal goals and planning behind the development of an exhibit. Reviewing such materials can help create a sense of the way the setting came to be the finished product described in the first three data sources. Wear spots also can provide clues for the way a place is used. Staff at the Ringling Museum of Art in Sarasota, Florida, speak of visitors' "two-step" wear spots on gallery floors. The spots reveal a typical movement pattern that could also be observed directly when visitors stepped forward to read a label and then back to view the entire painting. The spots could be found on the wooden gallery floors throughout the museum.

Interviews would follow the observation of the five data sources just described. Interviews would include staff and professionals, as well as visitors in the exhibit being studied. Wolf and Tymitz[13] have perfected an interview methodology to gain samples of visitor reactions to specific exhibits. In contrast to a structured questionnaire, interviews provide a rich array of responses to a wide variety of exhibit features. Typically, interviews make a good tool for discovering issues and general ideas that can be measured more rigorously with follow-up questionnaires and other evaluation instruments. Interviews make for a good pilot or first-effort evaluation, since they can unearth major negative and positive audience reactions to an exhibit. For example, in a study of a natural history exhibit, Wolf and Tymitz[14] discovered that visitors sampled had difficulty orienting to the exhibit because it seemed like an entrance-way to the museum. In addition, the main title to the exhibit was not clearly understood, and there was some confusion about the exact nature of the exhibit. The investigators also concluded that few visitors read the entry sign that explained the theme of the hall. These interview comments all pointed to orientation problems that are fairly common. An interview survey cannot find solutions to all of these problems, but it can be a first line of effort to *identify* problems contained in a specific exhibit.

Interviews can also help identify strong features of an exhibit. As an example, respondents in the Wolf and Tymitz natural history study praised the realism of the habitats and the art work, as revealed in the following interview response from their report:

standing so close to those fields . . . I get a kick out of pretending I'm there too. There's a feeling when you're standing there . . . I want to be quiet not to disturb them. I'd never feel that way if I was just looking at a picture or something.

The individual was describing a habitat installation, and it is important for staff to have feedback that their efforts are noticed and appreciated by visitors.

This writer has found the methods of behavior-setting and naturalistic evaluation very useful for exploratory studies designed to help identify exhibit goals. Their advocates would also feel these methods can be used to evaluate exhibits when goals are already known and can be used with either formative or summative evaluation efforts. Readers interested in this methodology will find John Zeisel's work *Inquiry by Design* very helpful for employing observation, interviews, and questionnaires to describe effectively the kinds of behavior-settings found in exhibits.[15]

Some Examples of Exhibit Evaluation Research

Once exhibit goals relating design to visitors have been prepared and evaluation goals have been identified, some research tasks intended to evaluate how well exhibit goals and actual visitor experiences/behaviors match must be completed. It is not possible to present every kind of task that could be used, since there are many potential goals. Below are selected examples of exhibit evaluation research that this writer has found helpful, with additional thoughts on summative and formative evaluation tasks and random examples of interesting findings.

What Do Visitors Expect?

Visitor satisfaction can be related to visitor expectations and Hans-Joachim Klein recently analyzed the things that people were interested in seeing in the automobile hall at the Deutches Museum.[16] This assessment of expectations through interests was part of a summative evaluation of the hall prior to reinstallation to commemorate the centennial of the first German-made automobile. Klein used a combination of spontaneous responses and patterned questions to assess interests. Specific interests (i.e., seeing "oldtimer" cars, seeing postwar automobiles, learning about famous automobile people) were assessed with a combination of visitor answers to the spontaneous question and a list of the content of exhibits currently in the hall. A second sample of visitors were unobtrusively observed to map the distribution of attention to different exhibits within the hall. In a third random sample, exiting visitors were asked to rate the quality of information provided in the current exhibit for each of the major interests identified in the first sample.

The automobile hall evaluation was a good example of using summative evaluation of existing exhibits to guide reinstallation planning by knowing visitor interests and expectations. At the same time, the evaluation guided planners by identifying ways of improving the exhibit design, the better to meet goals they had in mind. For example, it was hoped that visitors would learn about and take notice of the very first German automobile made, which was on display. Observations revealed that this exhibit received very little attention and needed to be more prominently displayed in the the reinstalled hall. In fact, while the interest profile showed that visitors *wanted* to look at vintage cars or "oldtimers," these objects received less attention-time than did many topics rated of less interest. The vintage automobiles were lined up in a row, and visitors tended to walk down the line of vehicles without exploring them in very much depth. One idea for the new installation would be to avoid grouping the cars so close together and provide more interpretation that would highlight unique features.

Visitors did spend time looking at more modern vehicles, and this behavior was consistent with indicated interests. One reason for the consistency was that visitors had personal memories of the recent vehicles, and those memories stimulated both interest and attention to that part of the hall.

The interest profile also identified topics not currently emphasized in the hall, and the exit ratings of information adequacy verified the lack of coverage of those interests. For example, learning about ways of making automobiles safer was a popular expectation unmet in the existing hall, but one that could be added in the reinstallation plans.

Visitor expectations for a specific object can be evaluated through the kinds of questions visitors would like answered. Rik Vos, at the Rijksmuseum in Amsterdam, Holland, interviewed a random sample of visitors after they had viewed Rembrandt's painting *The Nightwatch*. He inquired about questions they had about the painting and answers to the most commonly asked questions were later installed as text material displayed in an adjoining room. Visitors were then observed attending to the written text that anticipated their interests through the questions the visitors sampled earlier had asked.[17] Again, a summative evaluation task had made exhibit content more responsive to visitor needs and, in this instance, guided the development of interpretation that was definitely attended to by visitors.

Do Visitors Understand What the Exhibit Is About?

The question of whether visitors *do* understand what the exhibit is about requires evaluation that returns to the sort of visitor orientation discussed in chapter 5. The focus is now on individual exhibits, and it is important to know, especially if themes and concepts are an important part of exhibit design, whether visitors notice and understand the concepts in the way that the exhibit plan called for. Conceptual orientation also can help visitors learn and enjoy more about the exhibit by providing them with some psychological pattern or plan for what they are about to experience.

Exhibit designer Jean Jacques Andre compares a visit to a museum or to an individual gallery with eating a fine meal.[18] Visitors must be prepared, with an appropriate appetizer (orientation), for the feast to come and having partaken to the satisfaction of each, should leave, neither hungry nor stuffed. Exhibits can have major highlights analogous to the main course, and these highlight experiences should be limited to four or five that people can remember. Just as a meal has a dessert for conclusion, exhibits should also help the visitor come to a point of completion. Themes, concepts, and other kinds of messages should flow through the exhibit as a story-line that brings a sense of unity, as a well-served meal is a pleasurable and united experience in the diner's mind. Andre notes that all too often story-lines are overambitious and make it hard for the visitor to identify what is unique and to grasp the main message of the exhibit. While it may be necessary for some exhibits to have many objects on display, so that their visitors serve themselves as to the specific entres they will have, Andre's point is that conceptual orientation should be well-planned and the story-line not so ambitious as to overtax the visitor with information.

Andre's design guidelines for pacing a visitor's experience in an exhibit relates well with what evaluation research is discovering about exhibit orientation. A recent work by C. G. Screven identifies several kinds of *advanced organizers* that can help visitors decide where they are in the exhibit, what they want to see next, and what is of major importance to understand or remember[19] and thereby pace themselves in a manner envisioned by Andre. Screven's organizers include these:

1. *Conceptual preorganizers* placed at entrances and transition points in the form of words, objects, phrases, or symbols help the visitor anticipate the organization of what is to come and to identify key ideas.

2. *Overviews* can serve as an index or "menu" (to stay with Andre's analogy) and help the visitor identify what choices must be made to plan his or her stay in the exhibit.

3. *Topographic organizers* use spatial information in the form of simplified maps to inform the visitor of concepts that go with different areas in the exhibit.

4. *Postorganizers* help visitors consolidate what they have seen and also review and reinforce key ideas and exhibit highlights.

Screven explains that features like posters, information kiosks, films, self-testing devices, and labels that use questions can all serve to orient the visitor, and each feature can be evaluated for its effectiveness.

S. A. Griggs provides a nice example of a study with a goal of determining how well visitors were oriented to exhibits at the British Museum (Natural History).[20] Griggs's study revealed that conceptual and topographical (wayfinding) information needs must be planned for if visitors are to understand exhibit themes and move through an exhibit in a predetermined manner to follow a story-line. Visitors sampled confirmed a recommendation of Robert A. Lakota that orientation information should appear at the exhibit entrance.[21] Other findings supported the principle that (1) circulation patterns can be typed as radial or sequential, with the latter a better design for thematic-based exhibits; (2) that entrance orientation can be too complex and time-demanding to be comprehended and effectively used; and (3) that it may be easier to communicate wayfinding than conceptual orientation.

Griggs used variations of the basic methods of observation and interviewing discussed earlier. Interviews were centered on orientation-related tasks that measured visitor understanding of both exhibit conceptual and wayfinding information: visitors were asked to give oral descriptions of what they could remember about an exhibit's content and organization; to take the interviewer to a specific location point in an exhibit as a test of how well they understood the physical layout; were asked to locate objects and areas on an exhibit map as a measure of orientation; and visitors were given the parts of a story-line for a thematically organized exhibit in random order and asked to reconstruct the correct sequence of the story as it was presented in a gallery.

Griggs's study yielded summative evaluation findings for existing galleries, but it is also important to integrate some formative evaluation into the exhibit-planning stage, especially if a thematic exhibit goal is under consideration. Formative evaluation can fit well into the design process. For example, Arminta Neal, in *Exhibits for the Small Museum*,[22] mentions the importance of a story scenario or story-line that weaves together all the components of an exhibit and suggests preparing a story board with three-by-five index cards to review the development of major and minor topics. The board and cards provide flexibility, in that different sequences can be tried before a final outline is developed. The following tasks can provide some formative evaluation:

1. Prepare a story board (or exhibit outline) as suggested by Neal, but include statements about visitors' learning-objectives. What are the main topics? Subtopics? How will these topics be communicated to the visitor through key words, selected objects, images or design features, audiovisuals, written text, or other kinds of displays? The outline Neal suggests also enumerates the objects to be displayed and the specific exhibit materials used to cover each topic. It is important that each of these additional components fit into the learning-objectives planned.

2. Once the story board and/or outline is prepared, small groups of people can be asked to review the information, to determine whether the sequences of story or exhibit themes appear logical and easy to follow. One group could be made up of staff or other museum professionals. A small sample of visitors should also be asked to review the story outline. Ideally, this group should be selected

to represent a cross section of people who normally visit the museum. The story board could even be set up in an exhibit or a lobby area, and visitors walking by might be asked to participate. As simple as getting this type of feedback on an exhibit may sound, it can prove very useful. People can indicate points of confusion, lack of clarity, or parts of the story-line that are hard to follow. At this stage in exhibit planning, it is very easy and economical to change things.

3. Ideally, examples of objects should be arranged in the order in which they will appear in the exhibit and, once again, a small sample of visitors may be asked to describe what they think the exhibit is about and what classes of events or concepts best describe the objects shown. Photographs can be arranged by visitors, to get an idea of the way they would organize objects and the words they would use to describe categories of objects. Results from this sample can be compared with reactions to the story-line materials to see how well they match. Or the same sample of visitors might do both tasks and look at the objects (or photographs) and then review the exhibit outline as tentatively arranged.

Still another variation of this procedure is to have one sample of visitors react to objects, their pictures, in an intended order, with another sample asked to arrange the objects in an order they find most meaningful. Comparisons of the way each group reacts could suggest where the proposed outline should be changed to improve visitor understanding of the exhibit purposes and goals.

4. Key words to be used in gallery orientation can be tested directly as a means of finding words that are familiar and meaningful. It is possible to get estimates of words that will work best for orientation by conducting a small survey prior to writing orientation labels and signs. In one such survey made by this writer at Chicago's Field Museum, visitors were asked to rate a list of words selected from a thesaurus that described different exhibit content.[23] Each word was rated for familiarity and meaning. Visitors sampled did not have to define the words, but were asked to indicate how well they thought they knew the meaning of each word.

Results from the survey provided key words high in perceived meaning and familiarity. As might be expected, technical words often received low ratings. This finding does not mean that technical words should be avoided, but that familiar and easily understood words are best for initial orientation to exhibit subjects. Words on a more technical level can then be added and even associated with the familiar words as a way of helping visitors understand the technical terms.

Completing these steps is a fairly economical way of collecting some formative evaluation information about visitors' conceptual orientation. It should also be apparent that developing an outline that relates topics, objects, exhibit design features, and orientation/learning objectives helps to make decisions about the relationship between visitor needs and exhibit planning.

Knowing major groups or types of visitors is also important for anticipating exhibit orientation needs. For example, suppose the staff of a local history museum discovers, through a front-door-visitor survey, that 70 percent of the visitors to the museum are from the immediate community. During the summer, however, that figure drops to 50 percent, so that one out of every two people coming in is from out of the community. Imagine, further, that the survey reveals that one-third of those who indicate local residency report that they have lived in the community for less than three years. What first looks like an audience largely made up of people who should know something about the community is actually one that may not be familiar with local-history names and places. Orientation information, while it should not ignore the knowledge of residents *familiar* with the community, has to be effectively aimed at people who will have little personal acquaintance with local history.

What Are Exhibit-Circulation Patterns?

The fact that museums and other exhibit settings derive part of their uniqueness through use of three-dimensional space is axiomatic. Visitors must move across spaces to experience exhibits. The way visitors move through gallery spaces is not exactly "free" movement—many subtle factors can influence the paths visitors take through exhibits. It is important to understand those factors and to know whether commonly used circulation patterns fit well with object placement and interpretation planning.

A basic procedure for summative evaluation of circulation in an existing gallery, concluding with some potential problems (identified through research) in exhibit-circulation patterns, follows.

Describing circulation patterns. A simple floor plan can be drawn and used to record the route taken by a sample of visitors tracked or followed, using unobtrusive observation. Ideally, it is good to sample a few visitors at any one time and complete samples across a range of times and days when the gallery is open. A goal of one hundred randomly selected visitor observations is realistic. For museums where a low rate of attendance occurs, it will take a few more sample days to reach one hundred. Also, if a highly refined analysis of circulation patterns is desired and/or if the gallery has many exhibit stations or features, it may be advantageous to watch two hundred or three hundred visitors, if that count is not too time-consuming. It may also be advantageous to observe visitors during high and low or average levels of attendance or crowding. Visitor use of space can be influenced by the number of other people present and whether or not the gallery is crowded.

Some skill is needed for conducting unobtrusive observation success-fully, since the value of such observation is in learning about visitors without sensitizing them. If visitors know they are being observed, they may alter their exploration of a gallery. A good observer, like a good secu-rity guard, can watch people without making them feel they are being looked at directly. Assuming the role of another visitor in the gallery, watching people out of the corner of the eye or in the reflection of glass fronts in exhibit cases, and wearing clothes similar to those worn by visi-tors are practical ways of keeping observation unobtrusive.

Of course, the observer can be hidden, much like the security monitor-ing in stores and other public places. In one study, observers hid behind a fourteen-foot model of a grasshopper and observed visitor responses to that rather overwhelming exhibit.[24] Various kinds of hardware or equip-ment can be used, as the examples illustrated in a closed-circuit tele-vision study by James Taylor of a world's fair science pavilion.[25] It was possible in this study to monitor circulation patterns at major junctions through the complex of exhibition buildings. The researchers reported, however, that they experienced numerous technical difficulties with equipment. While breakdowns can be a problem, equipment has become more reliable in recent times. Robert Bechtel designed an ingenious floor-grid system that monitored visitor exploration of a small art gallery.[26] Visi-tors' scrutiny of individual paintings was recorded and the impact of different installations on movement in the gallery noted.

In this writer's experience, making use of security surveillance sys-tems that already exist is the most practical use of hardware; it also avoids costly investment in a system that may, or may not, work. In one situa-tion, it was possible to observe meaningful exchanges visitors had with different exhibits by watching the security camera system and also to video-record some sample observation episodes, so that another observer could verify the accuracy of the original observer.[27] For observing circu-lation patterns, however, it is hard to improve on trained human observers. Much as was done in original museum work, the observer can record circulation routes used, as well as exhibit stops and attention patterns. In many situations, using observers will prove the most cost-effective procedure. It is best to have a couple of observers draw independent sam-ples of the same exhibit space and then compare *overall* patterns. Nor-mally, the patterns will show general agreement, unless the gallery has very different audiences, different levels of crowding across time periods, or the observers are not using the same decision criteria for their obser-vations. Readers should also be aware of ethical concerns associated with unobtrusive observation.[28]

Key things to observe in visitors' activities include (1) direction of first turn made on entering a gallery, (2) percentage of gallery area explored, (3) total number of stops made, (4) total amount of time spent in *looking*, (5) stops and looking times for individual exhibits within the gallery, and (6) exit used. Figure 6.3 displays a sample observation protocol that could be used to collect this sort of information. Good observation can lead to some important questions: Are the majority of visitors moving in a direction consistent with story-lines and interpretation sequences? Are important objects being noticed and looked at by the majority of visitors? (If not, there could be a problem with the location of objects within the gallery.) Are visitors spending enough time viewing exhibits to sample the number of objects and text displayed? While it is unrealistic to expect visitors to look at and read everything on view, it is reasonable to expect them to invest more time at those displays designed to be crucial to the interpretation plan or with objects curators view as of most significance.

It is not necessary, or desirable, to make every visitor move in the same direction, stop at the same places, or devote their attention to a gallery in the same manner. What evaluation of circulation patterns can show is the way people move through a gallery; and the interpretation program can be modified to fit the most common patterns of movement. For example, suppose it is found that 70 percent of the visitors turn in a particular direction when entering a gallery and view most exhibits in a similar time sequence. That evidence would suggest that it is possible to set up a story sequence that most visitors could follow. However, it would also be wise to provide some interpretation for the 30 percent who come the other way, to prevent their being disoriented by the exhibit interpretation.

Identifying circulation problems. Evaluating circulation patterns can identify a number of problems that should be considered when designing new or renovated exhibits. A typical list of them follows.

1. Visitors tend to turn to the right unless the exhibit is designed to draw their attention to the center or the left. Often, gallery pamphlets or other interpretation aids are prepared *assuming* a left-to-right movement, with the result that the visitor is out of sequence with the story-line or interpretive materials. *It is important to sequence interpretation in the same direction that most visitors use to explore an exhibit.*

2. On the average, visitors will make more stops and invest greater amounts of time in the portions of the exhibit *first* visited than in sections reached later. People have incredible amounts of curiosity, but they also can become bored rather

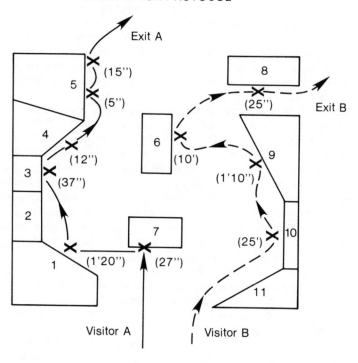

OBSERVATION PROTOCOL

Exhibit:

Date: Time:

Observer:

Fig. 6.3. Observation protocol forms such as the one shown here can be used to record the circulation patterns followed by museum visitors. The solid line with arrows at left and the broken line with arrows at right, here, show the routes of two different visitors. Each major exhibit is numbered, so that a descriptive summary can be made, to show the number of stops visitors make and establish the average holding time of each exhibit. Stops at various exhibits are indicated by X's, with the time of each stop noted in parentheses (minutes by an apostrophe, seconds by a quotation mark) beside the X. The notation "X (1'10")" written alongside the area marked "9" translates as "Visitor stopped at Exhibit 9 for one minute and ten seconds." Exits can also be labeled on these forms and exit use tallied. One hundred independent visitor observations are recommeded as a minimum, with a limit of three or four observations per protocol sheet. It is useful to record the exhibit title, the date and time of day the observations were made, and the observer's name.

easily. Thus, museum visitors will tend to look less at objects that appear similar and begin to search for something new unless they have very high intrinsic interest in the objects on display. Interpretation can also be used to sustain interest; and displays that occur farther along into an exhibit present a somewhat greater challenge for interpretation to attract and hold visitor attention. The visitor's known tendency toward a decreasing level of attention is also a good reason for planning a variety of objects for display and not exhibiting too many similar objects at one time for the average visitor.

3. Because of decreasing interest and attention within a gallery sequence, the exit often proves to be a very popular attraction. Arthur Melton first discovered this attraction to exits—not a particularly popular finding. Early on, Melton spoke of an "exit gradient" that would draw visitors' attention, the closer they came to an exit.[29] Visitors' attraction to exits needs to be understood as a curiosity to what's beyond the door of one exhibit and a sense of change or novelty. Most museums have more than one exhibit, and it is hard for visitors to suppress their curiosity about what is in the next room or gallery; their inclination is to push ahead and be sure to see the whole museum. Experienced visitors are likely to have an acquired sense of awareness that each gallery is designed with a self-contained plan and should be explored as an entity before moving along to other areas. Many occasional visitors, however, may not have that understanding.

4. One way to prevent exits from being unintended distractions in circulation routes is to plan galleries with few exits and use cul-de-sac exhibit arrangements. The cul-de-sac or curved exhibit bay tends to restrict the line of vision and naturally focus attention on the exhibits at hand.[30] A cul-se-dac located at the end of a hallway can be useful for turning visitors around so they will see exhibits on the other side of the hall. Furthermore, attraction to the exhibits placed in the cul-de-sac is likely to be high and somewhat systematic. In one evaluation, it was discovered that 70 percent of the visitors entering a cul-de-sac at the end of a hall went to the right and sequenced their movement to the left, stopping at almost every exhibit within the cul-de-sac.[31] This location would have proven very effective for telling a right-to-left-sequenced story. Beverly Serrell, in her studies, found that an entire aquarium laid out as a circle or cul-de-sac produced a highly predictable right-to-left movement pattern, with visitors exploring a high percentage of the exhibits.[32]

5. Controlling the line of vision can be very important in avoiding unintended problems in circulation. In one setting, it was planned that visitors would stroll into small side galleries of cul-de-sacs as they moved down a hallway in an exhibition.[33] Evaluation showed that the attraction toward dramatic exhibit spaces that could be seen down the hall proved irresistible, and visitors moved directly through the hall without stopping at the side exhibits. Dramatic objects on display, use of color, sound, movement, and lighting effects can all catch the eye and pull the viewer toward that point in a gallery. Such movement should be planned for, and it is valuable to know what sight lines exist in exhibit areas.

6. Related to line of vision is the tendency for visitors to take shortcuts or

choose the most direct route toward some point in the gallery they have visually noticed. This tendency to economize movement by taking a direct path toward a point of interest in the environment is basic behavior in both humans and animals.[34] It is an adaptive behavior for many situations, but not always for exploring an exhibit space. Blocking the direct line of vision, or designing a sequence of movement that is not on a direct path can be very desirable as a means to increase attention to specific objects and also increase the area of gallery toured.

Are Interpretation Features Working as Planned?

All interpretive features, from simple labels to a more elaborate participatory exhibit, can benefit from summative and formative evaluation to provide productive communication with visitors. There is no assurance that an interpretive feature (no matter how cleverly designed) *communicates*, short of collecting some kind of feedback from visitors.

Summative evaluation of aids in an existing exhibit can reveal how well they are working and may disclose that labels, for example, are being heeded by visitors and need only to be brought up to date and reworked with a fresh design to increase their effectiveness. On the other hand, summative evaluation may also show that labels are little heeded by visitors, seem confusing when read, and are in need of major change. Formative evaluation permits pilot-testing of new aids prior to the expense of installation. Before evaluating specific aids, one may find it helpful to make a global survey of visitor preferences for different aids and the ways they evaluate, in general, existing interpretive features. A global survey may suggest that specific aids such as labels or participative displays need to be investigated in more detail.

Global assessment of interpretation aids. One way to get an idea of how well the interpretation is working in an exhibit is to conduct some general assessments as people leave the gallery. Such an appraisal could be done as a simple interview or with a more detailed questionnaire (see fig. 6.4). An interview can start with a general question about visitor satisfaction with information provided and then ask visitors to comment on specific interpretation features. The questionnaire structures choices and, in the form shown in fig. 6.4, asks visitors to indicate both their preference for kinds of aids to be included for all visitors and the likelihood of those aids being used by the person answering the question. An alternative request would ask visitors to rate the quality of aids used in the exhibit visited. Each appropriate item from fig. 6.4 would be rated by visitors with the following answer choices:

Please indicate below the *quality* of the items listed for the exhibit you have just seen:

	Very good	Good	Average	Poor	Very poor	Did not notice
1. Object labels						
2.						
3.						

Please indicate how *helpful* the following items were in explaining the museum:

	Very good	Good	Average	Poor	Very poor	Did not notice
1. Object labels						
2.						
3.						

These global assessments made through sampling with a survey can identify existing problems and also suggest sources of information visitors would like to see added.

Evaluating labels. One of the most basic exhibit evaluation tasks is to find out whether visitors ever use labels. The presence of labels in an exhibit implies that some educational activity is to take place through reading, an implication not always made clear in exhibit goals.[35] For that reason, an evaluation could be set up primarily to evaluate labels. Four evaluation tasks can help improve labels:

1. Check to see whether labels are being read (or at least looked at).
2. Check to see whether labels deal with questions visitors are asking.
3. Check to see whether labels are readable.
4. Pilot-test new labels.[36]

If visitors pay little attention to labels, any other questions about them become academic. Observation can be used to determine the approximate number of labels the average visitor looks at and to rate the labels that are looked at the most and least. If circulation has been observed, earlier, researchers already have indications of the places where visitors are investing their attention-time and are likely to be reading labels. A caveat is in order, however: *it is hard to know, for certain, from observation, whether visitors are just looking at labels or are actually reading them.* A procedure modified from the work of Robert Wolf and Barbara

Response Scales

Interpretation Aid	Important to Include for All Visitors					Likelihood of Your Using				
	Not at all important	Somewhat important	Moderately Important	Very Important	Extremely important	Not at all likely	Somewhat likely	Moderately likely	Very likely	Extremely likely
1. Individual object labels	☐	☐	☐	☐	☐	☐	☐	☐	☐	☐
2. A panel with several object labels	☐	☐	☐	☐	☐	☐	☐	☐	☐	☐
3. General interpretation labels describing a gallery or collection	☐	☐	☐	☐	☐	☐	☐	☐	☐	☐
4. General interpretation labels that give background information beyond what is on display	☐	☐	☐	☐	☐	☐	☐	☐	☐	☐
5. Maps and graphics	☐	☐	☐	☐	☐	☐	☐	☐	☐	☐
6. Motion pictures (or video screen pictures)	☐	☐	☐	☐	☐	☐	☐	☐	☐	☐
7. Slide pictures	☐	☐	☐	☐	☐	☐	☐	☐	☐	☐
8. Photographs in exhibits	☐	☐	☐	☐	☐	☐	☐	☐	☐	☐
9. Self-guide pamphlets	☐	☐	☐	☐	☐	☐	☐	☐	☐	☐
10. Docent-led tours	☐	☐	☐	☐	☐	☐	☐	☐	☐	☐
11. Lectures or gallery demonstrations	☐	☐	☐	☐	☐	☐	☐	☐	☐	☐
12. Audio phone narratives	☐	☐	☐	☐	☐	☐	☐	☐	☐	☐
13. Computer terminal self-instruction	☐	☐	☐	☐	☐	☐	☐	☐	☐	☐

Fig. 6.4. *Sample questionnaire for a general assessment of exhibit interpretation aids. Visitors are asked to evaluate each interpretative aid twice: first, the appropriate box is checked, to indicate how important it is to include the aid; second, respondents check a box to show the likelihood of their using the aid.—Adapted from "Testing for Museum Literacy," unpublished paper by M. Kiphart, Ross J. Loomis, and P. Williams.*

Tymitz can make the observation of label reading more useful.[37] First, have someone read each label to be evaluated and note each reader's body position and head angle as he or she reads. An especially important item is the time needed to read sampled labels. For important labels, it is desirable to have a number of people read each label and calculate the average time used. The helper can be instructed to look at *objects only,* in a case, and then to look at objects and read their identifying labels, to estimate the additional time consumed in reading the labels. Once these preliminary observations are established, a second step requires establishing criteria for deciding whether a visitor is reading a label. The criteria should include stopping near the label and assuming a posture that permits reading the label. A minimum time (three to five seconds) for the stop should also be part of the criteria, and that time would be based on the preliminary observations. Visitors will sometimes provide other clues that they are reading, such as pointing to the label, removing or adjusting eyeglasses, leaning toward the label, reading the label aloud to another person, or commenting on label content as they move away from the exhibit.

Wolf and Tymitz prepared a summary map like the observation map shown above that distinguished between kinds of labels (i.e., orientation, conceptual explanation, object identification). A summary map provides an easy way to gauge the time visitors devote to the reading of various labels throughout a gallery. Another simple procedure can also be used to estimate label-reading. Labels can be removed or observations can be made before labels are installed, and a comparison can be made of visitors' time spent viewing the same exhibits, with and without labels. This procedure can be performed on a single display case or an entire gallery. The ratio of time spent before displays with labels and without should be greater than one if labels are drawing attention. The label-reading map and calculation of a no-label to label-present attention-time ratio can be used to determine whether labels are being used. Visitors will sample labels just as they sample exhibits. Only a rare visitor will read his or her way through the entire exhibit. It is especially important to determine whether major labels that provide conceptual orientation to exhibits are being read.

Minda Borun and Maryanne Miller provide another caveat for label evaluation in their summative study of adult label-reading at the Franklin Institute: use of labels is best evaluated by considering the whole visit and not assessing each label individually.[38] Visitors select certain labels to read that reflect personal interests and will show the highest rate of label use in galleries (or subareas of an exhibit) that they decide to study in more depth. Recall Jean Jacques Andre's analogy of a visit's being like a fine meal: Borun and Miller found that a majority of visitors selected a few "main courses" for their visit "meal" by spending more time and studying in greater depth a *few* selected exhibits. On the average, these visitors read almost 70 percent of the labels in an exhibit they chose to study.

Observation of visitor attention to labels can suggest interview questions for learning the reasons that visitors did or did not pay any attention to particular labels as well as what they like/dislike in text presentations. It is a good procedure to observe first and follow that with interviews to gain some explanation of what was observed. Beverly Serrell found, in her research, that this procedure identified successful labels in a study at Chicago's Field Museum.[39] She sampled three exhibits in Stanley Field Hall and, in contrast to the whole-visit study approach, concentrated on individual texts. This sampling of individual labels is fine, so long as it is not represented as a test of *overall* label reading for an entire visit.

Serrell's study found for the different texts sampled that successful labels attracted more than 50 percent of those who stopped at the exhibit, held the reader's attention long enough for the whole text to be read, and could be characterized as having fewer words and shorter sentences than other labels.

Interviews about labels can also disclose questions that visitors have about objects, period rooms, and other collections information that a label helps to interpret. Knowing what sort of questions visitors would like answered can suggest information to add to the label, appealing to the visitor's curiosity about the exhibit. The message in the label will be more interesting if the information not only relates to the objects shown, but also to questions that visitors have in mind. Label interviews can be structured around existing label text, with visitors being asked what else they should like to know that is not explained in the text. Or visitors can be shown an exhibit (or key objects) *without* labels and asked what questions they should like to have answered. Answers to those questions can be incorporated into new label text.

A third evaluation task is to assess reading difficulty of label materials. On the average, keeping written materials at the eighth-grade reading level accommodates a cross-section of the public that varies in age and education levels as reflected in the reading skills and experience evident. Since fatigue is also a problem for the museum visitor, it is important not to make label-reading more difficult than is necessary. Many tests of reading difficulty levels exist and can be used with museum materials. The distinction between difficulties with readability because of text level and difficulties with readability because of problems in comprehension should always be kept clearly in mind.[40] Assessing readability levels is very important when preparing written materials for children, and many of the existing tests report results by grade levels, which is convenient when writing for children. A reference source is available that reports words recognized by children and suitable for writing children's reading material.[41]

Table 6.2 presents a convenient test for readability that can be calculated without special tables or graphs. Use of the test with a few samples of label text from different parts of an exhibit will establish an estimate of the level of reading difficulty (by grade level) for the exhibit. One example of a computer readability program is the "Simplified Text Approach to Readability (S.T.A.R.)," developed by General Motors. It measures reading difficulty by considering the average number of syllables per word and the average length of sentences. Other versions of readability tests exist, and one test has been modified for analyzing passages of fewer than a hundred words. This latter test is useful for checking readability of shorter museum labels.[42]

Reading difficulty should not be confused with poor writing or text copy that offers little information to attract visitors' attention. Visitors may report that a label seems simple and written below their educational level when, in fact, *what they are responding to is the absence of information.* All readability tests do is provide a way of checking to see that written text material is within a range that can be grasped and made use of by most people in the audience.

The last label evaluation task is to pilot or pretest new label copy before it is installed. This simple and usually low-cost procedure can be very helpful in identifying problems and avoiding use of labels that fail to work well. C. G. Screven is a strong advocate of pretesting labels; he encourages placing simple mock-up labels in an exhibit and pretesting with fifteen or so interviews.[43] Visitors should be asked about the helpfulness of labels, their clarity, and whether the main ideas are understandable. A limited amount of pretesting can reveal problems in things like choice of words and clarity of explanations.

If it is not possible to put temporary labels in the exhibit, label copy can be read by a small sample of visitors—some fifteen to twenty-five, say—or people similar to visitors in levels of education, ages, etc. As men-

Table 6.2
Instructions for SMOG Grading Test for Readability

1. Select a passage of at least 30 sentences and select 10 consecutive sentences from the beginning, middle, and end of the passage.

2. For each of the 30 sentences selected, count every word of 3 or more syllables. Include any repeated polysyllabic word in the count.

3. Find the square root for the total number of polysyllabic words counted in the 30 sentences. The easiest way to determine square root is by using the square root function of a personal calculator.

4. Add 3 to the calculated square root, which will be the SMOG grade that represents the school reading-grade level a reader must be competent in to understand the passage tested.

Example: The four-step instructions contained in this table have 16 polysyllabic words. The square root of 16 is 4 (when rounded) and by adding 3, the estimated reading level is 7.

Source: Adapted from G. Harry McLaughlin, "SMOG Grading: A New Readability Formula," *Journal of Reading* 12 (1969): 637-646.

tioned earlier, this kind of pretesting is similar to consumer research in which panels of potential customers evaluate a new product. Pretesting labels is formative evaluation at its best, because it provides needed information in time to make constructive changes before final installation. The earlier task of finding out what questions visitors have in mind that could be answered in labels can also be included as part of pretesting.

As Screven would note, and as is consistent with goal-referenced evaluation, label pretesting can be done as an experiment. A sample of visitors seeing the exhibit and labels can be compared with a control sample who see only the exhibit. Comparisons between the two groups can test for differences in understanding of exhibit goals, amount of learning, and visitor satisfaction. Screven also suggests that a series of experimental changes may be necessary to get a label that clearly communicates an important message. This process of fine-tuning a label through successive changes and testing is crucial for conceptual labels that explain science, art, or history. Such labels are worth their space in a gallery only if they in fact do communicate the intended ideas to the visitor. Ideally, a group of staff members directly involved in preparing the exhibit and labels for it should take turns doing the short interviews with visitors. Direct feedback from visitors may not only cause staff members to change labels, but even bring about changes in some exhibit goals. While a series of modifications and testing takes time and effort, the results can be gratifying. One can know what information is being communicated (or what information is *not* being communicated) to those visitors willing to make the effort to read the labels.

These four label evaluation tasks can help improve communication potentials of text-based interpretation. Minda Borun and Maryanne Miller provide a number of good examples of label research at the Franklin Institute Science Museum, including formative evaluation using different label formats and content.[44] Beverly Serrell has a guide for label preparation that should be consulted as part of any label evaluation.[45] Also important to review is a summary by C. G. Screven, "Exhibitions and Information Centers," that combines evaluation with important guidelines for planning interpretive text.[46] In his summary, Screven mentions several reasons that labels fail to be used, including these facts: labels will fail if they are poorly located, placed too far from the object described; too difficult to read, either because of writing level and/or graphic design properties; too long or too wordy, conveying the impression that considerable time and effort will be needed to master them; overtechnical for lay readers; or so filled with information extraneous to what is on display that they appear to be a distraction to a busy, and perhaps tired, visitor.

Evaluating participative interpretation. Screven also discussed ways in which fairly simple modifications to a standard label can increase visitor involvement by presenting information in a more motivating and attractive format. For example, flip-panel labels are a low-technology way of providing more information without the visual clutter found in conventional labels with long passages of text. Visitors first see the top panel, which displays a limited amount of information, prompting one to lift successive underlying panels to acquire brief, controlled amounts of additional information, at will, at one's own pace and level of interest. This kind of interactive label uses what Screven calls *layering*, by dividing information into smaller units or chunks. This design avoids large displays of text that may appear overwhelming to visitors. Screven also describes computer-based information displayed on high-resolution, flat screens, opening up even more possibilities for providing depth of interpretation under visitor control without taking away from the visual quality of an exhibit by displaying too much text.

Evaluation of these participative or interactive displays requires finding out whether visitors pay attention to them and show the appropriate behavior to take advantage of the information they communicate. Evaluation, especially through formative pretesting, can disclose ways of making interactive displays work better and fulfill a role of interpretive aid.

As with evaluating any other interpretation feature, participative displays can be studied with a combination of observation, interviews, and questionnaires. Observation will not only reveal the attraction and attention-holding power of a display, but also any number of types of behavior that determine the kind of interaction taking place between viewer and display. For instance, this writer unobtrusively observed a hundred visitors, randomly selected, as they approached a push-button science exhibit.[47] Pushing the button activated a sequential narrative that was accompanied by a series of colorful graphics. Criticism of the display was that children simply pushed the button to watch the lights (and hear the sounds) and did not even wait for the narrative to be finished. Observations revealed that that criticism was wrong. Eighty of the one hundred visitors watched the exhibit go through its complete cycle, although several pushed the button again after the cycle had finished and *then* walked away. Children in the sample were just as likely to watch the complete display as were adults. It turned out that the exhibit had acceptable levels of attraction and holding power, but the narrative text was hard to understand. Systematic changes in the text and the substitution of less technical terms to convey technical meaning were needed. Results from short interviews guided the process of finding the right words and producing a simplified narrative text to enable the majority of people who watched the exhibit to understand it.

Planned changes in a participative display can be compared before and after the change, or comparisons can be made between alternate forms of an exhibit. Laurie Eason and Marcia Linn compared different science exhibit formats with each other and included a control group not experiencing either exhibit format.[48] Findings from their interviews indicated that students gained both information and skills at levels superior to the control students who did not visit and that the two formats were comparable. These researchers also stressed that formative evaluation during the development of a participative exhibit can greatly improve its final effectiveness.

People sometimes have strong opinions that participatory exhibits provoke too much excitement, encourage play behavior, fail to produce substantive learning, distract attention from objects shown (or even displace the objects as the focus of an exhibit), and appeal to a limited segment of the audience. While these criticisms have some validity, it is also true that participative exhibits are evolving into improved formats, and good summative and formative evaluation can help address these problems. Furthermore, interactive displays, like all other features in an exhibit, must have visitor-oriented goals and planning. There is a growing literature about participative exhibits to assist in the planning and evaluation of these interpretative aids.[49]

What Do Museum Visitors Learn?

Obviously, museum visitors learn as part of all the features just discussed. Visitors learn about orientation, as they read signs and remember some aspects of the pathways they used in exploring an exhibit. They also learn from looking at objects and reading the text of labels or taking part in a participative display. Setting an evaluation goal of measuring learning, however, requires some considerations in addition to the tasks already discussed. For such experienced exhibit evaluators as Harris Shettel and C. G. Screven, visitor learning has always been a factor separate from attraction (where do visitors stop or look?) and attention-holding power (how long do visitors view or study a particular exhibit?). (An early distinction between attraction, holding power, and learning that considered each as a separate factor of exhibit effectiveness appears in a 1968 research report.)[50] Assessment of learning is a task that has stimulated a tremendous amount of research, theory development, and debate among different investigators. Most of this research has been concentrated on such formal learning situations as schoolrooms or training related to industrial work. Screven distinguishes the unique challenge of assessing learning in an informal setting:

There are important differences between *formal* learning settings, such as schools, and the *informal* settings of museum environments, which are nonlinear, self-paced, voluntary, and exploratory. In schools, the primary teaching tool is the teacher, supported mainly by *verbal* media; in museums, the primary teaching tool is the exhibition, supported by objects and other visual media. These differences frequently require approaches that are radically different from those employed in schools and other formal settings.[51]

Museum visitors, on the average, are leisure-time audiences combining a visit to the museum with a larger social experience. As noted earlier, only a limited part of the audience is likely to consider learning a major reason for their museum visit. The majority are seeking a pleasant, highly social encounter that they can remember as a pleasant, entertaining event or activity.

Learning can never be completely separated from motivation, and Screven makes a very important point when he distinguishes between *formal* and *informal* learning environments. Museum visitors enjoy the freedom of the museum environment and the social occasion that is based on choice and not on required learning assignments such as one encounters at school or at work. Learning occurs, during a museum visit, to be sure, but not as a primary purpose of the visit, and not with a perception that one *must* learn something. For a major part of the visiting audience, Screven describes four aspects of visitor motivation that should be kept in mind when planning learning objectives for exhibits.[52]

1. Exhibits should be fun, and enjoyable, but designed to provide the most enjoyment when visitors attend and work at exhibit materials. Design features that simply excite or encourage play without a well-thought-out learning objective should be avoided. The experience of joy should be combined with a sense of mastery and the acquisition of interesting information.

2. As a general rule, visitors should feel no forced route for their visit. Here is where good orientation comes in, to help visitors pick a menu for their individual needs and interests. Visitors can adapt the exhibit to their own interests, learning styles, and time limitations.

3. On the average, individual exhibits and topic panels should be independent of each other, so that the visitor gets a coherent experience and sense of completion wherever he or she elects to stop and look. Each display or sub-unit of an exhibit should tell its own story, consistent with the radial or open-circulation design mentioned earlier. Sequential exhibit circulation should be used only when it is absolutely necessary to tell an exhibit story in an ordered sequence.

4. Consistent with the findings of the M. B. Alt and K. M. Shaw study of visitor descriptions of ideal exhibits mentioned earlier,[53] individual exhibit displays and panels should use good design principles that make them easy to understand by containing organization and logically coherent sequencing of information.

To be sure, these points emphasize the unguided or general-audience visitor. The highly motivated scholar-visitor is likely to be more interested in open-storage exhibits and study galleries. Whether museum exhibits should serve the learning needs of scholars or lay persons is an old and sometimes bitter debate.[54] Two considerations should be kept in mind regarding visitor motivation and learning. First, proper audience analysis through visitor surveys can suggest the relative mix of "advanced" visitors of serious intent and routine, casual lay visitors. A university museum may serve the former and develop exhibits with more advanced learning objectives, while a museum serving a broader cross-section of the public should keep general education objectives in mind. Second,

consistent with the idea of an exhibit menu, visitors can be given choices
of areas comprising different levels of complexity and interpretation. The
parallel-gallery concept provides areas for the general touring visitor and
other gallery spaces for study and display of more extensive collections.
Different levels or kinds of exhibit content can be kept separate through
alternate or parallel galleries designed for different degrees of visitor commitment; and exhibits themselves, within a gallery or a hall, can be aimed
at different levels of visitor learning and commitment.

Learning criteria. Deciding on what visitors can learn in an exhibit
is a special case of determining exhibit criteria and final goals. Taxonomies of educational or kinds of learning have been developed, but usually
are based on formal learning settings like the classroom. A basic, three-
way classification of learning criteria has been commonly used by psychologists and educators and is based on Benjamin Bloom's classes of
learning/teaching outcomes or goals:[55]

1. *Cognitive* criteria include facts, concepts, or relationship kinds of materials
that visitors would learn from viewing objects and attending to exhibit narratives.

2. *Affective* criteria are based on acquired emotional reactions to exhibit settings and materials, values, preferences, and—quite commonly—the acquisition
or change of specific attitudes. Technically speaking, attitudes also include some
cognitive learning outcomes.

3. *Sensory-motor skills* criteria include mastering a task like using a computer or other apparatus in a science display or trying to weave a fabric or play
a musical instrument in a cultural or historical demonstration. In general, skill-
learning is limited in exhibit environments, although learning to look effectively
and to explore an exhibit clearly involves some sensory-motor learning.

Each of these basic classes of potential learning criteria can be
organized into taxonomies or hierarchies to specify in much more detail
what learning outcomes can be planned. For exhibit-based learning,
C. G. Screven provides sources that readers can consult for more detailed
learning taxonomies.[56]

Finding learning criteria that fit the exhibit setting as well as other
kinds of experiences that museums provide will require research into
the ways in which people use museums and the kinds of skills they
develop. In time, this research could lead to learning criteria specifically
focused on museums. What are the special features of museum environments that promote learning? How do museums differ from other settings in the opportunities they offer for learning, and how do visitors
adapt to museums in ways that maximize their ability to learn? This last
question opens the possibility that museum-visitor learning cannot be

understood simply from the perspective of the setting or from what museum designers and other professionals can build into exhibits and programs. Learning also involves the ways in which visitors react to the setting and the kinds of *learning strategies* they bring with them. Those learning strategies may evolve, over time, and it is possible to enrich visitor experience by directly suggesting ways to study objects and visit exhibits. *Museum literacy*[57] is a term, growing in use, that describes the visitor's skill at coping with the museum environment. In a narrower sense, museum literacy refers to the visitor's "reading" or interpretation of museum objects. A broader use of the term encompasses the visitor's successful use of all information sources within the museum setting. Carol Stapp also sees museum literacy as a concept with its roots in the whole historical debate over whether museums are educational institutions that should make their holdings and environments accessible to the public.[58] She compares museum literacy to computer literacy as the acquisition of competencies that permit an individual to use successfully a complex information system. Stapp rejects the idea that museum literacy is spontaneous or innate and argues that thinking of museum literacy as innate has slowed progress in helping visitors to learn *how to learn* from the museum setting.

Recall from earlier discussions that one meaningful way to categorize the museum audience is in terms of level of involvement or use. Recall also that frequent visitors of museums tend to be more comfortable in the museum setting than those who visit infrequently. An interesting working hypothesis for future evaluation research would be that frequent visitors have achieved higher levels of museum literacy than have less frequent users. In fact, part of the reason that frequent users seek the museum environment with its objects is that they can experience subtle features or attributes that escape others, and they also get a sense of self-enhancement because of their ability to master the museum setting. Museum literacy, then, can be related to both visitor orientation and audience development, as well as to the topic of museum learning.

Just what *are* the skills that visitors need to receive the information found in museum objects as well as features and programs of the museum setting? Patterson Williams has identified four activities that can be taught to museum visitors to increase the effectiveness of their contemplation of objects.[59] Visitors can be coached to increase their skill in *looking* at objects or in using visual information about the unique properties of individual artifacts. Williams feels that museum experts over the years have cultivated specific skills in looking at and studying artifacts, and some of these skills need to be taught to visitors. Visitors also need to be encouraged to *react* and express feelings and monitor or understand those feelings as a legitimate part of museum visitation. It is important not only to know what kind of information museum visitors gain from their visits, but also to understand what reactions in the form of feelings, fantasies, and other non-intellective experiences museums offer to visitors. Williams also suggests that visitors learn to think about objects in *historical and cultural contexts.* Meaning can be enhanced by the context of background that surrounds objects; visitors need to use effectively the information offered on museum exhibit labels and, with other forms of contextual information, process their experience of museum objects into a more permanent memory. Finally, visitors need to know how to make *judgments* about museum objects. They need, like museum experts, to feel a sense of competency that they can evaluate and assess the quality and nature of things that museums exhibit. Williams's ideas about visitors learning to use the exhibit setting cut across the basic criteria classification of cognitive, affective, and sensory-motor skills.

Measuring learning. Examples of measuring each of the three basic criteria (cognitive, affective, and sensory-motor) follow. Readers are cautioned, however, that measuring learning is not always easy, and failure to document the occurrence of any learning may reflect difficulty in the evaluation process, as well as problems in the planned learning task itself.

The learning of such basic cognitive criteria as facts and concepts can be assessed with interviews and well-planned questionnaires. In this writer's experience, it is best to measure the same exhibit material with both open-ended interview questions and specific-content, patterned questionnaires (i.e., true-false, multiple-choice). Usually, separate samples are taken for each kind of measure, to avoid too much demand being placed on one visitor. Beverly Serrell used this procedure in her label evaluation study at the Field Museum.[60] The open-ended interview can include such basic questions as these:

1. Describe in your own words what you think this label (or exhibit) is trying to say.

or

2. What did you learn from this label (or exhibit)?

These general questions can get at more global or general learning, such as basic concepts or story-line sequences. Dominant factual content may also surface in the interview, and follow-up questions can request more detail, if appropriate, provided that the questions do not make the visitor feel uncomfortable or threatened.

Structured or patterned questions—those involving specific content—are obviously a form of quiz, and care must be taken to avoid queries that are either too detailed or too ambiguous. This format is good for assessing factual and conceptual content that is being communicated to the visitor. The quiz should be kept *short*, and the printed format should be made to look attractive. Alternate forms with different questions can be given to separate samples if there is a lot of content to be assessed.

Rapport with the visitor is very important when conducting learning evaluation. Although children are accustomed to taking tests and being held accountable for learning something, adults are likely to feel intimidated by questions about what they have learned. It is best to stress that the assessment is not of what they have learned, but of the degree to which the exhibit communicates its message. If visitors start to appear distressed at answering questions, it is best to let them stop, if they wish to, and ask the evaluation questions of another person.

Care must be taken to assure that apprehension over content-based questions does not create a biased sample. It is also important to define carefully the different kinds of sample groups used. For example, Serrell distinguished between groups of visitors who read labels that were easy to run through, those who read the difficult labels, and those who did not read labels at all. She also sampled visitors after they had been unobtrusively observed reading a label. Her interest was in getting some idea of what visitors learned when left on their own, to notice and read or *not* to notice or read labels. By contrast, one can ask visitors to look at exhibit content and then complete an interview or quiz to measure comprehension. These "cued" visitors will probably feed back more information about the exhibit, because their attention has been focused on it and their motivation increased, in anticipation of the forthcoming evaluation of their summing up of what they remember. The *cued visitor* provides an estimate of the potential for obtaining and retaining information from an exhibit and displays the highest level of such learning that might occur. Comparing cued and noncued samples can be a useful evaluation (see C. G. Screven[61] for discussion of this procedure).

Minda Borun provides a good example of the questionnaire administered through a temporary exhibit format to assess what visitors learn as an aspect of visiting a science museum.[62] The exhibit format helped make the questionnaire appear like a game; questions were administered through slides, and visitors responded with a push-button display. The strategy worked; refusal rate was low, and a sign had to be posted to turn away a great many visitors who were interested in participating, since a *controlled* random sample was what was needed.

This assessment of visitor learning also demonstrated the development of a hierarchy of cognitive criteria by (1) having some questions measure visitor vocabulary based on content of written labels, (2) having some questions measure recall of the kind of experience provided by different interactive displays, and (3) having other questions measure concept formation. Borun tested a random sample of entering visitors, to find out what people already knew, and also tested a separate sample of visitors known to have seen the appropriate exhibits (neither group knew they were going to be tested). Results from her testing disclosed that visitors had a cognitive gain in their knowledge of exhibit information. She combined her testing with some basic visitor survey data that enabled comparisons between age, amount of education, and number of previous visits. Her results were particularly encouraging for children, showing strong cognitive gain scores for children's visit experiences.

Some visitors might be uncomfortable with the idea of having their cognitive learning tested, since being questioned may have, for some, a schoolroom's disciplinary overtones. However, so long as exhibit designs contain didactic information in the form of factual and conceptual content, such testing is an appropriate evaluation tool. Furthermore, Borun's experience with testing at the Franklin Institute Science Museum suggests that incorporating testing as part of a visitor's exhibit experience reduces the avoidance reactions mentioned earlier in connection with using direct interviews and/or paper-and-pencil questionnaires. Computer hardware and software applications for participative exhibits are evolving in sophistication to such a degree that visitor learning could be assessed in conjuction with their participation.[63] For those who do not find the above-mentioned possibilities acceptable, the less direct conversational interview procedures used by Robert Wolf and Barbara Tymitz can identify the thematic, story-line, and conceptual content that visitors are acquiring from their time spent in a gallery.[64] S. A. Griggs used formative evaluation to test mock-up examples of information panels planned for new exhibits.[65] The mock-ups contained major conceptual ideas that were crucial to planned exhibit story-lines and major themes. In addition, the panels had sample texts so that the assessment could check readability and other text features. Samples of both visitors and staff viewed the mock-ups. Interviews and questionnaires not only identified learning potentials for the planned displays, but also identified areas of misunderstanding, confusing or difficult materials, and specific content that simply was not being communicated as planned. *Identification of these kinds of problems is at the heart of formative evaluation.*

It cannot be emphasized enough that exhibit materials can (and often do!) fail to communicate concepts and ideas that were intended and may even be misinterpreted by many visitors. Only by testing the displays with visitors can problems be identified. . . and then corrected. Systematic collection of staff review can also help to uncover problems.

This kind of formative evaluation is especially important when the goal is to communicate ideas or concepts as cognitive learning. Some reseachers use the term *schemata* to describe integrated bodies of knowledge focused around a limited topic.[66] Much of the learning that S. A. Griggs tried to assess, and that exhibit settings may communicate fairly well, are such organized bodies of knowledge. Conceptual orientation, exhibit themes, and unifying concepts presented in a specific exhibit could all be examples of schemata. It is thought that schemata may help us organize objects we find in the world by facilitating recognition and classification based on past learning. For example, Griggs found, in his research on exhibit mock-ups, that it was a mistake to represent a general concept with one specific example, since visitors tended to miss the unifying concept. It worked better to use an analogy or multiple examples. Griggs's finding is not surprising, in light of schemata theory. Visitors need to understand the schemata involved in a particular display as a means of organizing more specific content such as objects and facts presented.

Learning about schemata may be important in a couple of other ways. First, story-learning may be a special case of schemata use, in which individual facts, including new information, are made meaningful by putting them together in a sequence that is easy to anticipate and follow. Text that simply lists points of information is likely to be less effective than text that covers the same facts by telling a story. Second, researchers in reading performance suspect that the reader's use of schemata (or failure to use schemata, by reading from word to word) may determine how well he or she comprehends written material.[67] It is not surprising that Griggs found some of the label text hard for visitors to understand, since museum texts are often hard to organize into schemata.

Mock-ups or simulations provide a low-cost means of gaining formative evaluation feedback about schemata learning in time to guide final production. Harris Shettel found, some years back, that photographs could adequately represent key information elements of a planned exhibit and be used in formative testing.[68] While the mock-ups used by Griggs were more elaborate than photographs, Screven has demonstrated that simple cardboard trial label texts and graphics can serve as effective materials in formative evaluation designed to improve interpretation in an existing exhibit.

S. A. Griggs and Jane Manning provide some encouraging evidence that simulations or mock-ups of planned exhibits predicted quite well the way visitors would respond to the final exhibits.[69] This research, conducted at the British Museum (Natural History) revealed that both recall of conceptual story-line materials and perceptual reactions were similar for mock-up and finished exhibits. This finding is very important and suggests that formative evaluation of mock-up exhibit materials could be very useful.

C. G. Screven describes in some detail a series of experiences designed to measure visitors' factual and conceptual learning of exhibit content under different conditions of interpretive assistance.[70] This source will be helpful for readers who want to learn more about cognitive criteria for visitor learning. Two additional comments about learning cognitive types of information are in order.

First, most visitor research has emphasized acquisition of verbal or work-related information as present in written text. Cognitive learning can also include memory for objects seen without any text material present. William Barnard, Henry Cross, and I tested for memory of objects seen in a local history museum during a visit.[71] We were able to use displays that had not yet been labeled. While the subjects' ability to recall from memory the number of objects seen was very limited, their ability to recognize from photographs what they had viewed was much greater. Learning in museums should not be thought of as merely memory for text material, but should also be recognized as the ability to recognize visually things seen on past occasions. Visual-recognition memory is a well-researched area in psychology and a promising way of looking at visitor learning independent of word- or text-based interpretation.[72]

Second, care must be taken in using amounts of learning found in visitor research to decide whether an exhibit is working well. This word of caution is especially important for noncued or unguided visitors, with whom it is hard to know for certain the exhibit features they will be most attentive to. For this reason, it is important to use a *criterion-referenced* approach for deciding how much learning is a satisfactory outcome for an exhibit. Under a criterion-referenced approach, it is necessary to decide what specific exhibit content should be learned by most visitors. Orientation information and a major highlight exhibit probably should be mastered by 70 to 80 percent or more of the audience, while an out-of-the-way exhibit case illustrating an erudite or abstruse topic might be a source of attraction and learning to only 10 to 20 percent of the audience. In addition, visitors will not learn *everything* in an exhibit they choose to study. Good design and organization can increase the amount learned, but keep in mind that even a teacher in a highly controlled learning environment does not expect every student to learn every item of information.

C. G. Screven offers some guidelines for assessing whether acceptable levels of learning (of any kind) result from exhibit visits.[73] His guidelines are based upon general trends, rather than arbitrary percentages or statistical analyses, and they require testing random samples of visitors before they have seen an exhibit (pretests) and random samples of visitors right after their visit (post-test) and then comparing the test scores of these two groups. Visitor learning would be substantiated by:

1. Post-test scores that are two to three times higher than the pretest group scores.

2. Post-test scores of visitors cued by being asked to study the exhibit should be higher than those of a pretested group.

3. Ideally, score differences between post-test groups cued to pay attention and those of uncued visitors should not be too great. While cued visitors should score higher, if uncued scores are too low, that could indicate exhibits with poor attraction or holding power for the general visitor. Low scores might also suggest that interpreation is not communicating well.

4. Pretest scores for individual-content items should not be so high as to leave little room for learning from exposure to the exhibit. That is, high pretest scores for exhibit information would suggest that visitors already know the material planned for the exhibit. This level of knowledge might be true of only certain subgroups of visitors and suggest that exhibit plans should be modified to fit those visitors better.

Affective learning criteria have been studied far less than cognitive ones. It is important, however, to know how exhibits make visitors feel, as noted by Albert Parr:

Exhibits of contemporary poverty displayed by museum methods in a museum setting may also, quite possibly, have only the effect of making the terrible conditions appear less terrifying. By making them seem more impersonal, we may destroy their impact. Before being carried away by our indignant sympathies, we must be quite certain that our aid will help the cause and not hinder its advancement. For this we need some very sophisticated research into the emotional qualities of the museum ambience.[74]

Conversational interviews can sometimes reveal affective content centered on a particular exhibit. One way of obtaining this sort of information is to ask the viewer to write down emotion-related words or phrases that include perceptions of the way one feels at a particular place in an exhibit. Visitors can also be asked directly to assess their feelings when cued to look at a specific display. Again, their use of words denoting emotion can be listed and compared with the expected emotional reactions set forth in the exhibit objectives.

Spontaneous emotional reactions are probably best observed. The human face is a powerful communicator of feeling, especially when the individuals observed are unaware that they are being looked at. An observation protocol can be created, using standardized categories of facial emotion as defined in psychological research. Facial emotion has been studied extensively by psychologists, and it is possible to rate facial displays of emotion reliably.[75]

Minda Borun used a simple facial expression devised and drawn by Irving Faber[76] to assess overall feelings about a museum visit:

Fig. 6.5. Simple line drawings of expressive faces, such as these by Irving Farber, can be used effectively in questionnaires testing museum visitors' responses to the institution or the exhibit just visited.—Suggested by Minda Borun's "Measuring the Immeasurable" (Philadelphia: The Franklin Institute Science Museum, 1977).

Visitors are instructed to indicate which of the five faces sketched best describes the way they feel about their visit (or the way they feel about a certain exhibit). The device is a general sort of thing, but easy to do— and quick to complete. An adjective checklist, similar to that discussed in chapter 3, can also be used to denote feelings.

Although cognitive and affective learning have been discussed here separately, it is important to realize that both usually occur together. This combination may especially be true for museum learning that takes place as part of a social occasion in a unique setting. Visitor memories of the museum have both factual/conceptual and emotional content. When a visitor recalls something from a museum visit experience, the memory may have both *semantic* and *episodic* content—*semantic* indicating general knowledge based often on language communication of facts and schemata and *episodic* indicating personal-experience knowledge about a specific visit to a specific museum. Wayne A. Wickelgren has suggested that *episodic memory* may be the first recall of a unique experience, with *semantic memory* being used to enrich details of the remembered experience.[77] Gordon Bower believes that mood states are part of what is remembered.[78] Seeing cognitive materials such as pictures or words about something learned in a museum may bring back episodic memories of the visit and also the emotions experienced at the time. The converse may happen, also, with the memory of the way one felt in a particular place evoking some content or semantic memories. Perhaps it is not surprising that those who have studied visitor learning are emphasizing the unity or holistic nature of what is learned as a combination of social experience, feelings, schemata that ties specific information together, and some factual content, depending upon what interested the visitor.

Measuring visitors' attitudes toward an exhibit is one way to get both an affective and a cognitive assessment, since this concept combines both the way one feels and the way one thinks about something.[79] Attitudes also reflect the evaluations visitors make. Divining attitudes and, even more, determining whether exhibits influence or change attitudes requires an appreciable level of sophistication. Readers are referred to studies by Harris Shettel and by Minda Borun for examples of this kind of learning assessment.[80] While it is relatively easy to construct items that *appear* to measure attitudes, there often are difficulties in knowing for sure what the items indicate and whether people are really changing their attitudes.

Evaluating skill-learning, while not common in exhibit studies, can be useful in formative investigations of participatory exhibits. Laurie P. Eason and Marcia C. Linn present an example of using an interview to assess skills at manipulating mirrors, lenses, and prisms to solve science problems.[81] Students were given items of equipment and then asked to do different tasks that would reveal how well they had mastered certain skills. The interviewer could not only record individual success at the tasks, but could also observe specific skills present or not present in the process of completing the assignment.

Unobtrusive observation of visitors using participative displays in a gallery can sometimes reveal sensory-motor or skill-related problems. Failure to complete a task successfully—say, in a science-center display— may reveal skill problems. Observation can often identify the specific problem by noticing incorrect responses or significant skills that are missing or not used at the right point in a necessary sequence of acts. Evaluation may reveal the need for improved instructions, lowering the skills level required to improve performance, or perhaps challenging visitors by offering more than one skill-level difficulty for performing the task.

An Exhibit Evaluation Checklist

Preparing for an exhibit evaluation effort requires a number of tasks similar to getting ready for a visitor survey (i.e., anticipating costs and resources, planning a sample). Readers will find the information on planning tasks, in chapter 3, also useful for organizing an exhibit evaluation. Exhibit evaluation as a goal-referenced activity requires a flow of tasks that permit feedback of information at appropriate times, especially in the case of formative evaluation. To help with planning evaluation, readers are strongly encouraged to read C. G. Screven's discussion of goal-referenced exhibit evaluation, paying special attention to his flow-chart for the planning sequence of tasks.[82] Some topics in chapter 7, though oriented toward program evaluation, can also be a part of exhibit research. Readers might want to review appropriate sections for examples of evaluating audiovisuals and visitor self-guide interpretation materials. The following checklist—or a similar guide—can be helpful in planning an exhibit evaluation.

Checklist for Planning an Exhibit Evaluation

I. *Audience Definition*

    A.   Does adequate information about the visitors who will use the exhibit exist?

        ☐ Yes   ☐ No

        1.   Have attendance patterns been anticipated in exhibit planning?

            ☐ Yes   ☐ No

        2.   Have meaningful subgroups of visitors been identified and related to planned interpretation?

            ☐ Yes   ☐ No

            (If answers are no, consult chapters 2 and 3 for evaluation possibilities.)

B. Is a marketing or potential-visitor study called for to aid exhibit planning?
    ☐ Yes   ☐ No   ☐ Uncertain

    1. Are visitor expectations for the exhibit known?
        ☐ Yes   ☐ No

    2. Is a survey of potential groups interested in the exhibit needed?
        ☐ Yes   ☐ No
        (Consult chapter 4 for evaluation possibilities.)

C. Is current level of visitor knowledge about exhibit information known?
    ☐ Yes   ☐ No

II. *Visitor-Related Exhibit Planning*

A. Have exhibit plans been reviewed in light of visitor needs?
    ☐ Yes   ☐ No

    1. Have visitor learning opportunities been defined for the exhibit and related to specific design features?
        ☐ Yes   ☐ No

    2. Have specific design features of the exhibit (i.e., labels, planned circulation patterns) been prepared to provide effective orientation?
        ☐ Yes   ☐ No

        a. Does orientation explain exhibit purposes and concepts to the visitor?
           ☐ Yes   ☐ No

        b. Does exhibit orientation provide wayfinding information?
           ☐ Yes   ☐ No

        c. Has visitor comfort (i.e., control of noise, placement of benches for rest) been planned for?
           ☐ Yes   ☐ No

    3. Has exhibit circulation flow been planned?
        ☐ Yes   ☐ No

        a. Will intended circulation flow integrate well with interpretation goals?
           ☐ Yes   ☐ No

        b. Do circulation plans emphasize ☐ radial or ☐ sequential flow or ☐ a combination of both?

   4.   Has a review of visitor-related criteria for an effective exhibit been conducted?

      ☐ Yes   ☐ No

  B.   Will final goals (objectives) statements clearly show how visitors will be involved with the exhibits?

      ☐ Yes   ☐ No

III. *Planning Evaluation Goals*

  A.   Can evaluation goals be clearly stated?

      ☐ Yes   ☐ No

   1.   If *no*, is an exploratory study called for?

      ☐ Yes   ☐ No

   2.   If *yes*, will planned evaluation be:

      ☐ summative?   ☐ formative?   ☐ both?

  B.   What exhibit features will be evaluated?

      ☐ Visitor orientation

      ☐ Circulation/spatial planning

      ☐ Interpretation materials

      ☐ Other:_____

  C.   Is visitor learning to be evaluated?

      ☐ Yes   ☐ No

  D.   Do adequate resources (expertise, money, time, and effort) exist for the evaluation?

      ☐ Yes   ☐ No

   1.   If internal resources are not adequate, are external ones available?

      ☐ Yes   ☐ No

   2.   Are resources available for mock-ups to aid formative evaluation?

      ☐ Yes   ☐ No

NOTES

1. Lewis Thomas, *The Medusa and the Snail* (Toronto: Bantam Books, 1980), pp.6-7.

2. C. G. Screven, "Exhibit Evaluation: A Goal-Referenced Approach," *Curator* 19 (December 1976): 271-290.

3. Lothar P. Witteborg, "Exhibit Planning," *History News* 38 (June 1983): 21-24.

4. Screven, "Exhibit Evaluation: A Goal-Referenced Approach," pp. 274-275.

5. S. A. Griggs, "Formative Evaluation of Exhibits at the British Museum (Natural History)," *Curator* 24 (September 1981): 189-201. In addition to the Screven and Griggs articles cited here and in note 2, see C. G. Screven, "Exhibitions and Information Centers: Some Principles and Approaches," *Curator* 29 (June 1986): 123-124; Ellen Cochran Hicks, "An Artful Science: A Conversation about Exhibit Evaluation," *Museum News* 64 (February 1986): 32-39; and Mary Ellen Munley, "Asking the Right Questions: Evaluation and the Museum Mission," *Museum News* 64 (February 1986): 18-23.

6. R. S. Miles and M. B. Alt, "British Museum (Natural History): A New Approach to the Visiting Public," *Museums Journal* 78 (April 1979): 158-162.

7. Harris Shettel, "An Evaluation of Existing Criteria for Judging the Quality of Science Exhibits," *Curator* 11 (June 1968): 137-153.

8. M. B. Alt and K. M. Shaw, "Characteristics of Ideal Museum Exhibits," *British Journal of Psychology* 75 (1984): 25-36.

9. An extensive discussion of integrating evaluation and educational goals with exhibit design is found in R. S. Miles, M. B. Alt, D. C. Gosling, B. N. Lewis, and A. F. Tout, *The Design of Educational Exhibits* (London: Allen and Unwin Publishers, 1982).

10. R. G. Barker, "Explorations in Ecological Psychology," *American Psychologist* 20 (1965): 1-14; and R. G. Barker, *The Stream of Behavior* (New York: Appleton-Century-Crofts, 1963). And for an overview of a descriptive research approach, see Allan. W. Wicker, *An Introduction to Ecological Psychology* (Monterey, Calif.: Brooks-Cole, 1979).

11. Robert L. Wolf, "A Naturalistic View of Evaluation," *Museum News* 58 (September 1980): 39-45.

12. Robert L. Wolf and Barbara L. Tymitz, "A Preliminary Guide for Conducting Naturalistic Evaluation in Studying Museum Environments" (Washington, D. C.: Office of Museum Programs, Smithsonian Institution, 1979), pp. 5-9.

13. Wolf and Tymitz, "A Preliminary Guide for Evaluation," pp. 14-41.

14. Robert L. Wolf and Barbara L. Tymitz, "East Side, West Side, Straight Down the Middle: A Study of Visitor Perceptions of 'Our Changing Land' Bicentennial Exhibit" (Washington, D.C.: Office of Museum Programs, Smithsonian Institution, 1979), pp. 16-20; quotation from p. 18.

15. John Zeisel, *Inquiry by Design: Tools for Environment-Behavior Research* (Monterey, Calif.: Brooks-Cole, 1981).

16. Hans-Joachim Klein, "Das Auto Als Technisches Kulturprodukt," unpublished report (Karlsruhe, W. Germany, 1985).

17. Personal correspondence with Rik Vos, Rijksmuseum, Amsterdam, Holland.

18. Jean Jacques Andre, "Storyline and Exhibits," presentation for the 14th Annual Army Museum Conference, Fort Lewis, Washington, October 31, 1985.

19. C. G. Screven, "Exhibitions and Information Centers," pp. 123-124.

20. S. A. Griggs, "Orienting Visitors within a Thematic Display," *International Journal of Museum Management and Curatorship* 2 (1983): 119-134.

21. Robert A. Lakota, "Good Exhibits on Purpose: Techniques to Improve Exhibit Effectiveness," in *Communicating with the Museum Visitor: Guidelines for Planning* (Toronto: Royal Ontario Museum, 1976).

22. Arminta Neal, *Exhibits for the Small Museum: A Handbook* (Nashville: American Association for State and Local History, 1976), pp. 11-14.

23. Ross J. Loomis, "The Visitor and the Object:Some Formative Evaluation Considerations for Planning a Museum Exhibit," unpublished report (Fort Collins, Colo., 1981), pp. 11-28.

24. Paul G. Wiegman and Pamela M. Wiegman, "The Smithsonian Grasshopper," unpublished report (Washington, D.C.: Office of Museum Programs, Smithsonian Institution, 1973).

25. James Taylor, "Science on Display: A Study of the United States Science Exhibit, Seattle World's Fair, 1962" (Seattle, Wash.: Institute for Sociological Research, University of Washington, 1963).

26. Robert B. Bechtel, "Hodometer Research in Museums," *Museum News* 45: 7 (1967): 23-26; also Robert B. Bechtel, "Human Movement and Architecture," *Trans-Action* 4 (March 1967): 53-56. The hodometer was also used to assess color effects on movement by Rajendra K. Srivastava and Thomas S. Peel, in "Human Movement as a Function of Color Stimulation" (Topeka, Kans.: Environmental Research Foundation, 1968).

27. Ross J. Loomis, "Preliminary Study of the Learning Environment of the Museum of Atomic Energy," Report no. 5 (Oak Ridge, Tenn.: American Museum of Atomic Energy, 1977), pp. 8-16.

28. Ellen L. Ferguson and James P. Mason, "Human Subject Rights and Museum Research," *Museum News* 58 (January/February 1980): 44-47.

29. See Arthur W. Melton, *Problems of Installation in Museums of Art*, Publications of the American Association of Museums, New Series, no. 14 (Washington, D.C., 1935), pp. 92-156.

30. Arminta Neal, *Help! For the Small Museum* (Boulder, Colo.: Pruett Press, 1969), pp. 42-43.

31. Ray W. Cooksey and Ross J. Loomis, "Visitor Locomotor Exploration of a Museum Gallery" (Paper read at Rocky Mountain Psychological Association Meeting, Las Vegas, Nev., April 1979).

32. Beverly Serrell, "Visitor Observation Studies at the John G. Shedd Aquarium," unpublished report (Chicago, 1977), pp. 7-17.

33. Taylor, "Science on Display," pp. 129-146; and Robert S. Weiss and Serge Boutourline, "The Communication Value of Exhibits," *Museum News* 42 (November 1963): 23-27.

34. D. S. Olton, "Mazes, Maps, and Memory," *American Psychologist* 34 (1979): 583-596.

35. See Harris H. Shettel, "Exhibits: Art Forum or Educational Medium?" *Museum News* 52 (September 1973): 33-41.

36. Ross J. Loomis, *Four Evaluation Suggestions to Improve the Effectiveness of Museum Labels*, Technical Leaflet no. 4 (Austin, Tex.; Texas Historical Commission, 1983).

37. Wolf and Tymitz, "East Side, West Side, Straight Down the Middle," pp. 42-46.

38. Minda Borun and M. Miller, "To Label or Not to Label?" *Museum News* 58 (March 1980): 64-67.

39. Beverly Serrell, "Label Research Project: Field Museum of Natural History," unpublished report (Chicago, 1980).

40. George R. Klare, "Assessing Readability," *Reading Research Quarterly* 10:1 (1974/1975): 62-102. For a test of readability as a problem in comprehension, called the Cloze proce-

dure, see George R. Klare, H. W. Sinaiko, and L. M. Stolurow, "The Cloze Procedure: A Convenient Readability Test for Training Materials and Translations," *International Review of Applied Psychology* 21:2 (1972): 77-106.

41. E. Dale and G. Eicholz, *Children's Knowledge of Words*, Ohio State University, Bureau of Educational Research and Service, Project 153 (Columbus, Ohio, 1960).

42. The readability test for text of fewer than one hundred words is adapted from Edward Fry, "A Readability Formula that Saves Time," *Journal of Reading* 11 (1968): 513-516, 575-578, developed in *Teaching Content Area Reading Skills: A Modular Preservice and Inservice Program*, by H. W. Forgan and C. T. Mangrum (Columbus, Ohio: Charles E. Merrell, 1976), p. 33.

43. C. G. Screven, "Improving Exhibits through Formative Evaluation" (Paper read at ICOM/CECA Conference, the Netherlands, September 12, 1978).

44. Minda Borun and Maryanne Miller, *What's in a Name?* (Philadelphia: The Franklin Institute Science Museum, 1980).

45. Beverly Serrell, *Making Exhibit Labels: A Step-by-Step Guide* (Nashville: The American Association for State and Local History, 1983).

46. Screven, "Exhibitions and Information Centers," pp. 124-131.

47. Loomis, "The Learning Environment of the Museum of Atomic Energy," p. 15.

48. Laurie P. Eason and Marcia C. Linn, "Evaluation of the Effectiveness of Participatory Exhibits," *Curator* 19 (March 1976): 45-62.

49. For example, see Alan Friedman, Laurie P. Eason, and G. I. Sneider, "Star Games: A Participatory Astronomy Exhibit," *Plantetarian* 8:3 (1979): 3-7; Minda Borun, *Select-A-Label: A Model Computer-Based Interpretive System for Science Museums* (Philadelphia: The Franklin Institute Science Museum, 1979); Dan Fazzini, "The Museum as a Learning Environment: A Self-Motivating, Recycling, Learning System for the Museum Visitor" (Ph.D. diss., University of Wisconsin-Milwaukee, 1972); and Sherman Rosenfeld and Amelia Terkel, "A Naturalistic Study of Visitors at an Interactive Mini-Zoo," *Curator* 25 (March 1982): 187-212.

50. Harris H. Shettel, Margaret Butcher, Timothy S. Cotton, Judi Northrup, and Doris Clapp Slough, *Strategies for Determining Exhibit Effectiveness* (Final Report, Project No. V-011, American Institutes for Research, Pittsburgh, Pa., 1968), pp. 153-159.

51. Screven, "Exhibitions and Information Centers," p. 109.

52. Screven, "Exhibitions and Information Centers," p. 115.

53. Alt and Shaw, "Characteristics of Ideal Exhibits," pp. 32-33.

54. The potential conflict between exhibits as scholarly creations versus educational media is illustrated in Ira Jacknis, "Franz Boas and Exhibits," in *Objects and Others: Essays on Museums and Material Culture*, ed. George W. Stocking, vol. 3 of *History of Anthropology* (Madison, Wis.: University of Wisconsin Press, 1985), 75-111.

55. Benjamin Bloom, et. al., *Taxonomy of Educational Objectives: Handbook I: Cognitive Domain* (New York: David McKay, 1956).

56. Screven, "Exhibit Evaluation: A Goal-Referenced Approach," pp. 278-279.

57. Patterson Williams, "Museum Literacy: Theory into Practice" (Paper read at American Association of Museums, 1983 Annual Meeting); see also Carol B. Stapp, "Defining Museum Literacy," *Roundtable Reports* 9 (Winter 1984): 3-4.

58. Stapp, "Defining Museum Literacy," p. 5

59. Patterson Williams, "Object Contemplation: Theory into Practice," *Roundtable Reports* 9 (Winter 1984): 10-12.

60. Serrell, "Label Research Project," pp. 10-15.

61. Screven, "Exhibit Evaluation: A Goal-Referenced Approach," pp. 280-283; and Screven, "Exhibitions and Information Centers," pp. 119-121.

62. Minda Borun, *Measuring the Immeasurable: A Pilot Study of Museum Effectiveness* (Philadelphia, Pa.: The Franklin Institute Science Museum, 1977), pp. 20-43.

63. For a summary of computers and exhibit evaluation, see Borun, *Select-A-Label* and Screven, "Exhibitions and Information Centers."

64. Wolf and Tymitz, "A Preliminary Guide for Evaluation," pp. 14-41.

65. S. A. Griggs, "Formative Evaluation of Exhibits," pp. 189-201.

66. David E. Rumelhart, "Schemata: The Building Blocks of Cognition," in *Comprehension and Teaching: Research Reviews*, ed. John T. Guthrie (Newark, Del.: International Reading Association, 1981), pp. 3-26.

67. P. David Pearson and Rand Spiro, "The New Buzz Word in Reading is Schema," *Instructor* (1982): 46-48.

68. Shettel, et. al., *Strategies for Exhibit Effectiveness*, pp. 39-49.

69. S. A. Griggs and Jane Manning, "The Predictive Validity of Formative Evaluation of Exhibits," *Museum Studies Journal* 1 (Spring 1983): 31-41.

70. C. G. Screven, *The Measurement and Facilitation of Learning in the Museum Environment: An Experimental Analysis* (Washington, D.C.: Smithsonian Press, 1974).

71. William A. Barnard, Ross J. Loomis, and Henry A. Cross, "Assessment of Visual Recall and Recognition Learning in a Museum Environment," *Bulletin of the Psychonomic Society* 16:4 (1980): 311-313.

72. Two papers that illustrate well the research on visual-recognition memory are: R. N. Shepard, "Recognition Memory for Words, Sentences, and Pictures," *Journal of Verbal Learning and Verbal Behavior* 6 (1967): 156-163; and L. Standing, J. Conezio, and R. Haber, "Perception and Memory for Pictures: Single-Trial Learning of 2500 Visual Stimuli," *Psychonomic Science* 19 (1970): 73-74.

73. Screven, "Exhibit Evaluation: A Goal-Referenced Approach," p. 282.

74. Albert E. Parr, "Marketing the Message," *Curator* 12 (June 1969): 77-82; quotation from page 82.

75. See P. Ekman and W. V. Freisen, *Unmasking the Face: A Guide to Recognizing Emotions from Facial Cues* (Englewood Cliffs, N.J.: Prentice Hall, 1975).

76. Borun, *Measuring the Immeasurable*, p. 32.

77. Wayne A. Wickelgren, "Human Learning and Memory," *Annual Review of Psychology*, vol. 32, ed. Mark R. Rosenzweig and Lyman W. Porter (Palo Alto, Calif.: Annual Reviews, Inc., 1981), 21-52.

78. Gordon H. Bower, "Mood and Memory," *American Psychologist* 36 (1981): 129-148.

79. A basic overview of attitudes and influence is in Philip G. Zimbardo, Ebbe B. Ebbesen, and Christina Maslach, *Influencing Attitudes and Changing Behavior*, 2nd ed. (Reading, Mass.: Addison-Wesley, 1977).

80. Harris H. Shettel, *An Evaluation Model for Measuring the Impact of Overseas Exhibits*, Report no. AIR-F28-6/66-FR (Washington, D.C.: U.S. Atomic Energy Commission, 1966); Borun, *Measuring the Immeasurable*, pp. 26-43. See also Bob Peart, "Impact of Exhibit Type on Knowledge Gain, Attitudes, and Behavior," *Curator* 24:3 (September 1984): 220-237.

81. Eason and Linn, "Evaluation of Participatory Exhibits," pp. 50-52. In addition, see Minda Borun, Barbara Flexer, Alice F. Casey, and Lynn R. Baum, *Planets and Pulleys: Studies of Class Visits to Science Museums* (Philadelphia, Pa.: The Franklin Institute Science Museum, 1983), pp. 37-41.

82. Screven, "Exhibit Evaluation: A Goal-Referenced Approach," pp. 271-290.

7

Using Evaluation
to Improve Programs

"The purpose of evaluation research," notes Carol Weiss, of her work in that area, "is to measure the effects of a program against the goals it set out to accomplish as a means of contributing to subsequent decision making about the program and improving future programming."[1]

Modern-day museums provide their publics with much more than exhibits. Through membership associations, community outreach activities, media and communication departments, and education programs, museums provide a wide variety of public service and learning opportunities. Evaluation work on these public programs offered by museums is often administered by museum staff personnel or departments other than those working with exhibit design and preparation.

Such programs as exhibits can be made more responsive to their intended audiences through evaluation research. Goals must be stated in terms of the way a program relates to the people it is to serve and the outcomes that are hoped for from it. Finally, goals and more specific objectives must be defined in a manner that makes assessment of their usefulness possible.

Program goals often involve an event such as a docent presentation that may occur over and over again for a long period of time; or the event may be of short duration, as in the case of a one-time special presentation. *Duration* is only one characteristic of programs that researcher Carol Weiss suggests that planners should be aware of.[2] *Clarity of goals* is another characteristic that can vary from program to program. Some programs are marked by precise goals that result in clearly stated objectives, while other programs operate from more general or diffused statements of purpose. *Scope of coverage* can also vary. A children's presentation may be planned for a specific gallery in a museum and will occur only at that location. Another program may have as its scope schools throughout a large metropolitan area. This latter type of program will have to function under a variety of conditions. Programs also vary in *size of audience* and may be dependent upon repeat followers or serve a continually changing audience. Goals for programs can vary in *complexity.* Some programs have many subgoals that require a longer time span for their completion. Other programs have much less complex goals, such as teaching visitors a specific concept or skill, that can be accomplished in a short session. Finally, programs can vary in their *innovativeness,* with some using established procedures and hoping for conventional outcomes and others offering a high degree of novelty and uniqueness.

These diverse characteristics of museum programs and goals identified by Weiss can serve as points of focus for evaluation. It is important to keep them in mind as ways in which programs differ from one another. Specific objectives can be stated around them and around the following basic questions:

1. Who is the intended audience for this program?

2. Have specific objectives been prepared that clearly indicate the way the program relates to the audience and the impression on the audience that I expect the program to make?

3. What methods of measurement are most important to assess program effectiveness? Interviews? Tests of skill or knowledge? Observation?

4. Do I need to undertake summative evaluation to establish base rates of the way the program is currently working? Can I use formative evaluation to guide the development of a new or modified program?

Examples of Program Evaluation

The examples that follow are intended to sample the ways people have devised for evaluating a program. Programs sampled will vary in the characteristics of duration, size of audience, etc. Sometimes one feels that it is impossible to evaluate a specific program in any systematic manner. This is particularly true for programs of short duration and complex goals. Hopefully, the examples given will provide insights into program evaluation and encouragement for making the effort.

Evaluation of Living Presentation Programs

The use of live interpretation through docent presentations and demonstrations helps to make the museum more exciting to segments of the audience that are not deeply involved with museums. We mentioned earlier that occasional or nonvisiting members of the public are likely to respond to programming that emphasizes activity and to a museum visit as an event or excursion. Experienced visitors will find a presentation, such as a lecture or tour, a means of enriching their backgrounds. Changing presentations also provides a way of challenging repeat visitors with new information.

Live presentations are usually short in actual performance duration, but as a program can span many years. A museum constantly has to develop programs to match changes in exhibits and must, as well, recruit and train docents. Goals can be complex, especially in situations where a large number of different programs are offered. The size of the audience can run into thousands of children and adults served in a year. Evaluating this kind of program involves assessment of quality control, learning content, and the overall nature of the experience offered.

Quality control. Because presentations can be part of a program that lasts for years and involves many people, it is important to know the quality of what is being offered to the visitor, and also to know whether quality exists at a consistent level. Readers familiar with the popular *In Search of Excellence*, on high-level management, may recall that training of employees for Disney theme parks stressed the importance of attending to *little things*.[3] All Disney park employees who have contact with the public are to consider their time in the park as being onstage and their relation to visitors (who are regarded as guests) as a performance. This on-stage way of thinking applies not only to those who play such Disney characters as Mickey Mouse in front of visitors, but equally to concession stand attendants, grounds maintenance people, information guides, and everyone else who has contact with guests. *Live interpretation is a call to be on stage,* whether one is in the role of a park ranger, art museum docent, or role-playing a person from some other historical period than the present.

To make sure that the little things that add up to an effective, high-quality presentation are attended to, interpreter performance can be evaluated. Jim Reiss is correct in saying that traditional criteria for evaluating classroom teachers are not sufficient for live interpretation that must capture the attention of visitors who are not expecting to learn anything, have little reason to learn what is in the presentation, and see it as simply one part of the setting and visit experience.[4] Reiss is also correct in noting that live interpretation requires a level of interaction rather than straight didactic contact with the visitor and must be evaluated as such. While classroom teachers may have tests, papers, grades, required attendance, and even the threat of discipline to use as control over learners, docents or interpreters must rely on the strength of their personalities and presentations to draw and hold visitor attention. The challenge of live interpretation is to *involve* visitors, without the aids or controls available to classroom teachers and cause a learning episode to happen that is unique to nonclassroom settings. In well-prepared live interpretation, a visitor may learn something unexpected—may even acquire a new interest or hobby because of that experience.

A model for evaluation of live interpretation developed at the Edison Institute (Henry Ford Museum and Greenfield Village) was used to insure quality of presentations in the work of a large number of interpreters. Reiss describes the model as including performance criteria tailored to live interpretation and multiple assessments of an interpreter's work. Figure 7.1 reproduces an assessment form used by supervisors. Ratings included categories of communication and hand skills, two types of behavior very important to live performances. It was also of value to assess historical knowledge and behavior that included cooperation and ability to fit into an institutional setting. It is very important that specific criteria are spelled out and agreed upon both by supervisors and interpreters.

Ratings can increase in accuracy or validity by having more than one observation made and using two or more observers. As can be seen from figure 7.1, the supervisor and other staff members observe each interpreter and, in addition, comments from visitors are included in the personnel file. Interpreters are also asked to rate themselves, and then an interview is held with the supervisor. As a rule, interpreters rate themselves lower than others do, and this bias usually helps make the interview a positive experience (see fig. 7.2 for the interview form).

Jim Reiss points out that it is important to rate specific types of behavior and to use more than one source of information. The key to the evaluation is bringing management and staff interpreters into communication that shares information both ways. Interpreters need to know what is expected of them in concrete terms, so that they can incorporate the required elements in their presentations. Managers need to know what is going on in terms of the levels of performance being given, as well as the interpeters' problems that could be worked on by management. It is also important not to leave interpreters without any feedback or attention from the administration for long periods of time. Not only does such

SUPERVISOR'S SUMMARY RATING CHART

	SUPERVISOR OBSERVATION	LEAD INTERPRETER	INDEPENDENT OBSERVER	PERSONNEL FILE	SUMMARY RATING
INTERPRETIVE SKILLS					
Communication skills	3	3	5	5	4
Historical knowledge	4	4	4	5	4+
Hand skills	3	5	3	5	4
Cooperation	2	2	N/A	3	2 to 3
Responsibility, dependability, flexibility	3	3	N/A	3	3
Support of institutional policies	4	4	4	5	4+
Overall job performance	4	4	4	4	4

Rating Scale
1 = Consistantly inadequate performance in this area.
2 = Inadequate performance in this area; rarely achieves acceptable level.
3 = Adequate performance in this area; achieves minimum acceptable level.
4 = Good performance in this area.
5 = Outstanding performance.
N/A = Source not able to provide an accurate rating of this interpretive skill.

Fig. 7.1. Example of a rating chart for evaluating live interpretation. Ratings include several criteria and are made by more than one observer.—From History News 39:11 (1984): 14.

1984 INTERPRETIVE STAFF PERFORMANCE APPRAISAL
THE EDISON INSTITUTE
Official File Form — Final Interview

Interpreter: _____ *Date:* _____

Manager: _____

I. Interpretive skills:

	COMMENTS	RATING
Communication skills		
Historical knowledge		
Hand skills		
Cooperation		
Responsibility, dependability, flexibility		
Support of institutional policies		
Overall job performance		

Rating Scale
1 = Consistantly inadequate performance in this area.
2 = Inadequate performance in this area; rarely achieves acceptable level.
3 = Adequate performance in this area; achieves minimum acceptable level.
4 = Good performance in this area.
5 = Outstanding performance.

II. Manager's general comments on employee's strengths, weaknesses, and action taken to improve job performance:

III. Interpreter's comments:

Manager's signature _____

Interpreter's signature _____

Fig. 7.2. *An interview between supervisor and interpreter can be an important evaluation, as well as a management tool. The interview form shown here repeats some basic criteria (see fig. 7.1) for appraisal of staff interpreter performance and also is a means of comparing performance as noted by different observers, including the interpreter's own self-evaluation.*—History News 39:11 (1984): 15.

neglect increase the likelihood that poor performance will go undetected, but staff people are also likely to suffer from low morale occasioned by the belief that management does not care about them and their work. Live performance, by its very nature, is repetitious, and its practitioners are prone to fatigue and "burn-out." Supportive supervisory contact is needed, not just to deal with problems that threaten quality, but also to provide management's backing and insure positive feedback. People who do repetitive, complex tasks that involve continual contact with the public need feedback, from time to time, to reassure them of the importance of their work and encourage them to monitor their own performance to achieve and maintain top quality.

The evaluation program summarized by Reiss is fairly elaborate and time-consuming. Most museums would need to develop a fairly efficient means of evaluating live interpretation. One way of accomplishing some helpful evaluation is to encourage docents or other interpreters to engage in self-evaluation. A video recorder can permit interpreters to see themselves in action, presenting their talks and/or demonstrations. People are naturally self-conscious about viewing themselves on a video system and are inclined to be critical. Therefore, even self-evaluation needs some criteria of performance for guidance and positive social support from supervisors and peers. One stratagem for developing teacher-performance criteria and skills has used video-taped feedback. Once the teaching tasks needed are identified, video feedback can help in teaching specific skills that lead to performance of the desired tasks. Presentations can also be improved through evaluation focused on comparisons between docent methods.[5] Sometimes group review and feedback while watching a video tape can be a productive evaluation experience. Keeping that experience productive depends on its being conducted in a positive atmosphere based on support and constructive feedback. It may not always be possible to create that kind of environment, and supervisors may have to work with interpreters on a one-to-one basis to accomplish evaluation.

Because so many museums and historic sites depend upon volunteers to provide interpretation, it is important to build evaluation in as part of the management of volunteers. In general, making professional demands on volunteers will enhance the importance of their commitment, and undergoing evaluation is one way of developing professional standards. A cooperative docent program in Alexandria, Virginia, recruits and maintains, in a self-governing association, 175 volunteers who provide live interpretation at five historic properties in the area.[6] Each docent is expected to undergo evaluation during training and then once a year for each successive year served. The annual evaluation provides a continuing monitoring of performance and also establishes the expectation that presentations will be evaluated and standards of performance are required. The evaluation form used (see fig. 7.3) reveals some of the expected standards. Evaluation not only monitors the level of performance, but also is a process that helps communicate the standards of performance expected. We mentioned earlier that one of the primary benefits of evaluating interpretation and visitor experience is that the process itself induces thinking about goals and standards. It is very important that interpreters have specific ideas about what is expected and that they be shown ways of developing skills that lead to the desired performance. These skills should also be reflected in evaluation criteria; the evaluation summary in fig. 7.3 provides another working example. Notice that the evaluation is to be made using three basic criteria: tour logistics, tour content, and manner of presentation. The first category, tour logistics, is especially appropriate to docent presentations, since a tour group must be kept under control in a special setting, such as a historic building. We should stress that live interpretation must be evaluated with methods using criteria that are sensitive to the elements that make that kind of teaching and learning unique from other learning environments.

Learned content. It can also be important to assess what is learned, especially in terms of major conceptual understandings. While a docent can dispense facts, much of the thrust of modern interpretation and the use of live performances is to provide a framework of ideas that help individuals understand the setting (with its objects) that they are visiting. Barbara Carson and Cary Carson observe that learning to name objects, participating in demonstrations that illustrate functions of artifacts, and visually exploring a setting all combine to stimulate associations in a visitor's memory that will lead to a better understanding of current experiences.[7] This process of matching new experiences with older ones is at the heart of concept development. Carson and Carson are right in suggesting that if the match is a successful one, artifacts become more meaningful and also more likely to be a part of the visitor's memory.

Methods of evaluating what visitors learn from presentations are basically the same as those for exhibit-based learning, with the difference that the focus of evaluation changes from the docent's performance to the visitor's understanding of the information. For example, visitors might be given paper-and-pencil quizzes, or visitors' queries might be integrated

Fig. 7.3. Summary sheet for evaluation of volunteer docents that provides assessment in three categories important to live interpretation.—From History News 39:10 (1984): 32.

Historic Alexandria Docents Tour Evaluation

Name of Docent_____

Property _____

Name of Evaluator _____

Date _____

Tour Group Characteristics
(Adult group, school group, general tour, tour groups size, group behavior)

_____

Tour Logistics
Effective greeting _____

Rapport established _____

Sensitive to group (adjust to group level and interest)

_____

Logical continuity_____

Proximity to group and artifacts (is the docent using effective methods in addressing the group and indicating and explaining rooms and collection?)

_____

Request no touching_____

No touching - docent _____

No touching - group_____

Moves group as a unit_____

Security awareness _____

Maintains group attention _____

Use of time_____

Natural conclusion of tour _____

Tourist information (gives suggestions and directions) _____

Tour group participation (group interest, effective use of questions)

_____

Tour group final comments _____

Tour Content

Organized _____

Repetitive _____

Relevant _____

Helpful_____

Enjoyable_____

Informative (factual, detailed, covers basics)_____

Accurate _____

Presentation

Voice projection_____

Gestures _____

Enthusiastic _____

Hospitable _____

Group control_____

Suggestions_____

_____

into a participative display such as those discussed in chapter 6. To find out what the visitors learned, the focus of the tests would still be on the performance, but on the information listeners were receiving, rather than the giver's ability in presenting it.

Another method for using a test of conceptual and factual knowledge is to recruit small panels of people who have characteristics similar to different kinds of actual visitors. Panel members understand that they will be tested, will tour the exhibit, and/or will watch the demonstration prior to answering questions. Sometimes they are paid or given some other reward for their effort. Because volunteer panel members *know* that they will be tested, it is best to consider their performance as the maximum or optimal amount that a visitor could learn.

Some evaluators prefer to avoid a testing format of any kind and rely on unobtrusive observation made during and/or after a live performance. Comments and/or the frequency of key words overheard can suggest learning, especially when there is a repeated pattern of the same comments or words from several individuals in a sample of different visitors. Listening to the way visitors explain something from a presentation they have just heard to other members of their group can suggest concepts learned, and both children and adults can be encouraged to recite and ask questions during a demonstration. Content of the recitations and questions can be recorded and analyzed for developing concepts. An indirect way of measuring comprehension is by using estimates of the frequency with which visitors look at the interpreter during a presentation. Audience attention to a presentation can be estimated by unobtrusively scanning the listening group and judging what percentage of the group are looking directly at the speaker. Experienced speakers tend to make this sort of estimate almost automatically, but a nonspeaking observer can also be used to check and record the percentage of the audience looking at the interpreter at different times throughout the complete presentation.[8] This procedure yields a running record of visitor attention and can reveal times during the live interpretation when attention, and thereby comprehension, may be lowest. Frequent or extended periods when visitors' attention wanders from the interpreter can suggest that a presentation may be too long, too hard to follow, too repetitious, or that the interpreter is communicating fatigue or personal loss of interest. Unobtrusive observations cannot indicate in an absolute way how well a presentation is reaching the audience. For example, eye contact wandering away from a speaker does not necessarily mean that one is not listening to the spoken presentation and comprehending what is being said; but such indicators as that can suggest overall effectiveness or possible problems. Tests can be made to validate suggestions gained through the use of observation. Unobtrusive observation has the very strong advantage of collecting evaluation information without alerting visitors that they are participating in some kind of assessment.

Mary Ellen Munley used interviews to evaluate an experimental live interpretation that included a short drama performed in a museum period room.[9] An important evaluation goal was not simply that visitors were positively impressed overall, but that they were learning major historical themes from the drama. Statements made by visitors in the interviews were analyzed for content that could be matched to themes contained in the script. This content analysis is one way to look for basic ideas that visitors are using to organize their experience of the museum. Interview data did suggest that some visitors picked up on at least one of three major themes (a harder question to answer is what percentage of the audience should comprehend themes to consider a presentation successful).

Nature of experience. Munley's interviews also suggested that visitors sensed involvement with some of the emotions contained in the

historical setting being dramatized, as illustrated in this visitor's statement: "This [dramatization] gives the [period] room character. I was
involved in something emotional during that play, and I bet I remember
it when I leave here today." Such a sense of intimacy or involvement is
one of the tasks that live interpretation can perform well. Evaluation can
reveal a more global reaction that combines conceptual (cognitive) criteria
with emotional (affective), to give a general sense of visitor experience.

D. G. Hayward and A. D. Jensen emphasized experiential evaluation
criteria in a paper appropriately entitled "Enhancing a Sense of the Past."[10]
In their study of interpretation at Old Sturbridge Village, they emphasized the way visitors perceived the setting as a whole and acquired broad
interpretive themes or concepts. Of particular interest was whether visitors gained a sense of going "back in the past" and whether they thought
of the village as a real setting and not primarily a modern re-creation
of an imaginary past. Exit interviews were used; and, significantly, sampled visitors reported that both the physical setting and the activities of
interpreters contributed to a sense of the past. Visitors experienced in
visiting historic settings or re-creations of past settings seemed to have
an easier time getting into the mood or experiencing a sense of the past
than first-time visitors. In fact, first-time visitors reported that they
expected to find formal presentations about "colonial times," rather than
an opportunity to enter into and experience a historical setting intended
to take people back in time. Visitor-orientation experiences can also be
very important in making this transition between time periods. Interview
responses of Sturbridge visitors suggested that first-time visitors found
orientation materials such as films and brochures helpful in making the
transition.

Some studies combined multiple evaluation goals (criteria) with more
than one measurement method. Dennis O'Toole, in Williamsburg, combined observation with questionnaires, not only to measure visitors'
involvement and learning, but to ascertain whether changes in interpretation programs prompted by refurnishing and redecoration of a historic
building changed visitor experiences.[11] O'Toole described use of the
before-and-after comparison, which revealed that visitors became more
involved and paid greater attention to the revised interpretation program
at the historic facility. Visitors also showed more overall approval (i.e.,
gave higher ratings) to the newer program over the old. These kinds of
findings represent good news, evidence that constructive changes had
been made. Not all the Williamsburg news was good, however. The evaluation showed that visitors to the changed interpretation displayed a lower

level of acquired information when compared to earlier results. O'Toole states his concern at such a finding and reports that a task committee was formed to find ways to increase visitor learning from the newer interpretation formats. Modifications were made that enhanced both visitor-learning and the quality of performance by interpreters. A major reason that the modifications to the new interpretation program were successful was that the interpreters themselves got involved with the evaluation and were in a unique position to make substantive suggestions. In fact, O''Toole mentions that the information-evaluation feedback from staff people and other professionals was a valuable adjunct to the information gained from the formal analysis used. This example also points out that formative evaluation is as important for program development as it is for planning new exhibits.

Evaluation of Audiovisual Programs

Visitor use and comprehension of films, videos, slides, and other audiovisual materials can be considered a part of exhibit evaluation, to be included in evaluation goals. Evaluation of audiovisual presentations is discussed here, as they are often part of the museum's education or communications department programs.

Opinions about use of audiovisual materials in museums can vary from the position that they are inappropriate and should not be used at all to enthusiastic acceptance, in museums that schedule audiovisual presentations frequently in both exhibits and various program activities. Strong feelings about them, pro or con, usually lack evaluative information. M. B. Alt, having reviewed the debate over audiovisuals in museums, summarizes a study of visitor attention to a slide-tape program in an exhibit setting.[12] A random sample of visitors was observed viewing the display. Holding time, on the average, was for only 11 percent of the program's running time of thirteen minutes.

Holding times for an audience can be estimated a couple of ways.[13] For the audiovisual slide/sound program in the Alt study, holding time or power was calculated as a fraction:

$$\text{Holding time} = \frac{\text{time spent watching}}{\text{program running time}}$$

For this example, program running time was both the necessary time and the ideal viewing time. For other presentations, where there is not a program running time, necessary viewing times can be estimated by asking a few people to view the information long enough to get the main ideas presented. Ideal viewing times would include holding attention to a display long enough to study every feature. Either necessary or ideal times can be used for the denominator of the holding-time fraction.

Additional information from Alt's findings indicated that about half the sample of two hundred visitors attended for less than thirty-five seconds. Being seated, seeing the presentation from the start, and viewing during a time when the surrounding area was quieter and less busy tended to increase the length of viewing times, although the time of day the tape was run may also have influenced holding time. Visitors left the program at a fairly constant rate after the first minute of viewing, suggesting that they were deciding whether or not to leave independently of the length of time they had invested in watching.

This study did not assess the program's attraction power. That could be done by randomly observing a sample of at least one hundred visitors as they passed by the exhibit and noticing how many stopped and looked for at least three to four seconds. Attraction power can be estimated with the fraction:

$$\text{Attraction power} = \frac{\text{number of visitors stopping}}{\text{number of visitors passing by}}$$

Care should be taken to use the same area around the display as the sampling point for each observation.

Alt's findings emphasize that it is highly unlikely that visitors will stay for an audiovisual program that lasts for several minutes unless the production is very well done with a story-line that will hold the viewers' attention. Visitors may also be encouraged to watch longer programs as part of a rest break, if seating and some protection from noise is provided.

Estimating visitor comprehension of the content of an audiovisual presentation can be one of the goals of evaluation. Harris Shettel provides a good example of a procedure for evaluating visitor reactions to a film presentation, using a general-to-specific topic format of questioning to understand visitor comprehension and general reactions in a pilot test of films under preparation for a museum exhibit.[14] Three interviews were used to guide respondents' thinking about film content from general considerations (i.e., was the film too long? Did the film make the viewer think about the topic?) to very specific questions about content, assessing the main ideas intended for the film script. The middle interview was open-ended, so as not to suggest content-related topics to subjects. An initial question, for example, simply asked respondents to describe what they thought the basic message of a film was. A procedure that what they thought the basic message of a film was. A procedure that sequences questions from general to specific is very useful, since it provides for both open reactions, without ideas being suggested, and specific, searching questions on detailed topics. The content from the open interviews was evaluated by judges to determine the degree to which each respondent's answers to questions reflected good comprehension of major themes.

Shettel was careful to specify the limits of his pilot study. The fact is, however, that even a limited study based on interviews from a small sample of people who viewed interpretive materials indicated the key themes or salient points of information that were registering with viewers. Such pretesting of materials designed for presentations, whether live or in some media format, is an essential task that evaluation can perform. One convenience to live interpretation, as compared to film, is that pretesting results can be incorporated into new presentations fairly efficiently—and fairly quickly. And one should keep in mind that a presentation must sometimes be modified more than once before the desired points of information are effectively communicated.

In Shettel's example, a panel of recruited viewers evaluated the film after seeing it. This use of a panel is a common strategy in consumer research, and it is not unusual for the participants to be paid. It is also possible to test presentation materials on-site with a sample of pretested visitors who have *not* seen the film and another sample post-tested after having viewed the program. As with evaluation of learning from exhibits, post-test visitors should command more information than those who are yet to see the film. Keep in mind, however, that a clear understanding of film content in a setting where visitors may or may not give full attention to the presentation is also dependent on the film's power to attract and hold the visitor's interest. It may be necessary to cue a sample of visitors to view and listen to the presentation to estimate the audience's potential for learning—and then work on improving the film's attraction and holding power.

Evaluation of a Special Program

One characteristic of interpretive programs that must be given critical attention is their duration. A program may last only for the time period of a special exhibit—as was true of an evaluation of programs keyed to a temporary exhibit of master paintings. Daryl K. Fischer employed questionnaires to assess participant evaluation of the programs provided by an art museum.[15] Of particular interest was the way participants evaluated different kinds of art history information included in the educational presentations. Responses to this part of the questionnaire were coded into ten categories of art interpretation information, and it was possible to calculate the relative interest in each category of information from the replies of different respondents. Among the findings was the observation that respondents with educational backgrounds in art history and architecture preferred interpretation high in content that stressed materials and techniques used to create a painting. By contrast, people who participated in the programs because they came as members of a social organization, such as a church group, were more interested in expressive content and interpretation that brought out emotional responses. Interestingly, before the survey of that exhibit, the museum staff had not thought of churches as a strong community resource for participation in the programs. One of the benefits of the evaluation was the realization that churches should be notified about future programs of the type evaluated. Also, religious content in interpretation might have greater audience interest than realized.

What Fischer accomplished, in part, was an initial definition of specific content in art interpretation that reached a particular audience subgroup. This kind of evaluation effort, though simple in technique, revealed substantive information about the actual experience of art provided for a specific audience. Perhaps most dramatic among her findings was a consistent tendency for participants to indicate that the interpretation increased both general enjoyment or emotional experience and specific understanding of works of art. This finding, that gains in both enjoyment and knowledge resulted from interpretation, demonstrated that enjoyment and learning can be linked together.

Fischer also asked questions about other activities and opportunities related to interpretation of the special exhibit. This information was added to the reactions to art interpretation and to a series of visitor-description questions. Since some of the programs were offered away from the museum, Fischer also determined which of the participants actually came to the museum to see the exhibit. This project illustrates an under-used form of survey evaluation. Within a museum, any staff group responsible for special public programs could benefit from a continuing file of the type of survey completed by Fischer. Attendance and cost-income data should also be collected. Qualitative reactions to programs such as those collected by Fischer in her survey focused on art interpretation can be a valuable adjunct to the quantitative (i.e., attendance, fees collected) information. Staff people can assess the merits of different types of past programs in terms of available budget and consider the need to draw attendance and support or, on the other hand, the freedom to plan a program that is conceptually important but may not draw a larger house. Program projects and planning can include both popular offerings and more specialized events that will appeal to a limited audience. It is important that program evaluation results be kept on file so that staff turnover, or simply the loss of memory over time, does not result in a loss of useful information.

Evaluation of Visitor Self-Guides

Staff members working in publication or education sometimes administer a program of gallery guides as a supplement to exhibit interpretation. Frequently, the guides are available as leaflets that visitors can buy for a nominal fee and use to direct their visits. Both the rate of use and the content of such guides can be improved with evaluation. As with all evaluation, setting goals for the self-guides can help to determine the audience for whom the guide will be most helpful and its effectiveness as a map or suggested guide to exhibits as opposed to its use as a supplemental source of interpretation information.

Mildred Porter observed visitors with and without guides at Peabody Museum of Natural History and found that clear statements of suggested stops in an exhibit could influence visitors to look at those portions of a gallery.[16] While an old study, her work still serves as a good example of summative evaluation. Porter found that it was not only important to have a narrative that clearly suggested guidance, but in addition, one needs to call attention to specific attributes of exhibit objects mentioned in the guides. Guides should also provide information different from that available in exhibit labels.

One of the most important outcomes from Porter's evaluation was that few visitors picked up gallery guides unless prompted to do so by attendants. Her findings that those who used the guide did make stops may reflect the fact that visitors were often cued to attend more by the attendants. Even if cued, it is still important to know that the guide was used.

A contemporary study replicated Porter's finding that visitors seldom pick up gallery guides unless prompted to do so by an attendant.[17] While observations revealed a low rate of pick-ups, the gallery cash box for the guide being evaluated *did* fill up, after a period of time, and guides *were* being taken. A small sample of visitors was selected at random and asked to use the guides and then answer some questions about the information they provided (see fig. 7.4). Visitors' responses indicated that they found the guide useful and thought that guides should be available for selected exhibits in the museum. Perhaps most important, the sample produced as many responses saying that visitors would use the guide as a supplement to interpretation as there were responses saying they would use it as a self-guide. Visitors also perceived the guides as a bibliographic source of exhibit-related information and a keepsake from their visit.

Gallery guides probably serve more than one purpose, and C. G. Screven makes a good point in a current work when he observes that supplementary interpretation in the form of flyers or pamphlet guides may provide too much information for the visitor to use while in the exhibit.[18] It may also be true that visitors fail to pick up guides because they expect the exhibit labels to give them all the information they need. The two evaluation examples cited were done in a natural history museum and an art museum, respectively. Effectiveness of gallery guides may depend upon the particular setting, and evaluation results are limited to the setting they were derived from. Good formative evaluation is needed to find the best way of encouraging visitors to avail themselves of the guides and to use them in touring the galleries they describe. Without such evaluation, gallery guides may not be the *guides* intended at all, but will serve primarily as supplementary interpretation pamphlets or visit keepsakes.

One of the most common self-guide devices consists of audio narratives that visitors can rent to take along on their exhibit tour. C. G. Screven notes that these audio guides are seldom based on learning objectives or evaluated with a planned study. He reports on one research effort designed to provide guidance for visitors in a specific exhibit.[19] Samples of visitors were tested on a variety of self-guidance devices, including audio tapes. Visitors in each sample group received only one kind of guidance device. Visitors who used audio tapes with questions to guide their exploration of the exhibit were able to reach criterion test scores of 88 percent, or better, in mastery of the guide's information as measured by a post-test. Visitors using audio tape did much better than a sample of pretested visitors who took the same test, but had not seen the exhibit. Especially significant was the finding that visitors using audio tapes tested significantly higher than visitors observed spending five minutes looking at the exhibit (including reading labels) and then tested. Test questions were based on the exhibit and standardized for the various groups tested.

The audio tapes were prepared with instructional objectives intended to (1) provide a suggested order for viewing exhibit elements, (2) point out important relationships and visual features, (3) ask questions that

The following questions will ask you to evaluate the visitors' guide you have just read and used. Circle the appropriate answer.

1.	Did you find the guide helpful in understanding the exhibit?	Yes No	No opinion
2.	Did the guide make exhibit objects more interesting?	Yes No	No opinion
3.	Did the guide tell you things you didn't know before?	Yes No	No opinion
4.	Was the guide easy to read and use?	Yes No	No opinion
5.	Would you like to see guides similar to the one you have used available for selected exhibits throughout the museum?	Yes No	No opinion

The next six questions will ask how you would use guides if they were available for an exhibit you planned to see. Circle the appropriate answer.

1.	Would you use the guide as a source of more information about the exhibit?	Yes No	No opinion
2.	Would you use it as a keepsake of your visit?	Yes No	No opinion
3.	Would you use it as a bibliographic source of exhibit-related information?	Yes No	No opinion
4.	Would you use it as a self-guide to the visit?	Yes No	No opinion
5.	Would you use it as information to pass on to family and/or friends to encourage them to see the exhibit?	Yes No	No opinion
6.	Would you use it as part of a set of guides to collect and keep?	Yes No	No opinion

Fig. 7.4. Sample questions that could be part of a post-test survey of museum visitors who used a visitor exhibit guide. Questions focus on the visitor's evaluation of the guide itself and visitor comments on different uses for these hand-outs.

could be answered by observing objects or reading labels, (4) encourage label-reading, (5) provide feedback and encouragement following questions in the narrative, and (6) supplement label information in the exhibit that would enhance visitor understanding. The audio tape evaluation used an existing exhibit, and it was the instructional objectives listed here that enabled the tapes to be effective.

Off-the-street visitors were used in the study; and although the audio tape guidance devices made demands upon the visitor that not all visitors might accept, the findings from the study could be applied to the more popular types of audio tour guides visitors can rent. Screven did have visitors rate the acceptability of different guidance devices being tested, and visitors rated the audio tapes as among the most acceptable. Taking time to use the guidance devices was one of the major limitations, since the study concentrated on one exhibit within the museum.

Evaluating the School Group Visit Program

Many museums host visiting school groups as part of the museum's education programs. The school group visits are often part of a program that spans years and is complex in terms of the number of different kinds of group visits provided. Program goals can consist of specific learning objectives based on school curriculum for a given grade or more general plans for experiential learning. Often the visits are planned around innovative alternatives to classroom learning as a way of making the experience unique. Evaluation can identify how well the programming of the visit is working (i.e., are groups being provided with well-planned and coordinated visits?). Or evaluation can be used to determine what kinds of learning occur. An example of formative evaluation, done to see how well a new visit program was working out, follows, with examples of summative evaluation.

Formative evaluation of visit process. As is true of living interpretation programs, school visits require management, simply to handle the situation and take care of group needs. Museum teachers or docents have to keep groups under control and coordinate visits with both school and museum activities. Some of the criteria mentioned for live-performance evaluation would also apply to management of school groups.

Formative evaluation can be used to see whether a developing visit program is on target before a commitment is made to put the new program into full operation. In one example, a sample of both teachers and children were given a post-visit questionnaire, to see whether a new demonstration format developed for visits to an art museum was on target for reaching intended goals.[20] Planning for the visits included encouraging participation through the new demonstration format, developing enthusiasm for art and the art museum among grade-school children, and making sure that program content fitted school curriculum needs.

Teachers were asked to evaluate their students' interest in the visit and the program, and also to indicate how well the museum experience related to school curriculum objectives. In addition, open-ended questions asked teachers to list best and worst features of the museum visit, as a way to identify problems. Figure 7.5 lists some potential questions for a teacher survey.

The children's questionnaire used the facial-affect test mentioned in chapter 6, to measure the youngsters' assessment of the visit as a whole, and a word checklist (i.e., exciting-boring, too long-too short) to describe the children's reactions to the demonstration activity. Children were also asked to draw, from memory, an object or some feature that appealed to them from their visit.

Results from the survey provided feedback that substantiated staff perceptions that the new visit formats were appropriate for the grade levels planned and matched to teaching curriculum needs. Results also provided positive indicators that the visit process was working well and that teachers as well as students were positive about the visit. Because some children younger than the age level planned for were included in the sample, it was possible to show, through survey results, that the lower age levels should not be included in the regular program.

The sample drawn in this study was small, but adequate for formative evaluation purposes. Ideally a summative evaluation survey should be conducted after the new program has been operating for a while and a complete sample constructed that represents all grade levels and all types of schools served by the program.

Summative evaluation of student learning. In a major study of what children could learn through class visits for a science museum, four researchers—Minda Borun, Barbara Flexer, Alice Casey, and Lynn Baum—compared not only different types of visit experiences, but also different assumptions about what can be learned and ways in which children's learning should be measured.[21] A very important finding from this research was that affective learning growing out of an enjoyable and stimulating field trip may be the most consistent and salient aspect of school-group learning. School-group visits of short duration cannot be expected to compete with instructive classroom experiences in teaching

Fig. 7.5. Sample questions for a post-visit teachers' survey related to management of the school-group visit.

A. *Assessment of Interest*

    1. What was the level of interest your students had for the information you presented?

        ☐ Very high
        ☐ High
        ☐ Average
        ☐ Low
        ☐ Very low

    2. Would you recommend this program to other teachers in your school or district?

        ☐ Definitely yes
        ☐ Yes
        ☐ No
        ☐ Definitely no

B. *School-Visit Fit to Curriculum Needs*

    1. Were the information and concepts presented appropriate for the grade level of your students?

        ☐ Yes
        ☐ No, too elementary
        ☐ No, too advanced

    2. How well did the visit information and concepts relate to your curriculum?

        ☐ Closely related
        ☐ Somewhat related
        ☐ Vaguely related
        ☐ Unrelated

    3. Were the student work-sheet materials used appropriate for the grade level of your students?

        ☐ Yes
        ☐ No, too elementary
        ☐ No, too advanced

C. *Visit Management*

    1. Did the visit program hold the interest of your students?

        ☐ Yes
        ☐ No

    2. Was the length of the visit appropriate for your group?

        ☐ Yes
        ☐ No, too short
        ☐ No, too long

3. Was the visit leader well prepared? ☐ Yes

☐ No

4. Did the visit leader keep adequate control of the ☐ Yes
group's visit?

☐ No

5. Please list the *best* and *worst* features of your group's
visit:

Best

Worst

factual and basic information, even for group visits where carefully
programmed lessons are used. Some informative content will be learned,
but it is the unique experience of participating and experiencing a special setting that consistently impresses children and makes the museum
visit a learning experience different from that of the classroom.

The evaluation project of Borun, et al., at the Franklin Institute
Science Museum in this two-museum study is particularly worthy of note.
First, the evaluators defined and tested different visit conditions that
included control (no exhibit experience), exhibit visit; a more classlike
museum lesson; and a combined exhibit/lesson situation. Second, three
different tests of learning criteria were developed: (1) Cognitive learning
was assessed, both with visual-recognition items and conventional
multiple-choice, word-based questions. Student recognition, comprehension, and application of information contained in the exhibits or lessons
were assessed with these tools; (2) a short test measured affective
responses through carefully organized questions that asked about interest,
enjoyment, and motivation; and (3) a performance test asked students
to demonstrate skills and explanations using three-dimensional testing
materials. Figure 7.6 provides examples of questions prepared by Borun,
et. al., to measure the different learning criteria.

Results indicated that children did learn science concepts from the
exhibit experience, and learning was revealed across the visual, cognitive, and performance (skill) tests. Furthermore, their tour of the exhibit
seemed to produce as much learning as the museum instructional lesson. Significantly, the performance-based test turned out to be the most
sensitive measure of exhibit learning. This finding makes sense, since

Fig. 7.6. *Four testing activities used to measure what school children learned on a classroom visit to a museum. The first two items used visual and verbal types of questions to assess cognitive learning. Question 3 requires the child to perform some task to demonstrate skill-learning; and the fourth item measures feeling or effect.*—From Planets and Pulleys, *by Minda Borun, Barbara K. Flexer, Alice F. Casey, and Lynn R. Baum (Philadelphia: The Franklin Institute, 1983).*

1. Example of a visual-test item.

Students are to pick the picture that best answers this question: "Which ramp makes it easiest to raise the weight?"

(Students were also given a choice of indicating it would be the same for all three situations pictured.)

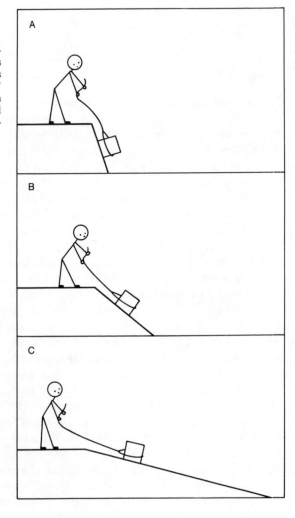

2. Example of a verbal test item.

> It is easiest to pull a weight up a ramp if the ramp is —
>> A. Very steep
>> B. Sort of steep
>> C. Hardly steep at all
>> D. The steepness has nothing to do with it.

3. Example of a performance test item.

> "This smurf has to move this weight to the top of the platform. He is too little to do the job without some help. Show me how the smurf could use one of these (inclined planes) to make the job easier."

> *Child is given a smurf figure and, in this example, miniature inclined planes of varied slopes. A miniature platform and weight are also part of the materials. Children are observed manipulating the materials, and their responses are scored in terms of how well they reflect understanding of information provided in the exhibit.*

> After the first basic activity to test the child's understanding of inclined planes, follow-up questions can seek evidence of more detailed learning:

> "Which one (inclined plane) would make it easiest to lift the weight to the platform?" *(Observer checks children's choice)*

>> ☐ Longest
>> ☐ Medium
>> ☐ Shortest

> "Why did you choose that one?" "What is this (inclined plane) called when it is used like this?"

4. Example of affective-learning test item. "Which face below describes how you feel about the exhibit?" (Circle one letter.)

A	B	C	D	E
"I love it!"	"I like it."	"I don't like it or dislike it."	"I dislike it."	"I hate it!"

the potential of an exhibit visit includes opportunity to interact with the content and combine skill and cognitive learning.

More than five hundred fifth- and sixth-grade students were sampled in the Franklin study, and teachers were surveyed about their expectations for classroom visits to the museum. Results indicated that science education was a major reason for bringing groups to the museum; and, in general, teacher expectations were being met. This study provided summative evaluation of both student learning and teacher reaction.

Evaluation results from the second study described by Borun and her colleagues were less informative, due, in this writer's judgment, to inadequate definition of learning criteria and methodology. The second study sampled more than five hundred sixth- and seventh-graders visiting the Museum of Science in Boston. Verbal, visual recognition and performance tests assessed learning in four different situations, similar to the Franklin study:

1. A *control* pretest group, tested before they saw an exhibit.
2. An *exhibit* group that visited the exhibit and then were tested.
3. A *lesson* group presented with a talk and then tested.
4. A group that received both an *exhibit visit* and *a talk* before being tested.

Criteria for demonstrating learning and tests used to determine the extent of it were much more open-ended in the Boston study than had been true for that of the Franklin Museum. While the idea of collecting more open-ended and student-suggested learning criteria was innovative, this writer should have liked to see some different approaches to the Boston study. First, it is important not to bias a study by selecting measurement tools that are thought to be most compatible with criteria selected and ignore other assessment methods. Staff at the Boston museum set as learning criteria perceptions and images and the ability to make connections and predictions, rather than the learning of facts and concepts of science. Because of the criteria chosen, more open-ended test questions were used. Results were much less clear in the Boston evaluation, and this writer should have liked to see items based on specific content in logical sequence used also. Contrary to what some may think, such test items (like those shown in fig. 7.6) can measure conceptual or integrative criteria, if they are well planned. They do require, however, making learning criteria fairly clear. A good stratagem, mentioned earlier, is to use open-ended questions to get global reactions and unique or spontaneous responses and items based on specific content to measure more concretely defined criteria.

Second, the Boston study would have benefited from more clearly defined schemata-based learning criteria. That is, staff people may have left criteria too vague to make assessment effective. Pilot-testing with a few students in the exhibit could suggest more detailed criteria. Using interviews in the pilot tests while viewing the exhibit with children can provide a way for hearing them talk about what they are learning as they visually explore objects and read labels. Analyzing the content of these interviews can suggest schemata or connected kinds of learning, as well as facts and specific concepts being acquired. In addition, the language used by the pilot-tested children could suggest formats for effective questions with a larger sample.

Third, attitudes can provide an important measure of what children learn on a classroom visit to a museum. And the Boston study could have measured more global learning criteria with attitude questions. By their very nature, attitudes sample both affect or feelings and cognitions (understandings), and summative evaluation of school visits clearly suggests that both affective and cognitive learning may occur. As mentioned earlier, attitude assessment is not easy, and measuring attitude change is even more difficult to achieve successfully. A basic use of attitude assessment, however, would be to measure students' attitudes on a topic before and after a museum visit.

In one study of visits to a historic Memphis house, students were given tests of their attitudes toward local history, historical houses, and school-group visits, both before and after their tour.[22] A goal of the evaluation was to see whether the visit changed student responses to such questions as these:

1. The people who lived in Memphis in 1850 have nothing in common with me.

2. There is nothing in the past I can use.

3. When you see something that is very old, it has something special to say to you.

Students indicated their level of agreement or disagreement with each question, by checking multiple-choice possibilities: strongly agree; agree; undecided; disagree; strongly disagree. For this study, there was some significant change toward increased, positive understanding of history. One major value of visiting a museum or historic setting is that students gain increased awareness of history and historical artifacts as shown through the feelings and perceptions measured by attitude questions. Results from this study of students touring a historic house in Memphis suggested that attitudes toward history and historical buildings did change as a function of the school-group visit. Students appeared more open to learning from history and placed higher value on past events and older objects because of direct experience with a historical setting. Consistent with Minda Borun's findings at the Franklin Institute on the importance of positive emotions being associated with a science museum visit, a major gain from visiting a historic house can be increased awareness that such a place exists and that the past is of value.

Some caveats about attitude assessment are in order. Often, a changed attitude about an individual question (i.e., "there is nothing in the past that I can use") is small in absolute magnitude; but if changes occur with a number of questions, it is possible to document school-visit impact on the young visitors' feelings and cognitions. Also, individual items are not limited to their obvious interpretation or face validity, since the pattern of answers to a series of items (organized into a test scale) may be a more dependable indicator of both the content of attitudes and the question of whether change is taking place.[23]

It is also necessary to make sure that differences in the amount of information evident in answers to the preliminary test and the post-visit test are not due simply to taking a test. That is, attitude items may sensitize respondents to the topic being studied and influence their answers on the post-visit test. This testing influence could be confused with effects due to the visit itself. In the Memphis study mentioned above, a control group of children took both the pre- and post-attitude tests, but did not visit the historic house. To establish whether the visit itself was changing attitudes, more change should occur for the visiting students than for the control ones. This problem of documenting the source of attitude change can also be handled by collecting independent or different samples of students for pre-testing and post-testing. Another solution is to give post-tests only, but include both a control and visit sample. For educational evaluation, post-test-only comparisons are sometimes necessary, because taking any kind of pretest can introduce students to the material included in the lesson or visit being evaluated. The pretest itself becomes a learning experience, and it is hard to prevent this learning from occurring. A post-test-only research plan can deal with these problems.[24]

Summative evaluation of visit methods. When Judith Sobol wanted to test whether or not an improvisional school-visit method taught art to children better than a traditional group lecture, she surveyed samples of children exposed to each of the methods and compared the two groups.[25] This basic strategy of comparing different methods of presenting the school-group visit can be very effective at yielding information about which methods work best at accomplishing school-visit goals. The school visit provides an opportunity to use nontraditional teaching methods, and for Sobol, the improvisional lead visit meant involving children in emotionally expressive activity as a way of communicating art and its meaning. School tours can be conducted in many different ways, and effective evaluation of each method should include the following considerations:

1. Development of specific evaluation goals and objectives for the way the methods tested should produce different outcomes. For example, will one method produce greater factual learning, while another method enhances skill learning? How do different types of tours match the kinds of objects presented or the galleries visited? How do methods relate to different student-age levels?

2. Selection of groups (different methods of presenting the tour) to be tested and compared.

3. Decisions to pretest before the tour and follow up with the post-test afterward or use post-tests only, as suggested above.

4. Determination of some kind of control comparison with children who do not experience any of the methods should be used, or a decision about whether a traditional instructive lesson is the desired comparison.

5. Standardization of the tour conditions (i.e., content, objects, number of galleries to be visited and order in which they will be seen), so that the only differences between them is the method of tour presentation used.

6. Employment of interviews, observations, and/or tests to assess selected learning criteria such as affective (enjoyment), cognitive, or performance (skill) behaviors.

Testing for differences between school-visit methods can be done as part of a more general evaluation of student learning. Even if there turn out to be a few major differences between visit methods, the effort will help staff people determine what is being learned and how well the tours are working. Knowing how well things are working is always an important reason for undertaking summative evaluation.

Program Evaluation Checklist

1. Have the goals of the program been defined?	_____ Yes	_____ No
A. Are goals complex?	_____ Yes	_____ No
Are there subgoals?	_____ Yes	_____ No
Have specific program objectives been written or stated?	_____ Yes	_____ No

B. Have they been defined in terms of
expected audiences?   _____ Yes   _____ No

C. Is the size of the expected audience known?   _____ Yes   _____ No

D. Have goals been defined in terms of program
duration?   _____ Yes   _____ No

E. Has program scope been defined?   _____ Yes   _____ No

F. Is this program a new or innovative one that
should be pretested with formative evaluation?   _____ Yes   _____ No

2. Has a survey of existing audience for the program been
completed?   _____ Yes   _____ No

A. If yes, is the program reaching intended groups? _____ Yes   _____ No

B. If no, would a descriptive survey determine whether
goals are consistent with actual participants using
the program?   _____ Yes   _____ No

C. Is a marketing survey needed to estimate size and
composition of potential audiences?   _____ Yes   _____ No

3. Have goals and objectives been prepared for an
evaluation of the program?   _____ Yes   _____ No

A. Is summative evaluation of an existing program
needed?   _____ Yes   _____ No

B. Could formative evaluation of a new or renovated
program promote successful development of the
effort?   _____ Yes   _____ No

C. Do visitor learning objectives need to be written and
tested?   _____ Yes   _____ No

D. Is a one-time evaluation called for?   _____ Yes   _____ No

E. Is a continuing monitoring of program quality
needed?   _____ Yes   _____ No

NOTES

1. Carol H. Weiss, *Evaluation Research: Methods for Assessing Program Effectiveness* (Englewood Cliffs, N.J.: Prentice Hall, 1972), p. 4.

2. Weiss, *Evaluation Research*, chapter 1.

3. Thomas J. Peters and Robert H. Waterman, Jr., *In Search of Excellence: Lessons from America's Best-Run Companies* (New York: Harper and Row, 1982), pp. 167-168.

4. Jim Reiss, "Judging the Voice of Your Museum," *History News* 39 (November 1984): 12-17.

5. See D. Allen and K. Ryan, *Microteaching* (Reading: Addison-Wesley, 1969); Adrienne L. Horn, "A Comparative Study of Two Methods of Conducting Docent Tours in Art Museums," *Curator* 23 (June 1980): 105-117.

6. Carl R. Nold, "Co-op Docents," *History News* 39 (October 1984): 31-33.

7. Barbara G. Carson and Cary Carson, *Things Unspoken: Learning Social History from Artifacts* (in preparation).

8. See Ronald E. Dick, Erik Myklestad, and J. Alan Wagar, "Audience Attention as a Basis for Evaluating Interpretive Presentations," Research Paper PNW-198, U. S. Dept. of Agriculture, Forest Service (Portland, Oreg., 1975). For a perceptive discussion of the pros and cons of docent evaluation and a detailed method for observing the interaction between docents and visitors, see Mary P. Flanders and Ned A. Flanders, "Evaluating Docent Performance," *Curator* 19 (September 1976): 198-225.

9. Mary Ellen Munley, "Buyin' Freedom: An Experimental Live Interpretation Program," Research Report, National Museum of American History, Smithsonian Institution (Washington, D.C.: 1982).

10. D. G. Hayward and A. D. Jensen, "Enhancing a Sense of the Past: Perception of Visitors and Interpreters," *The Interpreter* 12 (February 1981): 4-12.

11. Dennis A. O'Toole, "Evaluating Interpretation: The Governor's Palace, Williamsburg," *Roundtable Reports* 9 (Winter 1984): 15-16.

12. M. B. Alt, "Improving Audio-Visual Presentations," *Curator* 22 (June 1979): 85-95. See also Janet Landay and R. Gary Bridge, "Video vs. Wall-Panel Display: An Experiment in Musuem Learning," *Curator* 25 (March 1982): 41-56.

13. See C. G. Screven, "Exhibit Evaluation: A Goal-Referenced Approach," *Curator* 19 (December 1976): 281-282.

14. Harris H. Shettel, "Results of Film Evaluation Pretest for Man in His Environment," Research Report, Washington, D.C.: American Institute for Research, 1975.

15. Daryl Koropp Fischer, "New Data from Old Masters," *Museum Studies Journal* 1 (Spring 1984): 36-50.

16. Mildred C. B. Porter, *Behavior of the Average Visitor in the Peabody Museum of Natural History*," New Series, No. 16 (Washington D.C.: American Association of Museums, 1938), pp. 16-27.

17. Ross J. Loomis, "Evaluation of a Visitor Gallery Guide," Research Report no. 2 (Denver, Colo.: Denver Art Museum, 1982). Instead of a pamphlet, written guidance can be in the form of programmed learning cards prepared for specific exhibits, as evaluated by Richard J. DeWaard, Nancy Jagmin, Stephen A. Maisto, and Patricia A. McNamara, "Effects of Using Programmed Cards on Learning in a Museum Environment," *Journal of Educational Research* 67:10 (1974).

18. C. G. Screven, "Exhibitions and Information Centers: Some Principles and Approaches," *Curator* 29 (June 1986): 109-137.

19. C. G. Screven, "The Effectiveness of Guidance Devices on Visitor Learning," *Curator* 18 (September 1975): 219-243.

20. Ross J. Loomis, "Teacher and Student Reactions to a Pilot Program of Art Cart Demonstrations," Research Report no. 1, Denver, Colo., Denver Art Museum, 1982. Observation could also be used to evaluate children's reactions and the way they spend their time during a visit, as illustrated in R. W. Carlisle, "What Do Children Do at a Science Center?" *Curator* 28 (January 1985): 27-33. An older study that serves as a good example of combining observation and survey methods to study children's use of exhibits is Joyce A. M. Brooks and Philip E. Vernon, "A Study of Children's Interests and Comprehension at a Science Museum," *British Journal of Psychology* 47 (1956): 175-182.

21. Minda Borun, Barbara K. Flexer, Alice F. Casey, and Lynn R. Baum, *Planets and Pulleys: Studies of Class Visits to Science Museums* (Philadelphia: The Franklin Institute, 1983). Two other interesting examples of evaluating learning on school field trips are: John D. Balling and John H. Falk, "A Perspective on Field Trips: Environmental Effects on Learning," *Curator* 23 (April 1980): 229-240; and Jeffry Gottfreid, "Do Children Learn on School Field Trips?" *Curator* 23 (September 1980): 165-174.

22. Personal correspondence with Roger Van Cleef, Curator of Education, Pink Palace Museum, Memphis, Tennessee.

23. For a brief introduction to attitude measurement, see Robert Sommer and Barbara B. Sommer, *A Practical Guide to Behavioral Research* (New York: Oxford, 1980), pp. 135-153. A more advanced discussion of attitude scales is in *Research Methods in Social Relations*, 3rd ed., by Claire Selltiz, Lawrence S. Wrightsman, and Stewart W. Cook (New York: Holt, Rinehart and Winston, 1976), pp. 412-431.

24. Donald T. Campbell and Julian C. Stanley, *Experimental and Quasi-Experimental Designs for Research* (Chicago: Rand McNally, 1963), pp. 25-26.

25. Judith Ellen Sobol, "A Comparison of Two Methods for Creating Empathy with Art in Grade-School Children" (Thesis, George Washington University, June 1970). Early research on comparing different methods for conducting school trips still provides good working models for evaluation. For example, see Arthur W. Melton, Nita Goldberg Feldman, and Charles W. Mason, *Experimental Studies of the Education of Children in a Museum of Science*, no. 15, New Series (Washington, D.C.: American Association of Museums, 1936), pp. 9-23.

Bibliography

Abbey, David S., and Duncan F. Cameron. *The Museum Visitor: I. Survey Design.* Report no. 1, Information Services of the Royal Ontario Museum. Toronto: The Royal Ontario Museum, 1959.

———. *The Museum Visitor: III. Supplementary Studies.* Report no. 3, Information Services of the Royal Ontario Museum. Toronto: The Royal Ontario Museum, 1961.

Adams, G. Donald. *Museum Public Relations.* Nashville: American Association for State and Local History, 1983.

Ajzen, Icek, and Martin Fishbein. *Understanding Attitudes and Predicting Social Behavior.* Englewood Cliffs, N.J.: Prentice-Hall, 1980.

Alexander, Edward P. *Museums in Motion.* Nashville: American Association for State and Local History, 1979.

Alfano, Sam S., and Arthur W. Magill, eds. *Vandalism and Outdoor Recreation: Symposium Proceedings.* U.S. Department of Agriculture, Forest Service. General Technical Report no. PSW-1. Washington, D.C.: U.S. Department of Agriculture, 1976.

Allen, D., and K. Ryan. *Microteaching.* Reading, Pa.: Addison-Wesley, 1969.

Alt, M. B. "Evaluating Didactic Exhibits: A Critical Look." *Curator* 20:3 (1977): 241-258.

———. "Improving Audio-Visual Presentations." *Curator* 22:2 (1979): 85-95.

Alt, M. B., and K. M. Shaw. "Characteristics of Ideal Museum Exhibits." *British Journal of Psychology* 75 (1984): 25-36.

Andreasen, A. R., and R. W. Belk. "Predictors of Attendance at the Performing Arts." *Journal of Consumer Research* 1 (1980): 119.

Andrews, Kathryne, and Caroli Asia. "Teenagers' Attitudes about Art Museums." *Curator* 23:3 (1979): 224-232.

Annis, Sheldon. 'The Museum as Symbolic Experience." Unpublished paper. University of Chicago, Department of Geography. Chicago: University of Chicago, 1980.

Avery, David D., and Henry A. Cross. *Experimental Methodology in Psychology.* Monterey, Calif.: Brooks-Cole, 1978. Pages 180-183.

Babbie, E. R. *Survey Research Methods.* Belmont, Calif.: Wadsworth, 1973.

Baer, Ilse. *Zur Offentlichkeitsarbiet Der Museum.* Berlin: Verlag, 1978.

Balling, John D., and John H. Falk. "A Perspective on Field Trips: Environmental Effects on Learning." *Curator* 23:4 (1980): 229-240.

Barker, R. G. *The Stream of Behavior.* New York: Appleton-Century Crofts, 1963.

————. "Explorations in Ecological Psychology." *American Psychologist* 20 (1965): 1-14.

Barnard, William A., Ross J. Loomis, and Henry A. Cross. "Assessment of Visual Recall and Recognition Learning in a Museum Environment." *Bulletin of the Psychonomic Society* 16 (1980): 311-313.

Barton, Kenneth. "Recording Attendances at Portsmouth City Museums: The Method and Its Effect." *Museums Journal* 73:3 (1974): 167-168.

Bateman, H. M. "The Boy Who Breathed on the Glass in the British Museum." *Punch* (1916); *Curator* 11 (1959): 259-268.

Bechtel, Robert B. "Human Movement and Architecture." *Trans-Action* 4:6 (1967): 53-56.

————. "Hodometer Research in Museums." *Museum News* 45:3 (1967): 23-26.

————. "The Semantic Differential and Other Paper-and-Pencil Tests." In *Behavioral Research Methods in Environmental Design*, edited by William Michelson. Stroudsburg, Pa.: Hutchinson Ross, 1975.

Bertram, Susan. "Hard Times." *Museum News* 61:3 (1983): 20-25.

Bloom, Benjamin, et al. *Taxonomy of Educational Objectives: Handbook I. Cognitive Domain*. New York: David McKay, 1956.

Bloomberg, Marguerite. *An Experiment in Museum Instruction*. Publications of the American Association of Museums, New Series, no. 8. Washington, D.C.: American Association of Museums, 1929.

Boll, Heinrich. *Absent without Leave*. New York: McGraw-Hill, 1965.

Borun, Minda. *Measuring the Immeasurable: A Pilot Study of Museum Effectiveness*. Philadelphia, Pa.: The Franklin Institute Science Museum, 1977.

————. *Select-A-Label: A Model Computer-Based Interpretive System for Science Museums*. Philadelphia, Pa.: The Franklin Institute Science Museum, 1979.

Borun, Minda, Barbara K. Flexer, Alice F. Casey, and Lynn R. Baum. *Planets and Pulleys: Studies of Class Visits to Science Museums*. Philadelphia, Pa.: The Franklin Institute, 1983.

Borun, Minda, and Maryanne Miller. *What's in a Name?* Philadelphia, Pa.: The Franklin Institute Science Museum, 1980.

————. "To Label or Not to Label?" *Museum News* 58:4 (1980): 64-67.

Bower, Robert T., and Laure Sharp. "The Japanese Art Exhibit: A Study of Its Impact in Three Cities." Washington, D.C.: The American University, Bureau of Social Science Research, 1955.

Bower, Gordon H. "Mood and Memory." *American Psychologist* 36:2 (1981): 129-148.

Brehm, S. S., and J. W. Brehm. *Psychological Reactance: A Theory of Freedom and Control*. New York: Academic Press, 1981.

Bridge, Gary R. "Cultural Vouchers." *Museum News* 54:3 (1976): 20-64.

Brooks, Joyce A. M., and Philip E. Vernon. "A Study of Children's Interests and Comprehension at a Science Museum." *British Journal of Psychology* 47 (1956): 175-182.

Brown, Walter S. "The Economic Impact of the Public Visitor to the Seattle Art Museum's Tutankhamen Exhibit." Unpublished report. Seattle, Wash.: Seattle Art Museum, 1979.

———. "Member Survey of Seattle Art Museum, Part I." Unpublished report. Seattle, Wash.: Seattle Art Museum, 1979.

———. "The Public Visitor to the Seattle Art Museum's Tutankhamen Exhibition: Demographics and Behavioral Studies." Unpublished report. Seattle, Wash.: Seattle Art Museum, 1979.

Buhler, Leslie. "The Business of Membership." *Museum News* 59:3 (1980): 42-49.

Burnett, Leo. "The Art Institute Survey, Part 1." Leo Burnett Research Department, 1975.

Calver, Homer N., Mayhew Derryberry, and Ivan H. Mensh. "Use of Ratings in the Evaluation of Exhibits." *American Journal of Public Health* 33 (1943): 709-714.

Cameron, Duncan F., and David S. Abbey. "The Museum Visitor: II. Survey Results." Report no. 2, Information Services of the Royal Ontario Museum. Toronto: The Royal Ontario Museum, 1960.

———. "Toward Meaningful Attendance Statistics." *Bulletin of the Canadian Museums Association* 12 (1960): 6-10.

———. "Visits Versus Visitors: An Analysis." *Museum News* 39:3 (1960): 34-35.

———. "Museum Audience Research: The Effect of an Admission Fee." *Museum News* 41:11 (1962): 25-28.

Campbell, Donald T. "From Description to Experimentation: Interpreting Trends as Quasi-Experiments." In *Problems in Measuring Change,* edited by Chester W. Harris. Madison, Wis.: University of Wisconsin Press, 1967.

———. "Reforms as Experiments." *American Psychologist* 24:4 (1969): 409-429.

Campbell, Donald T., and Julian C. Stanley. *Experimental and Quasi-Experimental Designs for Research.* Chicago: Rand McNally, 1963.

Carlisle, R. W. "What Do Children Do at a Science Center?" *Curator* 28:1 (1985): 27-33.

Carson, Barbara G., and Cary Carson. "Things Unspoken: Learning Social History from Artifacts." (In preparation.)

Chase, R. A. "Museums as Learning Environments." *Museum News* 54:1 (1975): 37-43.

Chein, I. "An Introduction to Sampling." In *Research Methods in Social Relations,* edited by C. Selltiz, L. S. Wrightsman, and S. W. Cook. New York: Wiley, 1976.

Christensen, Erwin O. "Evening Hours for Museums: A Preliminary Statistical Survey." *Museum News* 43:11 (1964): 40-41.

Cohen, Marilyn S. "A Yale University Art Gallery Survey." Unpublished report. New Haven, Conn.: Yale University Department of Art History, 1972.

———. "The State of the Art of Museum Visitor Orientation: A Survey of Selected Institutions." Unpublished paper. Washington, D.C.: Smithsonian Institution, Office of Museum Programs, 1974.

Cohen, Marilyn S., Gary H. Winkel, Richard Olsen, and Fred Wheeler. "Orientation in a Museum: An Experimental Study." *Curator* 20:2 (1977): 85-97.

Cochran, W. G. *Sampling Techniques.* 2nd ed. New York: Wiley, 1963.

Coleman, Laurence Vail. *Historic House Museums.* Washington, D.C.: American Association of Museums, 1933.

———. *The Museum in America: A Critical Study.* Washington, D.C.: American Association of Museums, 1939.

Colorado Museum of Natural History. *First Annual Report.* Denver, Colo.: Colorado Museum of Natural History, 1901. Page 3.

Colorado State University. "Marketing the Arts in Fort Collins." Unpublished report. Fort Collins, Colo.: Colorado State University, College of Business, 1978.

Cook, S. W. "Motives in a Conceptual Analysis of Attitude-Related Behavior." In *Nebraska Symposium on Motivation, 1969,* edited by W. J. Arnold and D. Levine. Lincoln, Nebr.: University of Nebraska Press, 1970.

Cooley, William, and Terrence Piper. "Study of the West African Art Exhibit of the Milwaukee Public Museum and Its Visitors." In *The Museum Visitor,* edited by Stephan F. de Borhegyi and Irene A. Hanson. Milwaukee: Milwaukee Public Museum, 1968.

Cramer, Ted. "Marketing the Museum." *Museum News* 57:3 (1979): 36-38.

Cummings, Carlos E. *East is East and West is West: Some Observations on the World's Fairs of 1939, by One Whose Main Interest Is in Museums.* Buffalo, N.Y.: Buffalo Museum of Science, 1940.

Dailey, Daniel, and Roger Mandle. "Welcome to the Museum." *Museum News* 53:3 (1974): 45-49.

Dale, E., and G. Eicholz. *Children's Knowledge of Words.* Project 153, Ohio State University, Bureau of Education Research and Service. Columbus, Ohio: Ohio State University, 1960.

Dana, John Cotton. *The Gloom of the Museum.* Woodstock, Vt.: Elm Tree Press, 1917.

Daniel, T. C., E. H. Zube, and B. L. Driver. *Assessing Amenity Resource Values.* Washington, D.C.: U.S. Department of Agriculture, 1967. Pages 2-3, 27-32, 32-34.

David, G., and V. Ayers. "Photographic Recording of Environmental Behavior." In *Behavioral Research Methods in Environmental Design,* edited by W. Michaelson, pp. 235-279. Stroudsburg, Pa.: Dowden, Hutchinson and Ross, 1975.

de Borhegyi, Stephan F. "Space Problems and Solutions." *Museum News* 42:11 (1965): 18-22.

———. "Test Your Knowledge." *Midwest Museums Quarterly* 25 (1965): 10.

———. "Testing Audience Reaction to Museum Exhibits." *Curator* 8:1 (1965): 86-93.

de Borhegyi, Stephan F., and Irene A. Hanson. "Chronological Bibliography of Museum Visitor Surveys." *Museum News* 42:2 (1964): 39-41.

———. *The Museum Visitor: Selected Essays and Surveys of Visitor Reaction to Exhibits in the Milwaukee Public Museum.* Milwaukee, Wis.: Milwaukee Public Museum, 1968.

Denver Museum of Natural History. "1974 Survey of Visitors to the Denver Museum of Natural History." Unpublished report. Denver, Colo.: National Association of the Denver Museum of Natural History, 1974.

Denver Research Services. *Images of Denver's Civic and Cultural Institutions.* Denver, Colo.: Denver Research Services, 1982.

DeWaard, Richard J., Nancy Jagmin, Stephen A. Maistro, and Patricia A.

McNamara. "Effects of Using Programmed Cards on Learning in a Museum Environment." *Journal of Educational Research* 67:10 (1974).

Dick, Ronald E., Erik Myklestad, and J. Alan Wagar. "Audience Attention as a Basis for Evaluating Interpretive Presentations." Research Paper PNW-198, U.S. Department of Agriculture, Forest Service. Portland, Oreg.: U.S. Department of Agriculture, Forest Service, 1975.

Dillman, Don A. *Mail and Telephone Surveys: The Total Design Method.* New York: Wiley, 1978.

DiMaggio, Paul, Michael Useem, and Paula Brown. "Audience Studies of the Performing Arts and Museums: A Critical Review." Report no. 9, Research Division, the National Endowment for the Arts. Washington, D.C.: National Endowment for the Arts, 1978.

Dixon, Brian, A. E. Courtney, and R. H. Bailey. *The Museum and the Canadian Public.* Toronto: Culturcan Publications, 1974.

Downs, Roger. "Mazes, Minds, and Maps." In *Sign Systems for Libraries*, edited by Dorothy Pollet and Peter C. Haskell. New York: R. R. Bowker Co., 1979.

Downs, R. M., and D. Stea. "Maps in Minds: Reflections on Cognitive Mapping." New York: Harper and Row, 1977.

Driver, B. L., and P. J. Brown. "A Social-Psychological Definition of Recreation Demand, with Implications for Recreation Resource Planning." In *Assessing Demand for Outdoor Recreation*, pp. 63-68. Washington, D.C.: National Academy of Science, 1975.

Driver, B. L., Donald Rosenthal, and Lynn Johnson. "A Suggested Research Approach for Quantifying the Psychological Benefits of Air Visibility." In *Proceedings of the Workshop in Visibility Values, Fort Collins, Colorado, January 18-February 1.* General Technical Report no. WO-18, U.S. Department of Agriculture, edited by Douglas Fox, Ross J. Loomis, and Thomas C. Green. Washington, D.C.: U.S. Department of Agriculture, Forest Service, 1979.

Droba, D. D. "Effect of Printed Information on Memory for Pictures." *Museum News* 7:9 (1929): 6-8.

Eason, Laurie P., and Marcia Linn. "Evaluation of the Effectiveness of Participatory Exhibits." *Curator* 19:1 (1976): 45-62.

Echelberger, Hubert E., Donna Gilroy, and George Moeller. *1961-1982 Recreation Research Publications.* Washington, D.C.: U.S. Department of Agriculture, Forest Service, 1983.

Ekman, P., and W. V. Freisen. *Unmasking the Face: A Guide to Recognizing Emotions from Facial Cues.* Englewood Cliffs, N.J.: Prentice-Hall, 1975.

Elliott, Pamala, and Ross J. Loomis. *Studies of Visitor Behavior in Museums and Exhibitions: An Annotated Bibliography Primarily in the English Language.* Washington, D.C.: Office of Museum Programs, Smithsonian Institution, 1975.

Eisenbeis, Manfred. "Elements for a Sociology of Museums." *Museum* 24:2 (1972): 110-119.

Evans, Gary W. "Environmental Cognition." *Psychological Bulletin* 88 (1980): 259-287.

Fazzini, Dan. "The Museum as a Learning Environment: A Self-Motivating, Recycling, Learning System for the Museum Visitor." Ph.D. dissertation, University of Wisconsin-Milwaukee, 1972.

Fechner, G. T. *Vorschule der Aesthetic.* Leipzig: Brietkopf and Hartel, 1897.

Ferguson, Ellen L., and James D. Mason. "Human Subject Rights and Museum Research." *Museum News* 58:3 (1980): 44-47.

Fischer, Daryl Koropp. "New Data from Old Masters." *Museum Studies Journal* 1:3 (Spring 1984): 36-50.

Fisher, Jeffrey D., and R. M. Baron. "An Equity-Based Model of Vandalism." *Population and Environment* 5:3 (1982): 182-200.

Fisher, Jeffrey D., Paul A. Bell, and Andrew Baum. *Environmental Psychology.* 2nd ed. New York: Holt, Rinehart and Winston, 1984.

Flanders, Mary P., and Ned A. Flanders. "Evaluating Docent Performance." *Curator* 19:3 (1976): 198-225.

Forgan, H. W., and C. T. Mangrum. *Teaching Content Area Reading Skills: A Modular Preservice and Inservice Program.* Columbus, Ohio: Charles E. Merrell, 1976.

Friedman, Alan, Laurie P. Eason, and G. I. Sneider. "Star Games: A Participatory Astronomy Exhibit." *Planetarian* 8:3 (1979).

Fronville, Claire L. "Marketing For Museums: For-Profit Techniques in the Non-Profit World." *Curator* 28:3 (1985): 169-182.

Fry, Edward, "A Readability Formula that Saves Time." *Journal of Reading* 11 (1968): 513-516.

Gardner, Toni. "Learning from Listening: Museums Improve Their Effectiveness through Visitor Studies." *Museum News* 64:3 (1986):40-44.

Gasser, J. "Why Cities Need Museums." *Museum News* 57 (1979):26-28.

George, G. "Professionals Examine Future Directions for Texas Museums." *History News* 38:12 (1983): 14-17.

Gibson, J. J., and E. J. Gibson. "Perceptual Learning: Differentiation or Enrichment?" *Psychological Review* 62 (1955): 32-41.

Gibson, Katherine. "An Experiment in Measuring Results of Fifth-Grade Class Visits to an Art Museum." *School and Society* 21:5 (1925): 658-662.

Gilman, Benjamin I. "Museum Fatigue." *The Scientific Monthly* 12 (1916): 62-74.

Glass, G. V. 'The Growth of Evaluation Methodology." Research Paper no. 17, University of Colorado, Laboratory of Educational Research. Boulder, Colo.: University of Colorado, 1969.

Glass, Gene V., Victor L. Willson, and John M. Gottman. *Design and Analysis of Time-Series Experiments.* Boulder, Colo.: University of Colorado Press, 1975.

Goldberg, Nita. "Experiments in Museum Teaching." *Museum News* 10:2 (1933): 6-8.

Goldberg, V. "Business Buys into Arts." *Saturday Review,* September 1979, pp. 21-27.

Gottfreid, Jeffry. "Do Children Learn on School Field Trips?" *Curator* 23:3 (1980): 165-174.

Graburn, Nelson H. H. "The Museum and the Visitor Experience." In *The Visitor and the Museum,* edited by Linda Draper. Berkeley, Calif.: The Lowie Museum of Anthropology, 1977.

Grana, Cesar. "The Private Lives of Public Museums." *Trans-Action* 4:5 (1967): 20-25.

Greeno, J. G. "Psychology of Learning, 1960-1980: One Participant's Observation." *American Psychologist* 35:8 (1980): 713-728.

Griggs, Steven A. "Formative Evaluation of Exhibits at the British Museum (Natural History)." *Curator* 24:3 (1981): 189-201.

———. "Orienting Visitors within a Thematic Display." *International Journal of Museum Management and Curatorship* 2 (1983): 119-134.

Griggs, Steven A., and K. Hays-Jackson. "Visitors' Perceptions of Cultural Institutions." *Museums Journal* 2:3 (1983): 121-125.

Griggs, Steven A., and Jane Manning. "The Predictive Validity of Formative Evaluation of Exhibits." *Museum Studies Journal* 1:2 (1983): 31-41.

Harris, C. W., ed. *Problems in Measuring Change.* Madison, Wis.: University of Wisconsin Press, 1967.

Havelock, R. *Planning for Innovation.* Ann Arbor, Mich.: University of Michigan, Institute for Social Research, 1971.

Hayes, Martha G. "Demise of an Institution." *History News* 38:4 (1983): 14-16.

Hayward, D. Geoffrey. "The Quadrangle Research Notes: Springfield Library and Museums Association." Unpublished research report. Northampton, Mass.: People, Places, and Design Research, 1982.

Hayward, D. Geoffrey, and Mary L. Bryon-Miller. "Evaluating the Effectiveness of Orientation Experiences at an Outdoor History Museum." Unpublished paper, n.d.

Hayward, D. Geoffrey, and A. D. Jensen. "Enhancing a Sense of the Past: Perception of Visitors and Interpreters." *The Interpreter* 12:2 (1981): 4-12.

Heft, H. "The Role of Environmental Features in Route-Learning: Two Exploratory Studies of Wayfinding." *Environmental Psychology and Nonverbal Behavior* 3 (1979): 172-185.

Henderson, H. *Creating Alternative Futures.* New York: Berkley Publishing Corp., 1978.

Hicks, Ellen Cochran. "An Artful Science: A Conversation about Exhibit Evaluation." *Museum News* 64:3 (1986): 32-39.

Higgenbotham, James B., and Keith K. Cox, eds. *Focus Group Interviews: A Reader.* Chicago: American Marketing Association, 1979.

Hood, Marilyn G. "Adult Attitudes toward Leisure Choice in Relation to Museum Participation." Ph.D. dissertation, University of Toledo, 1981.

———. "Staying Away." *Museum News* 61:4 (1983): 50-57.

———. "Getting Started in Audience Research." *Museum News* 64:3 (1986): 25-31.

Horn, Adrienne L. "A Comparative Study of Two Methods of Conducting Docent Tours in Arts Museums." *Curator* 23:2 (1980): 105-117.

Hudson, K. *A Social History of Museums.* Atlantic Highlands, N.J.: Humanities Press, 1975. Pages 100-122.

Huszar, Paul C., and David W. Seckler. "Effects of Pricing a 'Free' Good: A Study of the Use of Admission Fees at the California Academy of Sciences." *Land Economics* (1974): 364-373.

Hutchinson, Charles L. "The Democracy of Art." *American Magazine of Art* 7:8 (1916).

Jacknis, Ira. "Franz Boas and Exhibits." In *Objects and Others: Essays on Museums and Material Culture*, vol. 3, edited by George W. Stocking. Madison, Wis.: University of Wisconsin Press, 1985.

Johnson, David. "Museum Attendance in the New York Metropolitan Region." *Curator* 12:5 (1969): 201-230.

Kaplan, Steven. "The Challenge of Environmental Psychology: A Proposal for a New Functionalism." *American Psychologist* 27:2 (1972): 140-143.

Kiphart, M., Ross J. Loomis, and P. Williams. "Testing for Museum Literacy." Unpublished paper. Denver, Colorado, n.d.

Klare, George R. "Assessing Readability." *Reading Research Quarterly* 10:1 (1974-1975): 62-102.

Klein, Hans-Joachim. "Barrieren Des Zugans zu Offentlichen Kulturellen Einrichtungen." Unpublished report. Karlsruhe, W. Germany, 1978.

————. "Analyse von Besucherstruktern an ausgewahlten Museen in der Bundesrepublik Deutschland und in Berlin (West)." Heft 9. Berlin: Institute for Museumskunde, 1984.

————. "Das Auto Als Technisches Kulterprodukt." Unpublished report. Karlsruhe, W. Germany, 1985.

Klein, Hans-Joachim, and Monika Bachmayer. *Museum und Offentlichkeit: Fakten und Daten-Motive und Barrieren*. Berlin: Verlag, 1981.

Kotler, Philip. *Marketing for Nonprofit Organizations*. 2nd ed. Englewood Cliffs, N.J.: Prentice-Hall, 1982.

Kresigberg, L. "The Museum Boom: America's Hunger for Culture." *Family Weekly*, 25 January 1981, pp. 4-7.

Krumpe, Edwin E. "Redistributing Backcountry Use by a Behaviorally Based Communications Device." Ph.D. dissertation, Colorado State University, 1979.

Lakota, Robert A. "Good Exhibits on Purpose: Technique to Improve Exhibit Effectiveness." In *Communications with the Museum Visitor: Guidelines for Planning*. Toronto: The Royal Ontario Museum, 1976.

Landay, Janet, and R. Gary Bridge. "Video vs. Wall-Panel Display: An Experiment in Museum Learning." *Curator* 25:1 (1982): 41-56.

Lehmbruck, M. "Psychology: Perception and Behavior." *Museum* 26:3 (1974): 191-203.

Leventhal, Howard, and Patricia Niles. "A Field Experiment on Fear Arousal with Data on the Validity of Questionnaire Measures." *Journal of Personality* 32 (1964): 459-479.

Levine, Marvin. "You-Are-Here Maps: Psychological Considerations." *Environment and Behavior* 14:2 (1982): 221-237.

Loomis, Ross J. "Evaluation of a Visitor Gallery Guide." Research Report no. 2, Denver Art Museum. Denver, Colo.: Denver Art Museum, 1982.

————. "Museums and Psychology: The Principle of Allometry and Museum Visitor Research." *The Museologist* 129 (1973): 17-23.

————. "Please! Not Another Visitor Survey!" *Museum News* 52:2 (1973): 21-26.

————. "The Visitor and the Collection: The Immediate Visual Experience of the Museum." *Mountain-Plains Museum Conference Proceedings* 7 (1976): 1-8.

————. "Getting to Know the Audience." *Longwood Program Seminars* 8: 8-11. Newark, Del.: Longwood Program Seminars, 1977.

————. "A Preliminary Study of the Learning Environment of the Museum of Atomic Energy." Report no. 5, American Museum of Atomic Energy. Oak Ridge, Tenn.: American Museum of Atomic Energy, 1977.

————. "Summer 1976 Survey of Visitors to the American Museum of Atomic Energy." Report no. 2, American Museum of Atomic Energy. Oak Ridge, Tenn.: American Museum of Atomic Energy, 1977.

————. "Visitor Floor Count in Selected Areas." Summer Working Report no. 6, American Museum of Atomic Energy. Oak Ridge, Tenn.: American Museum of Atomic Energy, 1977.

————. "The Visitor and the Object: Some Formative Evaluation Considerations for Planning a Museum Exhibit." Unpublished report. Fort Collins, Colorado, 1981.

————. "Teacher and Student Reactions to a Pilot Program of Art Cart Demonstrations." Research Report no. 1, Denver Art Museum. Denver, Colo.: Denver Art Museum, 1982.

————. *Four Evaluation Suggestions to Improve the Effectiveness of Museum Labels.* Technical Leaflet no. 4, Texas Historical Commission. Austin, Tex.: Texas Historical Commission, 1983.

Loomis, Ross J., and Carl F. Hummel. "Observations and Recommendations on Visitor Utilization Problems and Potentials of the Denver Museum of Natural History." Working Paper no. 1, Denver Museum of Natural History. Denver, Colo.: Denver Museum of Natural History, 1975.

Loomis, Ross J., Carl F. Hummel, and M. N. Hartman. "Archival Documentation of School Tour Utilization for a Natural History Museum." Working Paper no. 2, Denver Museum of Natural History. Denver, Colo.: Denver Museum of Natural History, 1981.

Loomis, Ross J., and M. B. Parsons. "Orientation Needs and the Library Setting." In *Sign Systems for Libraries*, edited by D. Pollet and P. Haskell, pp. 3-16. New York: R. R. Bowker Co., 1979.

Lovelock, C.H., and C. B. Weinberg. *Marketing for Public and Nonprofit Managers.* New York: John Wiley and Sons, 1984.

Madden, Michael. "Marketing Survey Spin-off: Library User/Nonuser Life Styles." *American Libraries* (1979): 78-81.

Mason, John T. *The Colorado Museum of Natural History: First Annual Report.* Denver, Colo.: Colorado Museum of Natural History, 1901.

Mason, Tim. "The Visitors to Manchester Museum: A Questionnaire Survey." *Museums Journal* 73 (1974): 153-157.

McCormick, Ernst J., and Mark S. Sanders. *Human Factors in Engineering and Design.* 5th ed. New York: McGraw-Hill, 1982.

McLaughlin, G. H. "Smog Grading: A New Reading Formula." *Journal of Reading* 12 (1969): 637-646.

Melton, Arthur W. "Some Behavioral Characteristics of Museum Visitors." *Psychological Bulletin* 30 (1933): 720-721.

————. "Studies of Installation at the Pennsylvania Museum of Art." *Museum News* 10:1 (1933): 8.

————. "Problems of Installation in Museums of Art." Publications of the American Association of Museums, New Series, no. 14. Washington, D.C., 1935.

———. "Distribution of Attention in Galleries in a Museum of Science and Industry." *Museum News* 14:6 (1936): 5-8.

Melton, Arthur W., Nita Goldberg, and Charles W. Mason. "Experimental Studies of the Education of Children in a Museum of Science." Publications of the American Association of Museums, New Series, no 15. Washington, D.C., 1936.

Mendenhall, William. *Introduction to Statistics*. Belmont, Calif.: Wadsworth, 1964.

Mendenhall, William, L. Ott, and R. L. Sheaffer. *Elementary Survey Sampling*. Belmont, Calif.: Wadsworth, 1971.

Miles, R. S., and M. B. Alt. "British Museum (Natural History): A New Approach to the Visiting Public." *Museums Journal* 78:3 (1979): 158-162.

Miles, R. S., M. B. Alt, D. C. Gosling, B. N. Lewis, and A. F. Tout. *The Design of Educational Exhibits*. London: Allen and Unwin, 1982.

Mitchell, Arnold. *The Nine American Lifestyles*. New York: Warner Books, 1983.

———. *The Professional Performing Arts: Attending Patterns, Preferences, and Motives*. Madison, Wis.: Association of College, University, and Community Arts Administrators, 1984.

Mittler, Elliot, and Walter Wallner. "A Membership Study of the Los Angeles County Museum." Unpublished report. Los Angeles, Calif.: UCLA Graduate School of Administration, 1967.

Mokwa, M. P., William M. Dawson, and E. Arthur Prieve, eds. *Marketing the Arts*. New York: Praeger, 1980.

Munley, Mary Ellen. "Buyin' Freedom: An Experimental Live Interpretation Program." Research Report, National Museum of American History, Smithsonian Institution. Washington, D.C.: National Museum of American History, Smithsonian Institution, 1982.

———. "Asking the Right Questions: Evaluation and the Museum Mission." *Museum News* 64:3 (1986): 18-23.

Murray, C. Hay. "How to Estimate a Museum's Value." *Museums Journal* 31 (March 1932): 527-531.

Museum News. "Pennsylvania Museum Classifies Its Visitors." *Museum News* 7:2 (1930): 7-8.

Nash, George. "Art Museums as Perceived by the Public." *Curator* 18:1 (1975): 55-67.

National Research Center for the Arts. *Arts and the People: A Survey of Public Attitudes and Participation in the Arts and Culture in New York State*. New York: Publishing Center for Cultural Resources, American Council for the Arts in Education, 1973.

Neal, Arminta. *Help! For the Small Museum*. Boulder, Colo.: Pruett Press, 1969.

———. *Exhibits for the Small Museum: A Handbook*. Nashville: American Association for State and Local History, 1976.

Newgren, Donald Andrew. "A Standardized Museum Survey: A Methodology for Museums to Gather Decision-Oriented Information." Ph.D. dissertation, Syracuse University, 1972.

Newman, Robert B. "I Wonder Who's Hearing It Now." *Museum News* 5:1 (1972): 20-22.

Newsom, Barbara Y., and Adele Z. Silver. *The Art Museum as Educator*. Berkeley, Calif.: University of California, 1978.

New York State Education Department. "The 1966 Audience of the New York State Museum: An Evaluation of the Museum's Visitors Program." Unpublished report. Albany, N.Y.: State Education Department, 1966.

Nichol, E. "The Development of Validated Museum Exhibits." Final Report, Project 5-0245, OEC 1-6-0502 45-1015, Bureau of Records, Department of Health, Education, and Welfare. Washington, D.C.: Department of Health, Education, and Welfare, 1969.

Nie, Norman H., et al. *Statistical Package for the Social Sciences*. 2nd ed. New York: McGraw-Hill, 1975.

Niehoff, Arthur. "Characteristics of the Audience Reaction in the Milwaukee Public Museum." *Midwest Museums Quarterly* 13 (1953): 19-24.

———. "Evening Hours for Museums." *The Museologist* 69 (1958): 2-5.

———. "Audience Reactions in the Milwaukee Public Museum: The Winter Visitor." In *The Museum Visitor: Selected Essays and Surveys of Visitor Reaction to Exhibits in the Milwaukee Public Museum*, edited by Stephan F. de Borhegyi and Irene A. Hanson, pp. 22-31. Milwaukee Public Museum Publications in Museology, no. 3. Milwaukee: Milwaukee Public Museum, 1968.

Nold, Carl R. "Co-op Docents." *History News* 39:10 (1984): 31-33.

O'Hare, Michael. "The Audience of the Museum of Fine Arts." *Curator* 17:2 (1974): 126-158.

———. "The Public's Use of Art: Visitor Behavior in an Art Museum." *Curator* 17:2 (1974): 309-320.

———. "Why Do People Go to Museums? The Effect of Prices and Hours on Museum Utilization." *Museum* 26:3 (1974): 134-146.

Olton, D. S. "Mazes, Maps, and Memory." *American Psychologist* 34:7 (1979): 583-596.

O'Toole, Dennis A. "Evaluating Interpretation: The Governor's Palace, Williamsburg, Pa." *Roundtable Reports* 12:2 (1984): 15-16.

Parr, Albert E. "Marketing the Message." *Curator* 12:2 (1969): 77-82.

———. "Museums in Our Milieu." *Mountain-Plains Museums Proceedings* 9:10 (1977): 1-10.

Parsons, Margaret Bouslough. "An Introduction to Museum Visitor Research." Master's thesis, Cooperstown Graduate Program, Oneonta, New York, 1975.

Pearson, P. David, and Rand Spiro. "The New Buzz Word in Reading is *Schema*." *Instructor* (1982): 46-48.

Peart, Bob. "Impact of Exhibit Type on Knowledge Gain, Attitudes, and Behavior." *Curator* 24:3 (1984): 220-237.

Peters, Thomas J., and Robert H. Waterman, Jr. *In Search of Excellence: Lessons from America's Best-Run Companies*. New York: Harper and Row, 1982.

Pollet, Dorothy. "You Can Get There from Here." *Wilson Library Bulletin* (1976): 456-462.

Porter, Mildred C. B. "Behavior of the Average Visitor in the Peabody Museum of Natural History, Yale University." Publications of the American Association of Museums, New Series, no. 16, pp. 16-27. Washington, D.C.: American Association of Museums, 1938.

Powell, Louis H. "How to Estimate a Museum's Value." *Museums Journal* 31 (1932): 527-531.

————. "A Study of Seasonal Attendance at a Mid-Western Museum of Science." *Museum News* 16:3 (1939): 7-8.

Prague, Rochelle H. "The University Museum Visitor Survey Project." *Curator* 17:3 (1974): 207-212.

Proshansky, Harold M., William H. Ittelson, and Leanne G. Rivlin. "Freedom of Choice and Behavior in a Physical Setting." In *Environmental Psychology: People and Their Physical Settings*, 2nd ed., edited by Harold M. Proshansky, William H. Ittelson, and Leanne G. Rivlin. New York: Holt, Rinehart and Winston, 1976.

Rados, David L. *Marketing for Nonprofit Organizations*. Boston: Auburn House, 1981.

Randall, Calvin. "Visitor Enhancement at Longwood Gardens." Unpublished paper. Longwood Program, Newark, Del., 1975.

Rattenbury, Judith, Paula Pelletier, and Laura Klem. *Computer Processing of Social Science Data Using OSIRIS IV*. Ann Arbor, Mich.: Institute for Social Research, 1984.

Rea, Paul Marshall. "A Directory of American Museums of Art, History, and Science." *Bulletin of the Buffalo Society for Natural Science* 10:10 (1910).

————. "How Many Visitors Should Museums Have?" *Museum News* 8:5 (1930): 9-12.

Reed, Vergil D. "Report and Recommendations on Research Methods Used to Determine the Impact of and Reactions to U.S. Official Exhibits in International Trade Fairs with Special Emphasis on an Evaluation of the Usual Methods as Applied at the Tokyo Fair." Washington, D.C.: Office of the International Trade Fairs, United States Information Agency, 1957.

Reekie, Gordon. "Toward Well-Being for Museum Visitors." *Curator* 1:1 (1958): 91-94.

Reiss, Jim. "Judging the Voice of Your Museum." *History News* 39:11 (1984): 12-17.

Robbins, J. E., and S. S. Robbins. "Museum Marketing: Identification of High, Moderate, and Low Attendee Segments." *Journal of the Academy of Marketing Science* 9:1 (1981): 66-76.

Robinson, Edward S. "The Behavior of the Museum Visitor." Publications of the American Association of Museums, New Series, no. 5. Washington, D.C.: American Association of Museums, 1928.

————. "Exit the Typical Visitor." *Journal of Adult Education* 10:16 (1931): 418-423.

————. "Experimental Education in the Museum: A Perspective." *Museum News* 10:2 (1933): 6-8.

Rosenfeld, Sherman, and Amelia Terkel. "A Naturalistic Study of Visitors at an Interactive Mini-Zoo." *Curator* 25:3 (1982): 187-212.

Ross, H. L., and D. T. Campbell. "The Connecticut Speed Crackdown: A Study of the Effects of Legal Change." In *Perspectives on the Social Order: Readings in Sociology*, edited by H. L. Ross. New York: McGraw-Hill, 1968.

The Royal Ontario Museum. *Communicating with the Museum Visitor: Guidelines for Planning*. Toronto: The Royal Ontario Museum, 1976.

Rumelhart, David E. "Schemata: The Building Blocks of Cognition." In *Comprehension and Teaching: Research Reviews*, edited by John T. Guthrie. Newark, Del: International Reading Association, 1981.

Schell, Suzanne B. "Self-Study." *History News* 38:10 (1983): 13-16.

————. "Taking a Hard Look: Strategies for Self-Study in Museums." *Museum News* 63:3 (1985): 47-52.

Schneider, David J., Albert H. Hastorf, and Phoebe C. Ellsworth. *Person Perception*. 2nd ed. Reading, Mass.: Addison-Wesley, 1979.

Schrodt, Philip A. *Microcomputer Methods for Social Scientists*. No. 40, Sage Publication Series in Quantitative Applications in the Social Sciences. Beverly Hills, Calif.: Sage Publications, 1984.

Schuman, Howard, and Stanley Presser. *Questions and Answers in Attitude Surveys: Experiments on Question Form, Wording, and Context*. New York: Academic Press, 1981.

Screven, C. G. "The Museum as a Responsive Learning Environment." *Museum News* 47:10 (1969): 7-10.

————. "Learning and Exhibits: Instructional Design." *Museum News* 52:5 (1974): 67-75.

————. *The Measurement and Facilitation of Learning in the Museum Environment: An Experimental Analysis*. Washington, D.C.: Smithsonian Institution Press, 1974.

————. "The Effectiveness of Guidance Devices on Visitor Learning." *Curator* 18:3 (1975): 219-243.

————. "Exhibit Evaluation: A Goal-Referenced Approach." *Curator* 19:4 (1976): 281-282.

————. "Improving Exhibits through Formative Evaluation." Paper read at ICOM/CECA Conference, The Netherlands, 1978.

————. "Bibliography on Visitor Research." *Museum News* 58:3 (1979): 59-88.

————. "Educational Evaluation and Research in Museums and Public Exhibits: A Bibliography." *Curator* 27:2 (1984): 147-165.

————. "Exhibitions and Information Centers: Some Principles and Approaches." *Curator* 29:2 (1986): 109-137.

Selltiz, Claire, Lawrence S. Wrightsman, and Stewart W. Cook. *Research Methods in Social Relations*. 3rd ed. New York: Holt, Rinehart, and Winston, 1976.

Serrell, Beverly. "Survey of Visitor Attitudes and Awareness at an Aquarium." *Curator* 20:1 (1977): 48-52.

————. "Visitor Observation Studies at the John G. Shedd Aquarium." Unpublished report. Chicago, 1977.

————. "Label Research Project: Field Museum of Natural History." Unpublished report. Chicago, 1980.

————. "Looking at Visitors at Zoos and Aquariums." *Museum News* 59:3 (1980): 36-41.

———. *Making Exhibit Labels: A Step-by-Step Guide.* Nashville: American Association for State and Local History, 1983.

Shepard, R. N. "Recognition Memory for Words, Sentences, and Pictures." *Journal of Verbal Learning and Verbal Behavior* 6 (1967): 156-163.

Shettel, Harris H. "An Evaluation of Existing Criteria for Judging the Quality of Science Exhibits." *Curator* 11:2 (1958): 137-153.

———. *An Evaluation Model for Measuring the Impact of Overseas Exhibits.* U.S. Atomic Energy Commission, Report no. AIR-F28-6/66FR. Washington, D.C.: Atomic Energy Commission, 1966.

———. "Atoms-in-Action Demonstration Center: Impact Studies: Dublin, Ireland; and Ankara, Turkey." American Institutes for Research, Technical Report no. AIR-F58-aa/67FR. Pittsburgh, Pa.: American Institutes for Research, 1967.

———. "Exhibits: Art Form or Educational Medium?" *Museum News* 52:9 (1973): 32-41.

———. "Results of Film Evaluation Pretest for Man in His Environment." Research Report, American Institutes for Research. Washington, D.C.: American Institutes for Research, April 1975.

———. "A Critical Look at a Critical Look: A Response to Alt's Critique of Shettel's Work." *Curator* 21:4 (1978): 329-345.

Shettel, Harris, H., Margaret Butcher, Timothy S. Cotton, Judi Northrup, and Doris Clapp Slough. "Strategies for Determining Exhibit Effectiveness." American Institute for Research, Technical Report no. AIR-E59-4/68-FR. Pittsburgh, Pa.: American Institute for Research, 1968.

Slovic, P., Baruch Fischoff, and Sarah Lichtenstein. "Behavioral Decision Theory." In *Annual Review of Psychology,* vol. 28, edited by M. R. Rosenzweig and L. W. Porter. Palo Alto, Calif.: Annual Review, Inc., 1977.

Sobol, Judith Ellen. "A Comparison of Two Methods for Creating Empathy with Art in Grade-School Children." Master's thesis, George Washington University, 1970.

Sommer, Robert, and Barbara B. Sommer. *A Practical Guide to Behavioral Research: Tools and Techniques.* New York: Oxford University Press, 1980.

Southworth and Southworth Architecture and Planning. *Lost in Art: Evaluation of the Visitor Information Center, Boston Museum of Fine Arts.* Boston: Southworth and Southworth Architecture and Planning, 1974.

Srivastava, Rajendra K., and Thomas S. Peel. "Human Movement as a Function of Color Stimulation." Topeka, Kans.: The Environmental Research Foundation, 1968.

Stake, Robert E. "Evaluation Design, Instrumentation, Data Collection, and Analysis of Data." In *Educational Evaluation.* Columbus, Ohio: State Superintendent of Public Instruction, 1969.

Standing, L., J. Conezio, and R. Haber. "Perception and Memory for Pictures: Singles Trial Learning of 2500 Visual Stimuli." *Psychonomic Science* 19 (1970): 73-74.

Stapp, Carol B. "Defining Museum Literacy." *Roundtable Reports* 9:1 (1984):3-4.

Suchman, Edward A. *Evaluative Research.* New York: Russell Sage Foundation, 1967.

Taylor, Frank A., and Katherine J. Goldman. "Surveys Surveyed." Informal publication. In *Opportunities for Extending Museum Contributions to Pre-College Science Education,* edited by Katherine J. Goldman. Washington, D.C.: Smithsonian Institution, 1970.

Taylor, James B. "Science on Display: A Study of the United States Science Exhibit, Seattle World's Fair, 1962." Seattle, Wash.: University of Washington, Institute for Sociological Research, 1963.

Thier, H. D., and M. Linn. "The Value of Interactive Learning Experiences in a Museum." *Curator* 19:1 (1976): 223-245.

Thomas, Lewis. *The Medusa and the Snail.* Toronto: Bantam Books, 1980.

Tversky, A., and D. Kahneman. "Availability: A Heuristic for Judging Frequency and Probability." *Cognitive Psychology* 5 (1973): 207-232.

Ullmann, Darrel A. *Attraction Sign Survey.* Lincoln, Nebr.: Nebraska Department of Roads and Nebraska Department of Economic Development, 1972.

Vandell, Kerry D., Thomas E. Barry, Jay D. Starling, and Philip Seib. "The Arts and the Local Economy: The Impact of 'Pompeii, A.D. 79'." *Curator* 22:3 (1979): 199-215.

Van Der Hoek, G. J. "Bezoekers Bekeken." Mededilingen, Gemeenttmuseum van den Haag 2:2 (1956).

Van Der Hoek, G. J., and Thea Van Eijnsbergen. "Audience Research in the Netherlands." *Museum's Annual* 2 (1970): 15-16.

Von Stroh, Gordon E. "Who Uses Denver Facilities?" 5th Report, Denver Urban Observatory. Denver, Colo.: Denver Urban Observatory, 1981.

Wainer, Howard. "Museums USA: A Type III Error." *Museum News* 53:4 (1974): 42-44.

Walker, S., and A. Walsh. "The Uses of Adversity." *Museum News* 61:3 (1983): 26-35.

Warwick, Donald P., and Charles A. Lininger. *The Sample Survey: Theory and Practice.* New York: McGraw-Hill, 1975.

Washburne, R. F., and J. A. Wagar. "Evaluating Visitor Response to Exhibit Content." *Curator* 15:3 (1972): 248-254.

Webb, E. J., D. T. Campbell, R. D. Swartz, and L. Sechrest. *Unobtrusive Measures.* Chicago: Rand McNally, 1966.

Weiss, Carol H. *Evaluation Research: Methods for Assessing Program Effectiveness.* Englewood Cliffs, N.J.: Prentice-Hall, 1972.

Weiss, Robert S., and Serge Boutourline, Jr. "The Communication Value of Exhibits." *Museum News* 42:11 (1963): 23-27.

Wells, Carolyn. *The Smithsonian Visitor: A Survey.* Washington, D.C.: Office of Museum Programs, Smithsonian Institution, 1969.

Wickelgren, Wayne A. "Human Learning and Memory." In *Annual Review of Psychology,* vol. 32, edited by Mark R. Rosenzweig and Lyman W. Porter. Palo Alto, Calif.: Annual Reviews, Inc., 1981.

Wicker, Allan W. *An Introduction to Ecological Psychology.* Monterey, Calif.: Brooks-Cole, 1979.

Wiegman, Paul G., and Pamela M. Wiegman. "The Smithsonian Grasshopper." Unpublished report. Washington, D.C.: Office of Museum Programs, Smithsonian Institution, 1973.

Williams, Patterson. "Object Contemplation: Theory into Practice." *Roundtable Reports* 9:1 (1984): 10-12.

Witkin, Herman A., Helen B. Lewis, Karen Machover, P. B. Meissner, and Seymour Wapner. *Personality through Perception.* New York: Harper, 1954.

Witteborg, Lothar P. "Exhibit Planning." *History News* 38:6 (1983): 21-24.

Wittlin, A. S. *Museums: In Search of a Usable Future.* Cambridge, Mass.: Massachusetts Institute of Technology, 1959.

Wolf, Robert L. "A Naturalistic View of Evaluation." *Museum News* 58:1 (1980): 39-45.

———. "Enhancing Museum Leadership through Evaluation." *Museum Studies Journal* 1:3 (1984): 31-33.

Wolf, Robert L., and Barbara L. Tymitz. "A Preliminary Guide for Conducting Naturalistic Evaluation in Studying Museum Environments." Washington, D.C.: Office of Museum Programs, Smithsonian Institution, 1979.

———. "East Side, West Side, Straight Down the Middle: A Study of Visitor Perceptions of 'Our Changing Land' Bicentennial Exhibit." Washington, D.C.: Office of Museum Programs, Smithsonian Institution, 1979.

Wright, G. A. "Some Criteria for Evaluating Displays in Museums of Science and History." *Midwest Museums Quarterly* 18 (1958): 62-70.

Yoshika, Joseph G. "A Direction-Orientation Study with Visitors at the New York World's Fair." *The Journal of General Psychology* 27 (1942): 3-33.

Zeisel, John. *Inquiry by Design: Tools for Environment-Behavior Research.* Monterey, Calif.: Brooks-Cole, 1981.

Zimbardo, Philip G., Ebbe B. Ebbesen, and Christina Maslach. *Influencing Attitudes and Changing Behavior.* 2nd ed. Reading, Mass.: Addison-Wesley, 1977.

Zube, Ervin H., Joseph H. Crystal, and James F. Palmer. "Visitor Center Design Evaluation." Report no. R-76-5, University of Massachusetts, Institute for Man and Environment. Amherst, Mass.: University of Massachusetts, 1976.

Index